Jane Caro is an author, novelist, journalist, ist, advertising writer and social commentator. In her thirty years in advertising, her creative work has won many national and international awards. She now serves on the boards of the Public Education Foundation and Bell Shakespeare, where she chairs their Arts Advisory Committee.

She appears in the media regularly, including weekly segments on *Sunrise* and *Weekend Sunrise*. Her six-part ABC radio series, 'For Better, For Worse' has been produced as a four-part TV series for ABC's *Compass*. Jane has also appeared on *The Drum*, *Q&A*, *The Project*, *Daily Edition*, *Mornings*, *Studio 10* and *Today*. She writes regular monthly columns for *Mt* (Management Today) magazine and the *Sun-Herald*'s Sunday Life. She is also in demand as a speaker, workshop facilitator and MC. *Plain-speaking Jane* is her eighth book.

jane caro

plain-speaking jane

MACMILLAN
Pan Macmillan Australia

Some of the people in this book have had their names changed to protect their identities.

First published 2015 in Macmillan by Pan Macmillan Australia Pty Ltd
1 Market Street, Sydney, New South Wales, Australia, 2000

Cataloguing-in-Publication entry is available
from the National Library of Australia
http://catalogue.nla.gov.au

Typeset in 12.5/18 pt Garamond Pro by Midland Typesetters, Australia
Printed by McPherson's Printing Group

*To Charlotte Catherine Clavering Grey & Henry Jones,
Alice Barlow & Edwin Booth, Edith Mary Rawlinson &
Thomas Edward Marshall, Eva Daynes & William Caro.*

*Without whom none of the following
would ever have happened.*

prologue

1995

I stepped out of the lift; the foyer was a hive of activity. People were rushing about with boxes and equipment. The receptionist was busy slotting files into her filing cabinets and shoving things into cupboards. Someone was drilling holes so they could hang the shiny new agency logo on the wall opposite.

'Morning,' I said. 'It's looking good already. Where's my new office?'

The receptionist gave me a bit of a look. 'Down the hall,' she said, inclining her head to the left. 'Right at the end.'

We'd spent the previous week packing the contents of our offices into boxes for the move from one office building in Sussex Street to another. The removalists had come in and moved everything over the weekend. Our new premises were only a couple of doors up the road but it was a newer skyscraper with better views so I was looking forward to seeing my new office.

I walked to the room she had indicated. It was small, windowless and dark. One desk stood at the rear of the room. At that desk sat my art director, Jane Evans. Boxes were piled up everywhere, filling almost all the available space.

'Is this your office?' I pulled a face. It wasn't at all what I had expected. 'So where's mine? I thought they said we'd all have team offices like we did in the old building.'

'Yeah,' said Jane. 'They did and we do. This is *our* office.'

'What?' I looked around me. The room was hardly big enough for one person, let alone two, and there was only one desk. 'Where am I supposed to sit?'

'There.' Jane pointed at what I had assumed was a guest chair. 'They said because you're only part-time you can just sit there on the days you come in.'

'You're kidding!'

Jane shook her head.

The year I had spent working at JWT was one of the most professionally satisfying of my life. I had come back into advertising after five years at home caring for my small daughters. Despite the fact that I was part-time (having – as far as I have been able to discover – virtually pioneered part-time permanent work in creative departments in ad agencies), Jane Evans and I had created a campaign for Drive laundry detergent that had won international acclaim and garnered prestigious awards from all over the world. I think it was probably the most-awarded campaign created in Australia that year. It had certainly done wonders for JWT's creative reputation and there was daylight between the number of awards Jane and I had brought into the agency and those the other teams had managed. The two of us now had strong creative reputations and credentials in the world of advertising. This gave us some clout. Yet here we were, being relegated to a poky back room, and here I was, being asked to work without a proper office or even a proper desk. The insult was gobsmacking.

Fortunately, I was no longer the easily cowed young woman I once was. I was a parent. I had been through some really tough experiences and survived them. I'd been in therapy for years and I had learnt a great deal. I was tougher and stronger as a result. There was no way in the world I was going to accept this disrespect without a fight.

I did not even put my bag down in that poky little room.

'I will not work in here.'

I gathered my computer and a box of my files and walked to reception. Although noisy, what with the drilling and people rushing hither and thither, the reception area was spacious. It was also light, airy and had a spectacular view of the harbour. I found a power point near the coffee table and plugged in my computer. I put the box on the floor and went back to get more of my stuff.

'What are you doing?' asked the receptionist as I unloaded another armful of papers.

'They don't appear to have allocated me a proper work space, so I'll be working from here until they do.' I gave the poor woman a big friendly smile.

'But . . . you can't.'

'Oh, I'm sure I can. There's much more room here and we

don't often have many people in reception. I'll get much more done than I will camping out in Jane's office. Just look at the light and that view . . . much more stimulating.'

As I went to fetch more of my stuff I noticed that the receptionist had picked up the phone. Good.

I continued to move all my boxes and files into reception. I was blithely typing some copy when the lift doors opened and a senior manager got out and walked towards me.

Only a year back in the workforce and I was causing trouble again.

one

I was born in June 1957 in London to an angry but determined young woman of twenty-six – Catherine (Kate) Caro nee Booth – and her young-man-in-a-hurry husband, Andy Caro. They had not intended to get pregnant so the first thing my father did when he heard the news was buy a TV set. He anticipated that my existence would mean a lot more evenings in and he was determined not to be bored. That was about the only concession he made to my imminent arrival. He continued to zip around London on a BSA Bantam motorbike and my pregnant mother crammed herself on the back.

Catherine and Andy had met four years earlier at a dance in Manchester, the industrial city where they were both born and brought up. Andy was studying history at Cambridge University and had come home to Manchester during the university holidays. Catherine was a secretary working at nearby Stockport. She already had a boyfriend, a handsome naval officer called Barry who was – fortunately for the rest of this story – away at sea at the time.

Catherine was a pretty young woman whose natural reserve hid a strong personality and a steely intellect. Andy was not handsome. He was short, boyish and very generously endowed with nose. At the dance he was also slightly full of his own importance as an Oxbridge man. On the plus side, he was quick-witted, funny and full of energy and charm. He spotted my mother across the proverbial crowded room and asked her to dance. My father was (and is – at eighty-four!) an excellent dancer. His mother, Cicely Caro (nee Marshall), was a professional dancer in the 1920s who – so the story goes – danced in the chorus of a musical starring Fred Astaire and his then partner, his sister Adele. This talent is one that all of us have inherited. If the music starts, the Caros – of all ages – are always the first on the dance floor.

Andy was feeling confident as he expertly steered this pretty but quiet young woman around the floor. He very quickly managed to drop his Cambridge pedigree (St John's College, like his father Jack, thank you very much) into the conversation and then proceeded to observe – rather loftily – that my mother reminded him of Jane Austen's Emma. Later, he quoted a line or two from Andrew Marvell's 'To a Coy Mistress' but (typically) got them wrong. My well-read mother immediately corrected him. To his credit, far from feeling embarrassed or annoyed, this piqued his interest. My mother was not just a pretty face and, while Andy liked pretty faces well enough, he liked good minds even better.

He asked her out and she accepted. Barry was going to be at sea for some time and, while her correction of the Marvell quote had increased my father's interest, it was the prospect of going to the upcoming Cambridge May Ball that had aroused my mother's. The May Ball was one of *the* social events of the year and Catherine, as the daughter of a shopkeeper, from a family in which no-one had ever gone to university, had never expected she would ever be invited. Reasoning that what Barry didn't know wouldn't hurt him, my mother decided that dating Andy was the best chance she was ever going to get to attend the only social function in the UK licensed by the Queen to serve cooked swan.

Like Cinderella, my mother did go to the ball. There was no fairy godmother, however, and my mother spent her entire savings – a whole twenty-five guineas – on a couture white-satin New Look gown. She kept that gown for decades, until its metal teardrop beading tarnished and the rust ruined the satin. I remember fingering it wistfully as a child.

Poor old Barry, he was much more conventionally handsome than my father, but he couldn't compete with my father's energy and determination or with the glimpse of new opportunities that Andy gave my mother. When Barry returned from his tour of duty, Catherine broke up with her naval officer and became engaged to my father.

This delighted my father's family and they immediately and permanently christened my mother 'Saint Kate'. (My father had renamed his girlfriend; she had previously always been called Catherine but from now on she would always be Kate or Katie.)

My mother returned the Caro family's affection wholeheartedly because they were interesting, lively and much more honest and open than her own rather repressed family.

Alfred Booth and his wife Eva (nee Jones) were not so impressed with Katie's intended. Alfred, in particular, found my father impossible to like. He thought Andy was a pushy, noisy, jumped-up little Jew. Alfred was an intelligent man who had been forced to leave school at thirteen. This lack of education notwithstanding, he had done well as a sales rep in publishing and enjoyed the industry. When Eva's father died just before their wedding, Alfred reluctantly left his job to take over the running of the Jones family shop. Once again, he had done well, expanding from one draper's shop to two and almost to three, only to be set back when he was called up during the Second World War in 1940, at the age of thirty-nine. He served in the Eighth Army as a tank transporter driver in the North African desert and returned home tight-lipped and embittered. Perhaps he also had a chip on his shoulder about Andy's privileged Manchester Grammar School, Cambridge University background. I suspect he had rather liked the idea of his youngest daughter becoming a navy wife. However, since my mother and her father were always at loggerheads, Alfred's dislike of her new boyfriend was just another mark in his favour.

If my father was Jewish – he had a big nose, his last name was Caro and he was expressive and uninhibited in a very non-English way – he certainly wasn't aware of it. The Booths were Methodists, but the Caros were completely irreligious. They didn't appear to be lapsed believers of any kind; there

was just no religion in the family. I suspect they prob
Jewish once – Manchester has a large Jewish population – but they appear to have left both faith and identity behind without a backward glance.

Despite her father's (unspoken but quite obvious) objections, Andy and Kate were married in 1955 after my father's graduation from university. They immediately moved to London where Kate continued to work as a secretary and Andy took a marketing traineeship with the paint division of ICI. Interestingly, he also took an application test for a job as a copywriter with a large ad agency and was offered a position. He chose marketing instead.

Then, late in 1956, a condom broke.

In the 1950s, reproduction was women's business and men – even my besotted father, who adores Katie to this day – were happy to keep it that way. My mother left her job and Andy, now the only wage-earner, redoubled his efforts at ICI. (The only legacy of that job, almost sixty years later, is that he still knows the right way to paint a wall. It is about the only practical household chore that he has a) mastered and b) likes to do. It must be said, however, that over the years, knowing how to paint a wall is something he has put to very good use in several of his own and his children's houses.)

Although giving birth was regarded as very much secret women's business back in 1957, it was, rather confusingly, also kept secret from women themselves. The medical professionals were the only ones who knew about birth. Fortunately, my mother had a friend, Millie, whose mother was a doctor.

Astonishing in itself – women doctors being very rare in those days – Millie's mum was also an enlightened practitioner with a particular interest in obstetrics. She gave my mother a book on childbirth. The book included advice on how to breathe through the pain of labour and other practical information that helped Kate to understand what was happening to her. My mother absorbed the advice so completely that when she had me – in a nursing home, as was the tradition in the UK – she refused to listen to what she saw as patronising advice from the midwives and gave birth to me in her own way.

At first the professionals sneered at both her book and the breathing techniques she used so conscientiously, but once I was born, they changed their minds. Rather sheepishly, the nurses asked my mother for the name of the book that had helped her to manage so well. Kate not only felt vindicated, but the sense of control her well-practised breathing techniques gave her was important, not just for managing the exacting business of birth, but for her dignity and her sense of herself. I am not sure my mother would have called herself a feminist at this point in her life, but perhaps it was from this moment that her feminist journey began.

Thanks to her stubborn defiance, I had an auspicious beginning. An easy birth to a mother who felt good about it is a great way to enter the world. It is not very common. According to my mother, most of my generation were born to terrified women who were ignorant about what was happening to them and were often made to feel ashamed. Indeed, I have had a couple of friends relate horror stories about their own births in

Australia in the 1950s. One told me that as her mother cried out in pain in a Catholic maternity hospital, a nursing nun said, 'Well, you made your bed and now you must lie in it.' In other words, you had sex and this is your punishment; good old original sin. No attempt appears to have been made to help or support birthing mothers. Indeed, in this case – and, no doubt, many others – they were treated as sinners, even though they were respectably married. God knows what it must have been like for so-called fallen women.

But it wasn't just Catholic maternity hospitals that treated birthing women with disdain. Another contemporary had an even worse story. As her mother laboured alone in a public hospital, hollering in pain, a nurse slapped her across the face and told her to stop making such a fuss.

My own mother, labouring in that nursing home in the UK, was surprised when she noticed an unused cylinder of nitrous oxide near her bed. It was the only pain relief offered to birthing mothers at that time.

'When do I get some of that?' she asked the nurse between contractions.

The nurse gave what my mother later described as a rather nasty grin. 'You only get some of that when you really start to scream.'

Not being stupid, my mother immediately began yelling her head off.

And they say we don't need feminism.

When I look back at women of my mother's generation facing the ordeal of childbirth, I am astonished by their courage. Of course, they had much less choice than we do – contraception in those days was very chancy. I am the result of a torn condom, as is my youngest sister. And no-one talked about any of this stuff – it was taboo. Maybe the medical profession hoped a woman's family would give her the information she needed. My mother had no family in London and, anyway, hers was a family that could never speak directly of such things. Even had they been less inhibited, they could have offered little help. As Kate laboured to produce me, on a midsummer's day in 1957, Alfred and Eva were busy caring for their first grandchild, my mother's older sister Margaret's son. I am not sure where Margaret's husband Tony was at that time – working, I suppose – and anyway, in the 1950s, men were never expected to care for their own children no matter what the circumstances. And in this case, the circumstances were exceptional. Margaret was unable to care for Nicholas herself because she was still recovering from puerperal fever.

Yes, you did read that right. Puerperal fever in the UK in the mid-1950s. Aunt Margaret was one of the last women in the UK to suffer from the disease that had once been the biggest killer of women after childbirth. Puerperal fever is caused by a lack of hygiene on the part of medical staff. If the birthing attendants don't disinfect themselves properly as they go from one birth to another, they can infect mother after mother. Birthing women are particularly vulnerable to infection because of their open cervix. My aunt was saved by a course of what were then experimental antibiotics. Without them, she would have died, as countless generations of birthing women had died before her. New-fangled antibiotics or not, the infection shredded my aunt's uterus and she was told that her son would be her only child. This was something my aunt refused to accept and a few years later she found a doctor who was willing to help her through a second pregnancy that resulted in my cousin Judith. Stubborn women run in my family.

My parents must have been shocked to learn of Margaret's illness. Improvements in hygiene meant puerperal fever was almost unheard of by the 1950s. It must have been terrifying to watch Margaret – previously a vibrant and healthy young woman – hovering between life and death, particularly after what had been a perfectly normal pregnancy. No doubt this would have played on the minds of my mother and my father when they received the – fairly unwelcome news – that they were pregnant with me. I think this makes my mother's decision to wrest control of my birth from the medical establishment both more understandable and courageous. She had not intended to be pregnant, but if she had to have a baby, she would do it her way. In fact, it turned out that she was good at giving birth, and she did so three more times in the next eight years, twice in her own bed at home.

Birth she had mastered, but actual child-rearing was a different story. She was not at her happiest with four children under seven. But I was her first child and – in the early days at least – a novelty.

two

I am not sure what my first genuine memory is. It might be going into my parent's bedroom after my brother Robert was born. I was not quite four. He was born at home like my sister Ann, although as I was only eighteen months old when she came along I don't remember her birth at all. In the UK at that time it was usual to give birth at home, particularly if it was a subsequent birth following an uneventful first birthing experience. By the time my brother was born, my parents had moved from London to the village of Swanland in Yorkshire; my father had left the paint company to work for the large British grocery manufacturing business Reckitt and Colman, based in Hull. And yes, Swanland did, in those days at least, have a pond with swans on it.

I remember Ann and I being ushered into my parents' bedroom and seeing my mother sitting bolt upright in her bed looking rather peculiar. Her hair was brushed and she may even have worn some lippie – which was not what she usually looked like in bed. The other detail that sticks in my memory is that her bed's top sheet was folded tightly back over the covers and tucked into the mattress very firmly (hospital corners, no doubt). The fact that she clutched a bundle whom I was told was my new brother and that the room was full of strangers (probably just a doctor and a nurse) made less impression on me than those rigid bedclothes. Obviously I knew something about how babies arrived because I distinctly remember wondering how the poor baby had ever managed to wriggle his way out and into my mother's arms.

I have other snippets of memory about our life in England. I remember the little village school I attended as a five-year-old. My teacher's name was Miss Horncastle and my mother's father, Grandpa Booth, used to tease me gently by insisting her name was Miss Hornblower. Sadly, that's almost the last nice memory I have of Alfred. He liked children until they got to the age of having their own opinions (six, from memory) and then he didn't like us much at all. My mother and her father were often at odds, too, and I suppose that tension and wariness rubbed off on me. And the fact that my father and his father-in-law still didn't like each other much didn't help my relationship with my maternal grandfather either.

It is the toilets at Swanland Village School that I remember most vividly. (Through my experiences as an advocate for public education, I know that it is often dread of the communal toilets that loom particularly large for little children when they first go to school.) In my case, the toilets were in an ancient building (sandstone, as I recall) with a high roof and no ceiling. The toilet cubicles were narrow but very tall, their walls ascending to the gloomy rafters. Worse, the rafters and walls were unlined and festooned with spider's webs. We still wrote on slates at my school in 1962, and we controlled our fear of these toilet-dwelling spiders by covering our slates with drawings of daddy-long-legs. There was a formula to our drawings; we started with a small dot in the centre of the slate for the body and then drew great spindly legs all the way out to the edge of the wooden frame. God knows why these drawings made such an impression on me. I must have been very afraid of those spiders – or those toilets.

Another memory from my early years in England is of being told off by Aunty Brenda for not flushing the toilet. I didn't like Aunty Brenda, a sharp-featured woman who was part cleaning lady, part mother's help. She was not really my aunt and she was always cross and I constantly felt ashamed of myself around her. I don't know why. Looking back on my childhood, I think I often felt a low-level sense of being bad. I don't know if that was just me or if it was a feeling that most children experienced around adults in the 1950s and 60s. It was a much more authoritarian time. Or is it just how kids always feel, even today, as they struggle to understand an adult world?

A nicer memory is of time spent with Granny Booth. Alfred and Eva moved from Manchester to Grange, in the Lake District, after my grandfather sold the shops. Their new house (I think they had it built for them) ran down to a railway easement and Granny used to read us the Thomas the Tank Engine books;

this was long before there was any TV show. When we went to the bottom of her garden, often to pick and eat the gooseberries that grew there in abundance, we would stand on that easement and identify the trains that went by as Thomas and his friends. We knew them by the different colours of their smoke, so I suppose there must still have been steam trains running at the bottom of Granny's garden. I loved doing that. Granny was the only one of my extended family who never made me feel bad, irritating, naughty or ashamed. She didn't judge you or tell you off; she just loved you and you knew it.

In place of my own scant memories of my early years, I have been told many stories. My favourite is of a photographer whom my proud parents hired to take shots of me soon after my first birthday. Apparently, to catch my attention, he dangled his wristwatch in front of me, calling it a 'tick-tock'. According to my mother, I looked him up and down. 'Watch,' I said. I like to think I was already handy with a put-down. Another example of my (supposedly) precocious language skills came from a stay in hospital when I had gastroenteritis at eighteen months. On one of her visits, my mother asked me what I had eaten for lunch. 'Coffeelower,' I replied. She regarded this as an excellent attempt for one and a half.

That coffeelower was probably the last time I willingly ate a vegetable until I was well into my teens. Although, given the authoritarian nature of nurses at the time, whether I ate the cauliflower willingly or not is a matter for speculation. My infant way with words may occasionally (only twice, as far as I know) have given my parents pleasure but, sadly for them, the characteristic that most marked my childhood was my stubborn refusal to eat.

Eating seemed to me to be an unpleasant and unnecessary interruption to what I loved to do most in the world, which was to read. I was also repulsed to the point of gagging by most flavours and many textures. My repertoire of acceptable foods was rigidly narrow. I would eat eggs, cheddar cheese, bread, apples, peanut butter, chocolate custard (not chocolate), strawberries, gooseberries, sausages, pastry and that was about it. I only drank water. To this day I loathe fizzy drinks – I don't like the sensation of the bubbles on my tongue and palate. I even hate sparkling mineral water, not that there was anything like that around when I was young. I remember how overwhelming quite bland flavours were at the time. I could not bear the meatiness of meat (I love it now) or the bitterness of vegetables. I loathed the coldness of ice-cream, the sweet intensity of chocolate. I hated the acid in oranges and tomatoes, the smell of melted cheese (it reminded me of vomit), the fishiness of fish and the sliminess of anything stewed or casseroled. I was the fussiest of fussy eaters. My mother (thank you, Dr Spock) decided not to fight my hatred of so many foods. Instead, she was strategic; putting eggs in my favourite dessert of chocolate pudding and just about anything else she could mix them into. She gave me fruit in place of vegetables and I would occasionally deign to eat raw carrots and celery. She gave me the bone from the roast leg of lamb to gnaw on every Sunday and I would occasionally eat a lamb chop but (shudder) not the fat. This strategy of not forcing me (I did not force my own fussy-eating children either) was much frowned upon at the time and remains so to this day but, if the outcome is anything to go by, it seems a wise one to me. I now eat and enjoy everything, except fizzy drinks. My husband, who was sent to boarding school at the age of six and was forced to eat everything on his plate, even if it actually made him vomit, remains a fussy eater to this day.

* * *

In 1963, my father was offered a better job in the Australian branch of Reckitts, which was based in Sydney, and so we migrated. My mother jumped at the chance to leave England. She still tells horror stories about trying to raise three children under five in Yorkshire, particularly in the winter. She didn't drive at that time and so had to walk to the village shops to buy the daily groceries. (My grandmother lived her whole life without a driver's licence. Indeed, Granny Booth couldn't even ride a bike. The one time she tried, as an adult woman with two teenage daughters, she lost control of the bicycle, careered down a hill, hit a kerb and flew off the bike into a field of nettles. That would be enough to put you off for life, I dare say.) This meant corralling one small child, a toddler and a baby in a pram, rain, hail, shine or snow.

'I would just manage to get the baby into his snowsuit,' she would later recall, 'when either you or Ann would need to go to the toilet, which meant getting you out of yours and starting the whole damn rigmarole all over again.' It was the winter of

1963 when my father was offered the job in Australia, one of the coldest for decades; no wonder she was so keen.

My sister, brother and I were too young either to be consulted or to have any feelings about the matter. I remember little about our departure from England and I am the only one of my siblings to have any memories at all of the UK. My mother does recall some snobbish anxiety among friends about what effect moving to Australia would have on us kids.

'How will you stop them getting that dreadful accent?' Kate remembers one woman saying. Given how Aussie we all sound now, that was a lost cause.

The journey by ship from England to Australia did furnish me with one happy memory of food. At one point on the voyage, we encountered stormy seas and everyone on the ship went down with seasickness, including my parents, sister and brother. I withstood the nausea for longer than most (not eating much has its upside) but finally succumbed and took to my bed. When I woke, I was ravenously hungry, which was not a common experience for me as a child. I pushed the call button in my cabin. (Unlike the Ten Pound Poms, we were full-fare-paying passengers, and even a five-year-old was entitled to the accompanying perks.) A steward arrived and I ordered a plate of dry toast. An enormous plateful was duly delivered. With an imperious wave of my hand, I dismissed the poor steward and demolished the lot.

Our arrival in Australia was not auspicious. My father became seriously ill on the trip over with pneumonia. He had to be carried off the ship on a stretcher and was taken by ambulance straight to hospital. I still remember seeing him way down below on the gangplank (I suppose we must have been up on the deck) being carried away from us. He looked very small and vulnerable. It was a strange and lonely feeling.

Yet the difficulty of our arrival was one of the reasons Kate loved the place so immediately. First, everyone at Reckitts Australia was aware of her situation and they rallied around to help. A house was rented for us in the Upper North Shore suburb of Gordon, I suspect because it was near where most of the Reckitts executives themselves lived. My mother didn't care where it was; she was just grateful that it had a fridge which had thoughtfully been stocked with food. My father's new colleagues and their wives (all his co-workers were blokes in those days) welcomed my mother – a young woman of thirty-two with three small children in tow – with warmth and kindness. And Kate remembers something else that made her feel that, far from coming to a strange country, she had actually come home.

'Every time I opened my mouth in England, I knew they heard my Lancashire accent and thought I was common. They looked down on me because of my class and where I had come from. When I opened my mouth in Australia, they just thought I was English.'

My mother's sense of belonging in Australia was no doubt enhanced by the fact that her sister Margaret and her family migrated to Sydney in 1964, when my Uncle Tony was also offered a job here. Eva and Alfred, with all their children and grandchildren settled 12,000 miles away, then gave up their purpose-built dream home in Grange, farewelled the gooseberry bushes and Thomas the Tank Engine trains at the bottom of their garden and, in their sixties, migrated here too. It must have been a wrench for them, and Eva – not being able to drive – was very dependent on Alfred and her daughters for mobility and company. Indeed, we got an inkling of what this move cost Eva at her funeral. She had asked that a few lines from a Rupert Brooke poem – 'The Soldier' – be read at her funeral: 'If I should die, think only this of me; / That there's some corner of a foreign field / That is for ever England.' Her daughters and grandchildren may have loved Australia, but I am not sure Eva ever did.

* * *

Alfred and Eva lived in Avalon, Margaret and Tony settled in St Ives and we bought a house in the cheaper suburb of Frenchs Forest, not too far from the Reckitts head office in West Ryde.

On virtually the first day we moved in to the unpretentious weatherboard bungalow (as Poms still refer to one-storey houses), Ann and I met the girls across the road, Julie and Lynne Spilsted. They were exactly our age and we became fast friends. It seems we had all not just landed in Australia, but landed on our feet.

Another positive memory of food is a result of our close friendship with the Spilsted girls. When I was about ten, Ann and I went to Harrington for a week's holiday with Julie and

Lynne and stayed with their grandparents, who lived beside the Manning River. We went fishing with Grandpa Spilsted and I caught a flounder. I don't think I ate any of it (ugh, fish!), despite Grandma Spilsted's coaxing. The next day, Julie and I walked along the river and found a rock covered in oysters. We sat on that rock smashing open the oysters with a sharp stone and eating them as we talked about all the mesmerising things that were occurring in our lives. They tasted deliciously of the sea. Poor Grandma Spilsted was terribly worried about how little I was eating. I didn't tell her about the oysters.

The long-term consequence of my very restricted diet may be my height – or lack thereof. (Mind you, all my family, apart from my brother Robert and my daughter Polly, are short.) I was always the kid in the front of the school photo holding the sign. In second class at Frenchs Forest Public School, my teacher (who disliked me as much as I disliked her) put together a class musical item for an assembly. It somewhat horrifies me to recall that the song all us white kids were singing was 'Mammy's Little Baby Loves Shortnin' bread'. Nothing wrong with a good Negro spiritual, perhaps, but we were doing it in black face. I was cast as one of the little 'picaninnies' (apologies, but it was 1964), which I knew meant baby. Being so undersized, I'd spent my life protesting that I was *not* a baby, so this casting horrified me. Without consulting the teacher (this may be why she did not like me), I swapped roles with my – much larger – friend so that I could play a mammy and she a picaninny. I irritated my teacher further by failing to bring the required long-sleeved shirt and so having to have black make-up rubbed on my arms as well as my face. They needn't have bothered. As a mammy, and standing at the back, no-one in the audience could see me anyway.

* * *

In 1966, aged nine, I sat for the IQ test held in New South Wales to decide which kids went to Opportunity Class (OC) for the final two years of primary school. I'm not sure why I sat the test; I had never done all that well at school, jogging along in the B class. My parents, particularly my father, had always given me the impression that they thought I was clever. The downside of this was I didn't feel it mattered about schoolwork or what the teachers thought, and I was hopelessly, endlessly, stubbornly bad at maths. Most of my teachers really didn't like me much, but in fourth class I was lucky enough to have a teacher called Mr Dan. He was very mean to the boys in his class – I remember him throwing the blackboard duster at them a lot – but he had a great sense of humour and was very nice to me. Perhaps that is why it was in Mr Dan's class that I wrote, directed and starred in a play I called 'The Witch's Crystal Ball' (I was the witch), about which I remember nothing except everyone died at the end. No matter, I bet it knocked 'Mammy's Little Baby' into a cocked hat.

Mr Dan was the first teacher to tell my mother that I was underperforming. It may be down to him that I got to sit for the OC test. In the event, I was successful. It meant transferring from Frenchs Forest to Chatswood Public, something I was happy to do. Apart from Mr Dan (as well as hurling blackboard dusters at the boys, he used to throw sweets to us when we gave an answer that pleased him), there was little I would miss from my old school. If memory serves me correctly (and I have no idea if it does), the attitude of most teachers towards kids in the 1960s was punitive and suspicious. The default assumption was that we were all about to do something wrong. I think it was called 'discipline' and we all got hit at some time or another, girls and boys – usually with a ruler while you held your hand outstretched, in front of as many eyes as possible. Schools and attitudes to children had vastly improved by the time my own children went to them.

At the beginning of the 1967 school year, my mother and I fronted up to my new primary school. My birthday is in June, so I was still nine, but I was enrolled in 5N, the OC class.

When we arrived, the person whose job it was to greet the new enrolments took one look at me and said, 'The infants school is down there.' She thought I was starting kindergarten. (I AM NOT A BABY!)

When my mother explained I was enrolling in fifth class, and OC at that, the woman looked at me with her mouth open. I think she thought I really must be an infant prodigy. Yep, I was that small.

I was so small that my mother took me to the doctor for a number of tests to see why I was not growing. I am fortunate that the doctor she took me to was another of my mother's sensible female GPs. Dr Margaret Mills performed all the requisite tests and informed my mother that I was just naturally small and, in fact, the perfect dimensions for my age if I had been born during the reign of Queen Victoria (I have always treasured that odd little detail). She told my mother that there was a new treatment for undersized children that involved the injection of a substance made from a pig's pituitary gland, however she did not see any need for it in my case. Neither Dr Mills nor my mother thought that being on the short side was either a disadvantage or something to be fixed. There was nothing wrong with me – that was all my mother cared about. Some short kids from my generation were not so fortunate. Those who were injected with that growth hormone often went on to develop Creutzfeldt-Jakob disease. Sufferers gradually lose their mental capacity and then die. It can lie dormant in your system for decades. It is the same disease that is caused by eating beef from cattle infected with mad cow disease. I was well served by Dr Mills and my mother and their calm good sense. I can't help wondering, though, what might have happened if I had been a boy.

Being so small did have its upside. There was a girl in my OC class who was my polar opposite. At ten, she was large in every dimension and looked like a grown woman. Easily as bright as I was (and much, much better at maths), people expected more of her because of her size and how mature it made her look. People expected much less of me, and so I was able to impress them by just being a perfectly ordinary ten-year-old. So – ahem – perfectly ordinary, in fact, that I was soon doing remedial maths in my OC class, something that would certainly never be allowed today.

I didn't enjoy OC. My teacher, Miss N, was a nervous woman with no sense of humour and, as far as I could see, no liking for children. I vividly remember being sent to get something from the top drawer in her desk only to find it full of Bex powders in little white folds of paper. She was always swallowing them down in class. The obsession with Bex powders among women in the 1960s was summed up by the advertising slogan 'A Bex, a cup of tea and a nice lie-down'. It was a headache cure, supposedly, but was marketed a bit like a tranquilliser. It was later discovered to destroy your kidneys if taken in excess. I sometimes worry about Miss N's kidneys.

Miss N did not like me. She marked me out as a misfit and sat me right up the front of the classroom where she could keep a sharp and disapproving eye on me. She thought I was a show-off, a loudmouth and lazy (all of which were true). To 'enrich' us, we were all supposed to learn a musical instrument and were duly issued with a small black piccolo. Once we learnt to play this, we were meant to transition to a flute. I know there is much research that says learning a musical instrument is terrific for children, just as there is research confirming the importance of playing sport. I am not disputing the benefits of either for most children, but they didn't work for me.

I had no interest in learning a musical instrument and – true to form – refused to practice. In two years of compulsory lessons, I never learnt to play more than the opening bar of 'An English Country Garden' (it consists of the note G repeated a few times). My classmates and I were all compelled to audition regularly for a place in the school flute ensemble. Eventually,

I was the last child standing. Reluctantly, the bandmaster allowed me to join, under strict instructions to move my fingers but not make a sound. I did as I was told. I wasn't musical, but I could act.

My father remembers coming to see me in a school concert and slowly realising I wasn't actually playing. 'Your fingers were moving differently from everyone else's,' he observed as we all emerged from backstage after the concert. 'Were you playing the instrument?'

'Oh no. I can't play at all.'

'I see. Well that's up to you, I guess, but tell me, why did I have to take time off work to come and watch you pretend?'

He had a point.

My acting ability gave me my only moment of triumph in OC. I had a lead role in the fifth-class play, singing an ode to 'My Old Black Billy' while dressed as a swagman. My performance was well received. The next year I auditioned enthusiastically for the lead role in the sixth-class play, but Miss N told me that, despite my excellent audition, I would be in the chorus. I'd had a lead role the year before, she explained, and, anyway, I was too small for the role. This explanation infuriated my father, who sent a letter complaining of height discrimination. Miss N then denied ever having said such a thing and explained it was only fair – as I'd had a lead role the previous year – to give other children in the class a chance to shine on stage. I have never understood this explanation. After all, do you prevent the fastest runner from winning the race two years in a row to give other kids a chance to win? Or is the smartest kid prevented from topping the class two years in a row to give others a go? No, it's only if you are good at drama that you have to share the limelight while at school.

My lack of height also contributed to another shortcoming (ha!) I had as a child at an Australian primary school: it emphasised just how completely woeful I was at any kind of sport. I couldn't run, jump or throw or catch a ball. Worse, I hated sport and still do. I cannot bear it when people wax lyrical about the wonderful things team sport does for kids. The only people who say so are those who are physically coordinated. Team sports enable a particularly smug kind of bullying when you are the kid that no-one wants to have on their team. And the shame attached to being a kid who is bad at sport is only made worse when well-meaning adults try to make amends. There is nothing more humiliating, after you have come stone-cold, motherless last in any kind of race – running, swimming, egg-and-spoon or sack – than to have some adult congratulate you by name for 'trying so hard' over a loudspeaker. All I wanted was for no-one to notice my failure. My mother – lousy at sport herself and with similar unhappy memories – always gave me a note excusing me from athletics and swimming carnivals.

The approved girls' sport at Chatswood Public was netball. I hate all sport but I reserve a special loathing for this ghastly game. I was subject to more relentless bullying (often disguised as 'helping') on the netball court than at any other time.

'Open your eyes when I throw the ball at you!' the other girls would yell at me, not realising that I was terrified of the bloody thing and closing my eyes and ducking was my instinctive reaction. Being yelled at didn't make me any braver, either. I knew I couldn't catch the bloody ball so it would likely hit me in the head if I wasn't careful – and those girls could throw a netball hard.

'You have Jane – we've got Heather!' the sporty girls would say when forced to pick a team. (Heather was another poor unfortunate uncoordinated misfit.) Oh, how I hated it and how I hated them. The smugness of those athletic schoolgirls set my teeth on edge. To this day, just the sight of a pleated netball skirt can make me feel nauseous.

Not to put too fine a point on it, I was a weird and unappealing child. Not only was I undersized and uncoordinated, I was mouthy and opinionated. I had a most unfortunate tendency to put my hand up in class and give my perspective on things. It was something that I was encouraged to do in the intellectual and argumentative atmosphere of my own home, but it was frowned upon everywhere else, even at school. I stubbornly resisted any attempts to get me to shut up or any attempt at improvement. Worse, I spoke like a grown-up, using – as I was told accusingly – 'big words'. You'd think this might have been encouraged in OC, but it wasn't; I think it was seen as showing off. I suspect being good at acting and performance was categorised in the same way.

I was also lazy, disorganised, scruffy and careless. My cardigan was always falling off my shoulders, my socks were always rolling down my ankles and my hair stuck up at odd angles. I had buckteeth. I was very unhappy about my lack of appeal. I knew I irritated people with my bumptiousness.

I wrote compositions for the fun of it but, far from impressing my teacher, she just saw this as another irritating attempt to get attention – as, I confess, it partly was. I volunteered to give a speech on Anzac Day. I was allowed to, but my pushiness met with disapproval. I wanted to be noticed and that drive in a girl was not seen as either acceptable or suitably modest. Girls who were neat, tidy, quiet and obedient – in front of adults, at least – were favoured. Their bookwork was always beautifully presented and their projects masterpieces of cleanliness and order. Mine were messy, untidy and often rushed.

This slapdash approach continued long after I left school. I remember helping my eldest – Polly – with one of her first school projects. I suppose she was about six or seven. It had to be on a sea creature. For reasons I cannot begin to fathom, Polly chose brain coral. At least we found a picture of said coral. We could not, however, find either a ruler or glue. In desperation, I mixed some flour and water into paste, just as my own similarly chaotic mother had done for me and my projects back in the day. I also copied her old trick of using the edge of a hardcover book to rule lines. We worked frantically on the damn thing for hours to no avail. It looked like a dog's breakfast by the time we had finished. It was due the next day, so what could we do? Polly handed it in. A few days later I was in Polly's classroom and saw that her brain coral project was proudly displayed on the back wall. It looked as bad as I had remembered it and the paste was starting to fail so all her pictures were slowly sliding down the cardboard. The other sea-creature projects displayed were computer-generated, neat as new pins and laminated to perfection. I had to ask the teacher about it.

'I notice you've got Polly's sea-creature project displayed on the wall.'

'Oh yes,' said Mrs Macdonald.

'I can't help wondering why,' I confessed.

'Well, she so obviously has done it all by herself.'

I stopped helping my daughters with their projects from that day on. I never did have any talent for them.

As it often is for misfit kids, my haven at school was the library. At Chatswood Public, it was run by Barbara Feinberg, mother of well-known novelist Anna Feinberg and now a successful novelist herself. Anna was in my year but not in my class. She was everything I admired and would never be: tall, athletic, popular and beautiful, with long curling black hair that was always neat. I don't think she ever addressed so much as a word to me in primary school, but I spent hours talking to her mother.

I escaped to the library whenever I could, knowing that I would receive a warm welcome. Barbara Feinberg encouraged my reading habit with all sorts of recommendations. I devoured the Anne of Green Gables books, the What Katy Did books, the Little Women books, *The Secret Garden*, *The Little Princess*, *Black Beauty*, *A Girl of the Limberlost*, *The Silver Sword*, the Heidi books and anything by Anya Seton, Catherine Gaskin or Mary Renault. I also tried more advanced authors – the Brontës, *Pride and Prejudice*, *Désirée* by Annemarie Selinko, *The Water Babies*, *Tales from Shakespeare*, *The Diary of Anne Frank* . . . to be honest, I have forgotten most of the books I read. I taught myself to speed-read without realising it. I didn't read word for word (I still don't, unless aloud) but swallowed the pages whole. I read long into the night. I was Jo March, Mary Lennox, Anne Frank, Anne Shirley, Désirée Clary, Jane Eyre (also plain and undersized) and Katherine Swynford, Duchess of Lancaster. I wasn't small and annoying when I read books, or bad at maths and sport. I wasn't 'me' at all.

three

One of the reasons supposedly 'gifted and talented' kids were sent to OC was so we could have an enriched education. As an adult, I have never been comfortable with that idea, particularly after my younger daughter, Charlotte, was accepted into OC at her primary school (not Chatswood but Artarmon). I resented some of the good stuff Charlotte got to do that Polly missed out on. I have never liked the idea of separating our kids into winners and losers, but when I was ten, I just went where I was sent. I certainly never gave my supposed advantages a second thought.

One of the ways we were being 'enriched' (apart from being obliged to learn a musical instrument) was with regular excursions. We went often to the Australian Museum, although all I remember was that we had to run about the museum finding answers to questions on gestetnered worksheets; it didn't feel all that enriching to me. What was really exciting was going on the annual excursion to Canberra. We travelled by bus and stayed overnight in a motel. The nice thing about that excursion was that it wasn't just for the OC kids. My class, 5N, was accompanied by our sister class, 5K, whose teacher was a man. In the way of schoolchildren (whether they have been designated as 'gifted and talented' or not), we decided that Miss N and Mr K were 'in love'. We had no actual evidence for this apart from the fact that he was a man and she was a woman (and a 'Miss') and they treated each other in a friendly manner. True or not, gossiping about our teachers made for a little subversive fun and allowed us to vent some of our spleen about being under their control.

The first evening, before dinner, all of us ten- and eleven-year-olds in 5N and 5K were playing in the motel car park. We were playing a game called 'Stuck in the Mud'. As events unfolded, it is clear we were also unsupervised.

'Stuck in the Mud' is a game of chasings where, if you were tagged, you had to freeze on the spot with your legs wide apart. The only way to get free was for someone on your team to crawl through your legs and so release you; hence, obviously, the metaphor of being 'stuck in the mud'. I quite liked this game because, while I was hopeless at chasing anyone, being small meant I was pretty good at slithering through people's legs. It was one of the few games where other kids actually wanted me on their team.

I was engaged in crawling through someone's legs when a cry went up from the other players.

'There's a car coming! There's a car coming!'

I have a distinct memory of looking up from my prone position and seeing a car driving through the car park. The picture that has imprinted itself on my brain is of the headlights – it was already dark – driving slowly through a crowd of children who are scattering in front of it. The car did not deflect from its trajectory, no matter who was in the way. It was heading directly towards me and the girl who was 'stuck in the mud'. We both hastened to get out of the way, but I tripped on her legs and fell backwards onto the bitumen.

The car rolled over the top of me. I still remember looking up at its black and greasy underside. I don't remember feeling much of anything as the world disappeared, just a kind of bewilderment that such a thing could be happening. Over the engine I could hear my schoolmates calling out in a panic.

'There's a girl underneath you! There's a girl underneath you!'

Then I heard the front tyres of the vehicle hit the kerb. The car stopped and I stared at the underside of the vehicle as it vibrated to the throb of the idling engine. Then the driver reversed, without moving the steering wheel, and the world came slowly back into view. I could see my schoolmates gathered on the kerb. Some of them were crying. Some had their eyes closed, perhaps in fear of what they might see. The car turned around and drove away into the Canberra night.

I was quite unhurt. The wheels of the car had not made contact with me. I was still lying on the ground in silent shock when Miss N and Mr K arrived. One of those smart kids had run off to fetch them.

Miss N helped me up and brushed me down.

'You're all right, you're not hurt. It's okay, nothing serious happened. It's okay.' She wasn't comforting me; there was irritation and alarm in her voice.

I felt a familiar pang of shame. Of course it would be me who was causing trouble and demanding attention – wasn't it always? I was still in a numb state of bewilderment. What had just happened? Had I really just been run over? By a car? I couldn't quite make sense of it.

The two teachers hurried me off to my allocated motel room. The kids sharing with me were the only other children allowed in. Then the teachers gave us the special privilege of watching the TV – something that had previously been explicitly forbidden. It was a TV with a meter – I had never seen one before nor have I seen one since – and I remember them loading it up with coins. Despite the shame I had felt at causing trouble, now I felt rather special and important. I was the centre of attention; in a very odd way, I was sort of a hero. I quite enjoyed the fuss.

What I did not think about at the time but certainly have since, particularly after having my own children, was why there was no follow-up. Who was that person who drove their car through a crowd of children in a motel car park, scattering them as they went? How could they actually run over a child and then just reverse off and drive away without stopping to see if I was all right? Why weren't the police called? I don't doubt for a second that quite a few of those gifted and talented kids had taken special note of the car's registration number, yet nothing was done. The adults in charge downplayed the event. Indeed, my parents were never officially told that it had happened. I suppose the teachers were frightened – they had left us unsupervised, after all – and so just wanted the whole thing to go away. And it was the way things were done around kids back then. If there were no visible signs of injury, better to pretend it hadn't happened. No-one – apart, perhaps, from the car's driver (was he or she mad? doped to the eyeballs? demented?) – actually meant me any harm.

When I returned from the excursion, my mother asked me if I had a good time. I told her that I had been run over. She gave a horrible little moan and I immediately felt awful. I had clearly upset her, and over nothing; after all – as the teachers had said – I was unhurt. I had absorbed the minimisation of the experience so effectively that I hastened to do the same thing for my mother. Nothing had happened, I reassured her, I was just fine. The car hadn't touched me. And since that was the era of never making a fuss, this was the last that was said about it. For a decade or two, anyway.

* * *

Of course, most of the games I remember playing had no such bizarre outcome. I have very vivid memories of the fun I had as a child in Frenchs Forest. There was a gang of us, all girls. Me and my sister Ann; Julie and Lynne Spilsted; Kim, who lived over Julie's back fence; and Mary-Ann Haydock, who was a few years older than we were but one of those lovely, motherly girls who liked playing with younger kids. Mary-Ann was an only child, while Julie, Lynne and Kim all had brothers. Ann and I, by this time, had our little brother Robert and our baby sister Ruth, but we certainly didn't waste any time playing with them. Us girls all lived within a block of one another on either side of Yarraman Avenue, a road that for many years remained unsealed. Next door to Julie, Lynne and Kim was a small patch of remnant bushland that became our playground.

There were bad things about being a child in the 1960s, but there were some wonderful things about it too. First among these was how much freer we were to roam and have adventures without the anxious and controlling presence of grown-ups. We built cubbies in that bush and explored every inch of it. We gave names to its prominent features – Spilsted Rocks and Caro Caves – and we wandered the neighbourhood at will. We walked for miles along the Pipeline (that's what we called it) eating lollies and talking. Nobody worried about us. No-one asked us where we were going or when we would be back or where we had been. When we were hungry or, in my case, when it got dark we came home. We were neglected, by modern standards, but it had its advantages.

When we weren't playing in the bush, we played in our backyards. We tied skipping ropes around our waists and one another, and then inched our way around the Spilsteds' paling fence, our toes clinging to the narrow bottom horizontal rail and our fingers to the top one. In our imaginations, we were climbing Mount Everest and we called out to each other about the wonderful sights we could see. On hot summer days we turned the Spilsteds' above-ground pool into a swirling whirlpool by running round and round and round. On Cracker Night (yep, it still existed) my mother built a bonfire with a proper Guy Fawkes and invited all the neighbours. The loud explosions that accompanied even many of the 'pretties' (what we called the purely decorative fireworks) may have driven the cowardly Caro kids into the house to cower under their bedcovers, but it was a grand occasion.

None of my siblings or I were physically very brave. It was another source of secret shame for me that I was often afraid to do things other kids my age took in their stride. But it wasn't just actual risk I was afraid of; I was at the mercy of my imagination too. One night we watched an episode of *Walt Disney Presents*. It related the legend of Ichabod Crane and the headless horseman. At one point, the show personified Death as a horseman in a black cloak on a rearing black horse. When the cloak fell away from Death's head, they used 1960s special effects to render a bizarre and chaotic explosion of colours and effects rather than a face, to an accompaniment of thunder, lightning and appropriately dissonant music. My brother, sisters and I dissolved into a shrieking mass of utter terror. None of us could sleep. I remember seeing the vision of the headless, faceless horseman every time I closed my eyes. Every shadow in my bedroom hid the spectre and I even got up to shove a chair against my wardrobe door in case Death was hiding in there. My poor mother was so infuriated by her four hysterical children she rang Channel Nine to complain about the unsuitability of such a program (*Walt Disney Presents*!) for children.

We were – all four of us – terrible cowards. But I was the most ashamed. I was the oldest. I ought to be the bravest.

All four of us sucked our thumbs. Shamefully (there's that word again), I sucked mine until I was nine. It is probably why I was so bucktoothed. I slept with a nightlight until I reached puberty.

I was (usually) braver in the daylight hours. On rainy days my all-girl gang and I repaired to the Haydocks' garage. Mary-Ann's mother had kept all her old dresses from the 1950s and we would raid the box they were kept in and play dress-ups for hours. We were queens, princesses, the little Goose Girl (Julie had a tantrum about not getting the part she wanted in that production, declaring, 'Well, I'll be the horse then, that gets its head chopped off!' – a remark that made us all, including Julie, laugh till we cried), movie stars and the characters in our favourite books. We were all readers and were obsessed with the Famous Five. When Julie and Lynne got a puppy they called him Timmy, after the dog in Enid Blyton's books. He turned out to be a bad-tempered cattle dog rather than a friendly golden retriever, but never mind.

We held a fete in our backyard at which we sold our old toys to other neighbourhood kids, and when they ran out of money we gave their money back so they could buy some more. The point of the fete was the game, not the money. We put on puppet shows. We giggled and squirmed over Mr Spilsted's collection of *Man* magazines that we found in the bottom of his wardrobe. We played Doctors and Nurses without anyone thinking we were perverted (apparently my mother overheard every word of one such game and just laughed her head off). We created societies (literary, dramatic, poetry) that had books of rules and fancy names but never lasted for more than a day. We squabbled (see the headless-horse anecdote above) and competed over ideas, stories and costumes, we had rivalries and jealousies and we were not always very nice to one another, but my overwhelming memory is of the enormous amount of fun we had.

We had an old gentleman's wardrobe in our spare room with odd-shaped, built-in compartments and boxes for storage. That became a mansion for our Barbie dolls, and we spent hours and hours decorating it with doilies and bobbins of thread and any odd but appropriately sized objects we found. *The Borrowers* was another favourite book; I suppose that wardrobe was the 1960s version of 'The Sims'. On my own, I wrote terrible, melodramatic stories and drew and drew and drew. I had a biscuit tin in which I kept my collection of paper dolls and the clothes I painstakingly designed, drew, coloured in and cut out for them to wear. That task could keep me busy and happy for hours. I was also a bookworm, famous for refusing to come out to play if I was absorbed in a particularly good story.

Even walking to and from school was an adventure. It was quite a long walk and I can remember us catching cicadas and Christmas beetles in the summer. Now I only ever see them in the country. Dogs could be a bother. No-one ever kept them behind fences or on leashes in the 60s and they'd chase cars and random children at will. The school playground was alive with dogs after recess and lunch, searching through the bins for leftover food. Their scavenging often resulted in overturned bins and a favourite punishment was to get us to clear up the mess they left. On our walk home from school we'd gossip and lolly-gag, and, again, no-one ever bothered very much if we were late.

When I moved from Frenchs Forest Public to Chatswood (Julie was accepted into OC too but decided not to go – which was quite normal in those days), I walked to the bus stop on my own. It wasn't as much fun as being with the rest of the kids, but I used to pass the time composing poems and stories in my head and writing them down once I arrived home. One of them – a school project called 'On Myself' – was published on the back page of *The Australian*. That was the one and only time my work has ever appeared in that publication.

On the way home from Chatswood, my friends and I would dawdle down Victoria Avenue from the school to the Forest Coach Lines bus stop near the station. Maybe my appetite was growing because I clearly remember we would buy two potato scallops for a cent from the fish-and-chip shop. Potato scallops were slices of potato covered in batter and deep-fried – bloody marvellous, they were. I used to smother them in vinegar and salt. We could also buy quite a decent-sized slab of dark or milk chocolate from the chocolate shop for about the same sum. They'd carve it off a big block – presumably made on the premises – with a guillotine, wrap it in tissue paper and you'd eat it almost like an ice-cream. My favourite was Barratt's liquorice sherbets, bought from the sweet shop; the lemon sherbet was wrapped in waxed paper and you sucked it up through a liquorice straw. We'd gorge on one or other of these treats, then we'd run full tilt for the bus home.

Once home, forget homework. I'd throw myself down on my belly in front of the TV. Like all children of the 1960s, TV played a very big part in my childhood. It was the era of the American sitcom with the explanatory opening song. To my shame, I can still sing all the words of the intro to my two favourite shows, *The Patty Duke Show* and *The Addams Family* (especially when drunk). I also loved *Bewitched* and *I Dream of Jeannie*, two programs that are particularly interesting in retrospect. They both featured lead female characters with special powers; Samantha Stephens was a witch and Jeannie Nelson was a genie. The point of both sitcoms was that their male protagonists – Samantha's husband Darren and Jeannie's 'master' Captain Nelson – spent their entire time trying to repress and control the women and stop them using their powers. I leave it to you, dear reader, to decide what the scriptwriters may have been picking up in the zeitgeist.

My younger siblings preferred *Gilligan's Island* and *The Brady Bunch*. From my lofty position as the eldest (but pretty quickly the shortest), I despised such puerile rubbish. I also adored *Doctor Who* with William Hartnell. In those early days of the series, the Doctor didn't just take the TARDIS through space and into the future but also into the past. Those were my favourite episodes. Yes, I loved the Daleks and the Cybermen, but it was the trips back into history that gripped my imagination. There was one storyline, however, that seared itself on my brain. It was 'The Celestial Toymaker'. The eerie and terrifying games that the Doctor and his companions were forced to play had me on the edge of my seat. I still remember a giant chessboard where one false move could bring disaster.

I also devoured *Lost in Space*, Looney Tunes cartoons, *Fractured Fairy Tales*, *Rocky and Bullwinkle* and *The Flintstones*. I spent many a Saturday afternoon watching the midday movie, but I drew the line at the Three Stooges or the Marx Brothers. That kind of physical comedy just made me squirm. In fact, I was so influenced by my copious consumption of afternoon television that when I was seven and my mother announced she was pregnant for the fourth time (to everyone's astonishment, not least her own), I imagined our family was going to be joined by a baby like Pebbles Flintstone or Bam-Bam Rubble. I was bitterly disappointed after I ran all the way home from school, knowing that my new baby sister Ruth would be home from hospital, to be greeted by a scrunched-up, motionless lump that did very little but eat, cry and poo. No cute 'goo goo ga ga' like Pebbles, or even a boisterous 'bam bam bam bam'. From memory, I hardly looked at her again for about eighteen months. I left her to my mother and made myself scarce.

I liked some Australian TV too. *The Magic Circle Club* and *Adventure Island* were favourites but we soon became addicted to *Bellbird* and *GTK*. My mother turned off the TV the minute *Bellbird* had finished and served dinner.

Though I didn't much like being a child – particularly at school – I loved the freedom I had with my friends and my parents. My parents were not authoritarian. My mother was laid-back and mostly good fun. She was firm about mealtimes and bedtimes (I drifted off to the theme music of *This Day Tonight*) but not much else. I was very close to my mother. I think that as she began to feel overwhelmed with the work of raising four children virtually on her own (my father was working long hours climbing the corporate ladder, so he wasn't around very much), she turned to me – as her eldest – for support.

I remember sitting at the dinner table one evening while my mother was serving strawberries for dessert. We all loved strawberries but they were very expensive in those days and, on the rare occasions they were served, my mother doled them out in strictly equal but miniscule quantities. My father might not have been around very much (he was never home in time for dinner during the week, for example) but his lively, straight-forward – sometimes to the point of rudeness – manner had rubbed off on us all. My mother counted out an equal number of strawberries for each of us (including cutting the last one into four) while my siblings were all yelling at her, 'Me first! Me first!' Suddenly, aged seven or eight, I had an epiphany. I saw how harried my mother looked and an idea dawned.

'I don't mind when I get served,' I said. My mother looked up at me with real gratitude and (of course) gave me my straw-berries first. My siblings just looked at me with disgust, for good reason; I was being both smug and manipulative. Perhaps this was when my family – as I experienced it – began to divide into two camps. By realising that I would benefit by making my life easier for my mother, I became aligned with my parents. My brother and sisters were aligned with one another.

four

I was four foot one when I started first form at the Forest High in 1969, the year I turned twelve, and the smallest uniform my mother could find for me was far too large. In those days, Forest High girls wore a pale green belted tunic over a short-sleeved white shirt in summer and a bottle-green serge version over a long-sleeved white shirt in the winter. It was the era of the miniskirt, so that belt came in very handy. When we left home in the morning our tunics were a suitably modest length, only to get hitched up the minute we were out of sight of our parents. The Forest High uniform of that era did not feature box pleats as so many others did. It had one pleat right down the front and it was de rigueur to obsessively fold and refold that one pleat continuously. Allowing it to billow out over your hips (as it was designed to do as the wearer developed curves) was to be terminally uncool. But curves were not something I had to worry about at that point in my life.

When I started at Forest High I was automatically put into 1A because I came from Chatswood OC and so was just assumed to be bright. Here I was reunited with Julie and some of my old Frenchs Forest Public friends, but most of the kids in the class were as new to me as I was to them. We spent our first day being introduced to our timetable and our teachers. At some point we went to our first science class in a proper science classroom. In those days (perhaps they are still like this), science classrooms didn't have rows of desks and chairs. They were furnished with large heavy tables with sinks in the centre. We sat around the tables facing the front of the class – two in the middle, two on each end – on high, square stools.

We all tumbled into this unfamiliar room and found places as near to our friends as possible. Once we were seated our teacher explained the class rules. One rule was that every time an adult entered we were to stand up quietly and courteously. As if on cue, the head science teacher (or science master, as he was called then) came through the doorway. We all dutifully got off our stools. Our teacher, Mrs Lesnie, who had turned to greet Mr Rogers, turned back to us with a smile. Then her smiled faded and she glared in my direction. Everyone was silent. Mrs Lesnie's stare grew more angry and her colour rose. Mr Rogers, too, was staring accusingly. I didn't dare look around but wondered what terrible thing someone behind me was doing.

Eventually, a furious Mrs Lesnie spoke. 'We are all waiting for YOU to stand up!' Her voice was trembling with rage and she was pointing directly at me; my legs were hidden by the heavy table.

'But I *am* standing up!'

* * *

We had moved house between primary and high school. My parents had decided to sell the modest weatherboard in Frenchs Forest and build a brick Habitat house in Terrey Hills. My father was moving rapidly up the corporate ladder at Reckitts. He was now the managing director of their subsidiary company, Samuel Taylor, makers of Mortein, Aerogard, Preen and Pure & Simple. As a result, despite the six of us all living on his one salary, financially we were a little better off. It would take a year to build the house on the block of land my parents had purchased so, in the meantime, we were renting a house on a six-and-a-half-acre block in Duffys Forest.

This meant I had to get up early to get the one school bus that travelled from semi-rural Wyong Road to Forest High, picking up kids from Terrey Hills and Belrose along the way. This area, jam-packed with new housing developments, was to be my teenage stomping ground, with occasional forays to the more established suburbs of Chatswood (for shopping) and Queenscliff, Long Reef and Harbord (for posing on towels in a bikini). Basically, I went where the buses went.

Leaving my old gang behind – even though I saw Julie and Kim every day at school – was a wrench, but the acreage that came with our rented house was a kids' paradise. We even had a muddy dam where we were allowed to swim – though perhaps we shouldn't have been. I took five-year-old Ruth to that dam one hot day. She had become a little more like Pebbles as she got older and I was now quite fond of her, albeit in a superior big-sister sort of way. When I dived into the muddy water, she was standing on the steep dam bank. When I surfaced – maybe five seconds later – she had disappeared. Panicking, I plunged my hands into the opaque water to try to find her. Immediately I felt a mass of hair, grabbed it and pulled hard. She came up, coughing and spluttering. She had tried to follow me into the water without realising how quickly and steeply the bank fell away under the surface. I never took her swimming in that dam again.

What I most liked to do on that bushy block of land was take my Barbie dolls and play quietly with them on my own. I knew it was shamefully babyish for a high school kid to still be playing with dolls and would have stoutly denied doing such a thing had anyone asked, but I loved using my Barbies to make up stories.

When I wasn't stealthily playing with my Barbies, there was a girl close to my own age who lived nearby – Lynne. Her family reminded me a bit of Kim's family. Both were dominated by the dark presence of a silent but frightening father. Not only was I scared of these men and avoided crossing paths with them as much as possible, I could see that their wives and children were also frightened. Kim's mother was forbidden to wear make-up and her movements were very restricted. Even then I knew this was wrong and disturbing. As Kim grew older, her father attempted to control his daughter's behaviour in the same way, never letting her go out and forbidding her to speak to boys. As Kim blossomed into a spectacularly beautiful young woman, he was fighting a losing battle. Kim's dad spent most of his time (I don't know if he had a job or not; I have a residual memory that he may have once been a policeman) sitting in a shed in their back garden – maybe it was an office. I still remember how chilled I felt if ever I sensed his eyes resting on me from the shed window through which he surveyed everything.

Lynne's father, whom I will call Mr F, had a similarly chilling effect. The family lived on a returned serviceman's block thanks to his war service, and tiptoed around him whenever he was present. They relaxed visibly whenever he left the room. Perhaps Mr F suffered from PTSD – who knows? Perhaps Kim's dad did too. So many men did in those days. It was a new experience for me, seeing cowed wives and children. No-one was afraid of my father, not even when he yelled at us to GET THE HELL OUT OF THE WAY or SHUT THE EFF UP if the cricket was on TV. My mother certainly never took a backward step where he (or anyone else) was concerned. When Dad started travelling a great deal as his career took off, leaving my mother to cope at home, she made no secret of how much she resented his absence. One day, in a fury, she made a sign and stuck it on our front lawn (this was back in Frenchs Forest). It read: MOTHER CARO'S BOARDING HOUSE. The neighbours thought it was hilarious and we kids were mortified. I am still not sure what my father thought.

Julie's dad wasn't scary either; he was distant and mostly absent, though friendly enough when he was around. But my father and Mr Spilsted were younger than Mr F and Kim's father and they'd never gone to war. My father had done a couple of years of National Service in the UK before he went to Cambridge, and told us many humorous stories about his career as Britain's most inept soldier, but he'd never raised a fist in anger. Nor had one been raised against him. He could be quite verbally aggressive, particularly during debates about ideas, but physical violence was alien to him.

Lynne, being less fortunately fathered, stayed out of the house as much as possible. She and I spent a lot of time in the Ku-ring-gai Chase National Park that surrounded Duffys Forest and Terrey Hills. We soon discovered that just over the back fence from Wyong Road was Waratah National Park, the home of Skippy the Bush Kangaroo. Following on from the phenomenal international success of *Skippy* the TV show, the producers had taken the set of the fictional Waratah National Park and turned it into a modest theme park devoted to the show. It was moderately popular at that time and cars queued up to enter most weekends. They had to pay a fee to see the sets, some of the many Skippys and enjoy a few carnival rides. We, however, could just climb over my back fence and mingle with the paying customers free of charge, which, as you can imagine, we often did.

* * *

By the end of 1969, we were finally able to move into our newly built house in Burraga Avenue in Terrey Hills, a few kilometres closer to civilisation. I was, however, still at the mercy of that one bus out of the place in the morning and that one bus back in the afternoon. Despite this drawback, I was much happier as a high school kid than I had ever been in primary school.

When I entered second form in 1970, I not only put the things of childhood behind me (bye-bye, Barbie), I also made a conscious effort to change the way I related to my peers. I now think the decision I made at thirteen to make myself more palatable to people of my own age was one of the most pivotal of my life.

I knew that I had annoyed my schoolmates at primary school, so I watched my peers at Forest High carefully. One of the advantages of the way public schools divide primary and secondary into completely different schools is that it gives kids the chance to reinvent themselves. I noticed that swearing and slang were important to my peers, so I took them up. I noticed that using big words was not helpful, so I stopped using them. I noticed that wearing my skirts short, my hair long and a boy (any boy) on my arm was approved of, so I adopted all three. I learnt to be (mildly) rebellious in class and by the time I was in third form (the equivalent of today's notorious Year 9) I had taken up smoking. I also noticed that to be accepted by the cool kids (Julie was cool, so that helped) I had to be seen as no threat. So as not to threaten anyone else's position in the gang, I had to arrive with my own best friend. Fortunately I met another minor misfit like me – Becky M – and we bonded over our secret enjoyment of good books, politics and issues of social justice. Together we got to hang with the cool crowd and, even if our status in that group was fairly lowly, it still gave us higher status than most of the rest of our peers. I also genuinely liked most of the cool crowd. They were interesting, they were adventurous, they were not compliant and they had more fun.

There may be some people reading about my deliberate transformation with horror and seeing it as confirming everything they ever feared about public schools – the whole 'hanging out with the wrong crowd' paranoia. They may see what I did as dumbing myself down. But I disagree. My successful reinvention of myself (helped by the fact I developed the generous tits I still carry around today and the tiny waist and slim hips that I no longer do) taught me something very profound. It taught me how to adapt my communication style to my audience.

In the early 1970s, the so-called youthquake was well underway. Young people, particularly uni students, were demonstrating – usually against the Vietnam War – at the drop of a hat (not that anyone wore one of those anymore). School students were not left out. I remember the controversial *Little Red Schoolbook* being handed out to us as we poured out of school at 3 pm one day. It was all about sex and so had scandalised the media, the church and conservative politicians everywhere. The fact they wanted it banned made us all the more determined to read every word. For some of my peers, it may well have been the only book they actually read cover to cover. Then some subversive group somewhere organised a school students' strike. I can't remember what we were meant to be striking about, but Becky and I were determined to attend.

The teachers at school had threatened us all with dire consequences if any of us dared to skip out of school and meet at Sydney's Town Hall steps as requested. Becky and I didn't care; after rollcall we went straight out the front gate and caught a bus to Chatswood then a train to Town Hall and arrived just in time for the demo. I remember we were led in a chant:

'What do we want?'

'Students' rights!'

'When do we want them?'

'Now!'

What those rights were I no longer recall. If I ever knew. But that was beside the point. It was subversive. It was cool. It was fun.

At one point, standing on those steps in my school uniform, I saw a TV camera pointed in my direction. I was smoking a cigarette at the time so, quite deliberately, I took a deep drag and blew the smoke all over the camera lens.

That night, my family and I were sitting around the table having dinner. As far as my parents knew, I had just finished a perfectly ordinary, uneventful day at school. The TV news was on and suddenly, as the announcer talked about that day's school students' strike, the screen filled with smoke. As it cleared, there I was, insolently blowing cigarette smoke at the camera. Talk about sprung.

I got into trouble, of course, although my parents were more concerned about me smoking and wagging school than attending the strike. The school huffed and puffed (ahem) at us for a bit, but I don't remember too many of the aforementioned dire consequences. The unforeseen benefit of this fifteen seconds (probably literally) of notoriety was what it did for my image with my peers. Just for a few days – a week at most – Becky and I were seriously cool.

I had begun to learn how to use my uncool interest in politics, ideas and things of the mind in a way that did not annoy my peers. I had learnt how to say what I wanted to say, but to say it in a way that enabled my audience to hear it. I didn't stop reading voraciously. I didn't forget my advanced vocabulary – indeed, I expanded it, though not perhaps with language that would have been approved of by adults – and I didn't even stop participating in class. I just learnt how to be myself without getting up the nose of my peers (though I may have been correspondingly more likely to get up the nose of my teachers). It was humbling, it was necessary, and I use the skills I acquired from that conscious makeover to this day.

By the end of my second year at high school, I had grown breasts and developed curves. I had also grown eight inches in a year. There was even some hope I might make five foot. I also, probably not coincidentally, had my first steady boyfriend. My tenacious flirting with my cousin Nick's Barker College friends (Barker was a posh private boys' school on the Upper North Shore) eventually paid off. David was Nick's best mate and he was sweet, dark, quite nice-looking and tall – very tall. In fact, he was well over six foot. To kiss we either had to sit down or lie down (don't panic, it was all very innocent). We must have looked very funny together, but at the height of our romance we neither noticed nor cared. We went to the pictures (we saw

Woodstock, if memory serves me correctly) and spent a lot of time wandering around Paddy's Markets buying cheap scarves and other hippie shit. Paddy's Markets were in Haymarket in those days, so I'd meet David, who lived in Pymble, on the train at Chatswood and we'd head into the city from there. We had no money but lots of time as the summer holidays stretched before us. It was when the holidays ended that our romance hit a snag.

David was a Barker boy. This meant that the week before the school term started (he was going into fourth form, I was going into third), he had to get his hair cut. This was the 1970s. It was impossible for a socially ambitious girl to be seen going out with a boy with (shudder) short hair. I struggled to push my shame aside but I simply could not do it. The short hair was a deal-breaker. Sweet guy that he was, I broke his heart, breaking up with him by phone two weeks after the visit to the barber. If there had been text messages in those days, I would have used one to dump him. I knew my reasons were shallow, immature and vain, and I was ashamed of them – but not quite as ashamed as I was to be seen with a gangly boy sporting a short back and sides. I returned to school that summer an older but no wiser woman. I was also on the hunt for another boyfriend.

The year of 1971 was a year of triumph. I had left that dorky, bucktoothed (I had braces), big-word-using, show-off far behind. By the end of the year I'd had three steady boyfriends. There was poor David, of course, and two Chris's – one another Barker boy and one an eighteen-year-old who played drums in a rock band. Not a famous rock band, I hasten to add, but any drummer was cool in the 70s. He dropped me, which was a first, and I cried – from the humiliation more than anything. It was the hunt I liked most; the thrill of wondering whether he would or wouldn't succumb to my charms. I was ruthlessly realistic, too. I knew my limits. I don't know where I got this pragmatism from – maybe my mother, maybe my phlegmatic northern English cultural heritage – but I set my sights on the boys I thought I could get. There were lots of girls who were more glamorous than I was and I left the really gorgeous guys to them. That was another useful lesson I learnt: the secret to success lies in having realistic expectations. I had friends – my Terrey Hills next-door neighbour Margaret, in particular – who ate their heart out over boys who were out of reach. Cold-hearted little monster that I was, I could see no use or joy in that. If a boy I liked didn't appear to like me, I moved on.

The next few years of high school were a veritable blizzard of steady boyfriends. (I know, I'm bragging, but it was a long time ago.) I remember Jim, Robert, a stunningly good-looking but utterly corrupt hippy called Barry and Brenton. In between there were flirtations, snatched kisses and boys I held relentlessly at arm's length. Despite my best intentions not to reach too high, I also had some unrequited crushes. I remember one in particular. Margaret from next door had a sister who was a year younger. Beth was slender, sexy and effortlessly popular. Future cartoonist and painter Bill Leak was in the year above me and already a star. His caricatures of our teachers decorated our annual school magazine. He was also a wonderful jazz pianist and a brilliant painter of portraits. His major work for

HSC art was a painting of his English class, with every one of the students accurately depicted. He was very attracted to my charismatic next-door neighbour and offered to paint her portrait. I had a crush on Bill and so found excuses to go next door whenever she was sitting for him – just to hang out, you understand. How I yearned for him to notice me and offer to paint my portrait. I don't think he so much as looked in my direction.

Beth liked Bill well enough and she certainly liked having her portrait painted (I wonder if she still has it), but there was another guy hanging around that she liked even better. His name was Tim Farriss and he and his best friend Kirk Pengilly were in her year. In the end, Beth went out with Tim. Eventually they were married. He went on to world fame as the lead guitarist in INXS. To both their considerable credit, they are still together after all this time. There can't be many fifteen-year-olds who get to choose between talents like Bill Leak and Tim Farriss.

Decades later, Bill, by this time a famous newspaper cartoonist, was a speaker at the (now late and lamented) Caxton newspaper advertising awards. I went up to him after his excellent keynote and reintroduced myself. He vaguely recalled me from school. As he knew no-one and I knew most people, he hung out with me a fair bit throughout the weekend conference. An ad I wrote won a Caxton award at the Saturday night dinner and I was thrilled that this had occurred in front of Bill. (What is it about the insecurity of your school days that stays with you forever, no matter how confident you may become in the wider world?) The celebrations after the dinner went on into the small hours and I remember drunkenly confiding in Bill that I'd had a crush on him when I was sixteen. He had the grace to respond by saying that he'd wished he'd known because he remembered me being quite attractive back then. Well, what else could the poor bastard say?

Later still in that raucous evening – or early morning, as it had become – we were all much the worse for wear and getting a little maudlin. Bill turned to me and said, 'I'm glad I didn't know you were interested in me back then because I would have broken your heart.' Drunk as I was, I remember feeling a little put out by his presumption. How did he know I wouldn't have broken his?

five

I was only fifteen but it was a great party. I had been drinking large quantities of a deceptively sweet concoction called Blackberry Nip. So much so, that when I went to the bathroom the sink seemed to rise up to meet me, rather than the other way around. A friend's parents had gone away for the weekend and she and her older brothers and sisters were taking advantage of their absence to throw a party. Most of the guests were much older than we were and I had only managed to wangle permission to go to the party by concealing the fact that any such event was planned and by implying that I was merely spending the night at my friend's house appropriately supervised by her parents.

I spent my adolescence blithely and convincingly lying to my parents. As far as they knew I spent a great deal of time at a church-run coffee shop called Pact Folk. In reality, I only went once to provide myself with the accurate details I needed to compose a convincing alibi. I then roamed the pubs and unsupervised parties of the hinterland of the northern beaches. Like many of my friends, when fully made-up and wearing the platform shoes that were fashionable then I could pass for a much older girl. The generous breasts helped considerably. True to my natural cowardice, however, when an older boyfriend took me to the local pub (the President in Belrose) I sat in the car and he ferried vodka and oranges out to me. Just the possibility of being asked my age terrified me. I needn't have been so nervous. Underage friends of mine regularly ran into some of our teachers at the President, particularly on Friday nights, and the teachers' response was to shout their students a drink. In these more puritanical times, a teacher would get the sack for such behaviour, or, at the very least be publicly humiliated on Facebook.

But, to return to my pubescent friends and myself, we were not nearly as sophisticated as we seemed. Maybe that was why I was so moved by Mena Suvari's character – Angela Hayes – in the film *American Beauty*. She conveyed the same false worldliness that my friends and I did back in the 70s. Like Angela, we were naive and innocent beneath the dirty talk. Our determination to appear older than our age led us into many situations that we could not handle. I was more fortunate than most, mainly because, beneath my bluster and big-talk, I was cautious. As with the vodka and oranges downed in the car, if there was a chance of getting caught, I found a way not to be there. That's why I was quite happy at the unsupervised party, downing Blackberry Nip. I knew there was little or no chance I would get caught.

In the small hours of the morning, somewhat the worse for wear, my friend and I went to bed. We were sharing a double bed and, moments after we had switched out the light, one of my friend's sister's uni friends entered the room. He made a beeline for my friend. In hushed tones, he began to try to persuade my friend to have sex with him. Paralysed by embarrassment and fear (this was way too grown up for me), I did the only thing I could think to do and lay absolutely still, pretending that I was either asleep or unconscious. I listened as he wheedled and took all sorts of liberties. My friend tried weakly to resist but, perhaps simply to be rid of him, or maybe because she wanted to – I don't know – she gave in and the two of them had sex while I lay right next to them. It wasn't erotic. It wasn't remotely fun or exciting. It was terrifying and mortifying.

The next morning, I was furious with my friend but far too self-conscious to let her know that I had been awake and fully aware of everything. Now, as a grown woman, I look back on that memory and wonder if I was the observer of a rape. That man, so much older than my friend, would not take no for an answer and – from what I overheard – she appeared to feel that it was easier to give in to him than cause a scene. It never crossed my mind to reveal that I was awake and so get rid of him. I wish I had. What kind of a man creeps into a teenage girl's bedroom and pushes his advantage in that way? And yet we both accepted it at the time as almost reasonable and it was her I was angry with afterwards, not him. If he had pushed his luck with me, would I have caused a scene? I hope so, but he didn't, I did not know him, he was not a friend of an admired older sister and I gathered – from some of what they whispered to one another – that this may even have happened before. It is also interesting that my presence did not deter him. I was clearly no threat. Maybe it even added an extra thrill.

Girls were then – and many still are – very vulnerable to predatory men. Less obsessively protected than their mothers had been but without permission to stand up for themselves, many of my friends had sexual experiences they did not want. They would not have identified them as rape and they universally took the blame for the encounters. If sex went wrong, they always saw it as their own fault. We really had bought the idea that it was up to us to control men – and if we couldn't, the failure was ours.

I can only recall one friend who actually used that word – rape – to describe her experience. Sue had strict parents who would not let her go out with her friends in the evenings. She quickly found a way around their rules: she went to bed at the appointed time then climbed out her window. One night, while her parents believed her to be safely tucked up in bed, she was brutally raped. She then made her way home and climbed back into her pyjamas and into her bed. She got up the next morning as if nothing had happened, saying nothing to her parents. She was convinced that, far from helping and supporting their daughter, her parents would blame and despise her if they knew what had happened. Her school friends were the only people she felt able to confide in.

I now suspect that many young women, throughout the generations, have had similar experiences. Thanks to the pill, which we all went on around the age of sixteen (the age when the doctor was no longer obliged to inform your parents), my generation of young women were the first to have a pretty good chance of avoiding the complication of pregnancy. But contraception – even when available, even when it's the best so far invented – can fail and many of my school friends had to arrange a discreet termination, sometimes with the help of their parents, sometimes without it. In fact, unlike their older sisters and aunts (and mothers and grandmothers, if any of them had told us the truth), not one of my friends had a child while a teenager. The spectre of the unmarried mother (as they were then called) was fading fast, thanks to the pill, but it had not receded altogether.

And despite the women's lib movement that was in full cry in my later years of high school, radicalising our mothers and our female teachers, we were still sometimes threatened with the charge of being 'in moral danger', which meant being sent to a girls' home. We didn't actually know what girls' homes were like, but we knew they were where bad girls were sent – girls who had shamed their family and were destined for horrible, sordid lives on the edges of respectable society. It is, of course, most likely that the term 'girls' home' was a euphemism for 'home for unmarried mothers', where they worked you to death in the laundry until you gave birth, then sedated you and took your baby away. Or maybe it referred to reform school. It didn't matter; we were just scared of them.

What 'in moral danger' actually meant was never quite specified either, but we all believed it had something to do with losing your virginity. Such threats didn't stop us having sex, of course. They just stopped us telling anyone about it and so getting any helpful advice and guidance. The male equivalent (apparently boys couldn't be 'in moral danger') was to be charged with carnal knowledge – which meant having sex with an underage girl. A boy I knew vaguely who went to a Catholic boys' school was rumoured to have been charged with this offence. True or not, we immediately saw him as Frenchs Forest's own Lord Byron. It goes without saying that any girl involved in such a scandal would have been the opposite of glamorous. She would have been despised as a slut.

As fast as sex was changing – or at least the accessibility and safety of it (remember we were the generation with the pill but without AIDS) – so were sex roles. When I was young, hair was the symbol of that change. Many young men had beards, but it was the flowing long hair they cultivated that caused the most trouble. In the 1970s, gender stereotypes were smashed. Boys and girls dressed alike in high-waisted jeans that were skin-tight over our bums and bellies and wide and flaring from upper thigh to some inches past our feet. We all wore huge platform shoes and our hair long. Men of the older generation were horrified by this (though some joined in with a fashion for mutton-chops) and complained that you could no longer tell boys from girls. Young men of my generation were often told to 'get a haircut, son' by strangers.

I have never thought that fashion is accidental. What is popular at a particular time appeals because it expresses something of importance. For us, it was the blurring of the previously rigid differences between men and women. It brought more physical, sexual and intellectual freedom for women and more emotional freedom for men.

The other symbol of rebellion for my generation was illegal drugs. Many of my friends experimented with all sorts of substances. To my secret shame, I was afraid of putting unknown chemicals into my body. I avoided everything except alcohol and nicotine while trying (no doubt unsuccessfully) not to appear uncool or (insult of insults) 'straight'.

When I turned fifteen, Becky's parents were away from home so a few of us gathered there, ostensibly to celebrate my birthday. It was really an excuse to muck up without our parents. Becky's older brother, who was also my boyfriend at the time, had some marijuana. I had smoked it a few times without any discernible effect and said so. Jim and Becky decided it was time to get me properly stoned. They packed a pipe with some dope and gave it to me. I dragged away at it and then, because I was claiming I couldn't actually suck up much smoke because it was so tightly packed, Jim blew down the pipe as I sucked on it. Whoa! That worked all right and I spun out of control. I don't remember much about the experience except that my heart was racing and I felt so dizzy with anxiety and fear I wondered if I might die. I was also verbalising these feelings at a million miles an hour and I vividly remember Jim, Becky and the rest of the crowd rolling about laughing at my motor-mouthed, hypercharged paranoia. I don't blame them. They were all stoned too and all they had meant to do was include me in the good time they were having. How were they to know that my response to marijuana would be to have a full-scale panic attack? And there was an upside: it put me off the stuff for life.

My friends were much less cautious than me. Forest High had been built in the early 1960s in response to the baby boom and the burgeoning development of suburbs like Frenchs Forest, Belrose and Terrey Hills. We used to call the large intersection between Forest Way and the Wakehurst Parkway 'the blinking light' because it was literally the only traffic light in the suburb. Since its inception, Forest High, now overflowing with 1300 students, had had a tradition of annual school trips. My year – the class of '74 – had the honour (?) of behaving so badly that we ended two of those annual excursions forever. I don't think the class of '75 ever forgave us.

The first trip was to Jindabyne National Fitness Camp, organised by the most wonderful and long-suffering science teacher. On the way to the camp by bus, we stopped at a petrol station and somehow eleven cigarette lighters were stolen. I was not involved; not because I can claim any moral superiority, but because of my perennial fear of getting caught. The lighters weren't stolen for any good reason. They were nicked because they could be and because it was seen as an anti-authoritarian lark – a kind of middle-class adolescent machismo. Given that we were very fond of our teacher, we were soon very sorry for what we had done. After the humiliation of the police being called and our rooms at the National Fitness Camp being searched (the police failed to find a single lighter – perhaps some of us had potential as future criminals), we guiltily gathered all the contraband and returned it to our teacher with apologies.

It was too late, however. Forest High would not be welcome in Jindabyne again.

The second trip, in fourth form, was to the snow, a celebrated junket that was much anticipated. On our first night, the teachers took us to see a double bill at the Cooma cinema, which was screening *Count Yorga, Vampire* and *Psycho*. It was the days of horror movies and with no internet and usually only one TV per household – invariably dominated by Dad – teenagers flocked to the cinema and that hotbed of steamy sexual encounters, the drive-in. (There was a Skyline Drive-In at Frenchs Forest for years. I remember it with great affection.) That night in Cooma, things were much more innocent. We delightedly screamed ourselves hoarse.

The next night, no activity had been organised, and a bunch of the super-cool girls decided it would be a really terrific opportunity to drop some acid (LSD). This might have gone undiscovered if they had been the only students involved, but for some reason a rather straitlaced young woman decided this was the night she should kick over the traces and drop some acid too. As there is nothing those who use drugs like better than other people using them too, her participation was welcomed. It was a delightful scandal for those of us who were in the know. We whispered and giggled as our friends – whom we were both shocked and impressed by – confused our teachers and the students not in on the secret with their odd behaviour. Nothing terrible happened and by the next morning the young women involved had slept off the chemicals and the excursion went on as normal.

Unfortunately, on our return to school, the straitlaced young woman was overcome by an attack of conscience. Breaking the unspoken rule of the Australian school students' code, she told her mother what she and the other girls had done. Worse, she named names. Her mother marched up to the school and all hell broke loose. Anyone who had shared a motel room with any of the named culprits was hauled into the deputy principal's office and interrogated. To a girl, they kept mum. Then the authorities tried a different tactic, interviewing the prefects and other goody-two-shoes who had been on the excursion. They also kept their mouths shut. It seemed that none of us knew anything. None of us had seen anything. It was all news to us. I say 'us', but I was not interviewed. I had not shared a room with any of the accused and I was neither a prefect nor a goody-goody, so I was left alone. Had I been interrogated, I would have kept my mouth shut. Coward I might have been, but idiot I was not.

Unable to prove their case, the school had to content itself with hounding the girls at the centre of the scandal, dragging them in front of the deputy for any minor infringement. Two of them left school at the end of fourth form. Two others stubbornly refused to give up their dreams of gaining their HSC. I still remember seeing them responding wearily when called out of class for yet another upbraiding as late as halfway through fifth form. Eventually, the school administration got bored and the scandal was allowed to die. Sadly for the year groups who followed us, there were no more excursions to the snow.

The young woman who had blown the whistle never recovered her status. No-one was actively mean to her, I am pleased to say, but the stink of her betrayal clung to her until we all finished school. I feel sorry for her now. Presumably she was working through something very complex that she – like the rest of us – was just too young to handle. The pity is that two of our school friends paid a high price for her emotional problems and, of course, their own stupidity. They lost their chance for a higher school certificate. One of the girls bullied out of the school (by the teachers, I might add) had been at OC with me. She was a very bright girl. Someone ought to have tried to hold on to her. I think they would try much harder now.

Despite (or perhaps because of) the various scandals, I was very happy at Forest High. I had friends. I had boyfriends. I felt that I had finally learnt to fit in. I didn't do brilliantly at school academically – except at English – but I felt safe and accepted as a teenager in a way I never had as a child.

six

I did well enough at school to get into arts at Macquarie Uni. While a Bachelor of Arts was not my first choice of degree, I didn't get an offer to study social work at Sydney Uni in the first round. At first I was disappointed but then got excited about the range of subjects I could choose at Macquarie. Just as I started to make my subject selection, I got a second-round offer from Sydney Uni. I thought about it for a day or two and then – probably to the long-term benefit of all concerned, particularly any future clients – decided I'd stick with the arts degree. My total HSC mark was not spectacular, but my English mark was top-notch and I had noticed that one of the prerequisites for many second-year English literature subjects at Macquarie was a nine-decile HSC result in English. I made up my mind to skip English 101 and go straight to the much more exciting second-year subjects.

In the New South Wales school year, there is a long break between the end of the HSC and the start of university, so my friends Di and Leanne and I had decided to take a trip around Australia. We intended to stay at youth hostels in Melbourne, country Victoria, Adelaide, Victor Harbor and Perth, and booked our travel (plane, bus and train) and accommodation accordingly. My parents were going to Melbourne at the same time – probably to watch the cricket – and agreed to drive the three of us down so we could start our great adventure. I was as excited as my friends as we planned, organised and booked our trip. I felt grown-up and independent – even a bit sophisticated. I could not have been more deluded.

We interrupted the drive from Sydney to Melbourne at a motel along the way and, for the first time in my life, I simply could not sleep. In the room we shared Di, Lee and I had pushed the twin beds together for the three of us, and as I tossed and turned I tried to tell myself it was discomfort that was keeping me awake. To be honest, I had no idea what was wrong with me. I was simply awake and oddly unhappy. I knew I should be excited, but that was not what this unpleasant and unfamiliar feeling seemed to be about. What my disturbed state was saying, shamefully, was that I wanted to go home.

The next day I was tired, of course, and uneasy, but I kept my feelings to myself. The closer we got to Melbourne, a city I had never visited before, the more uncomfortable I felt. When we arrived at the youth hostel, my misery intensified. In those days – this was late 1974 – the Melbourne Youth Hostel doubled as a boarding house for down-and-outs. It was sleazy, dirty and very rundown. There were tragic-looking old people shuffling about its decrepit corridors; most of them seemed to be heavily medicated. The communal bathrooms were filthy, the floors covered in slime. That's my memory of it, anyway, and we certainly wore our thongs in the shower.

I was a nice, naive seventeen-year-old North Shore girl, and the place scared the shit out of me. When my parents drove away, I couldn't contain my feelings any longer. To the horror of my friends, I burst into desperate tears. The only word I could find to describe my inner turmoil was 'homesick'. How pathetic, how weak, how babyish! My friends tried to comfort me, but I could see that they were as bewildered by the depth of my misery as I was. And I was devastated. I found a public phone and called my parents at the hotel where they were staying. I went to see them, sobbing my heart out. But I could see that their reaction was very like that of my friends. What did I have to be homesick about?

'But you've been planning this trip for months,' my mother said.

'And you were so excited about it,' my father added.

'I know,' I said miserably. I didn't blame them for being perplexed. I was too.

'You've known Di and Lee since primary school.'

I nodded, but the tears kept falling.

'There's nothing to be afraid of.'

'I know that, but it doesn't help!' I wailed.

'You say you didn't sleep very well last night?'

I nodded again and blew my nose.

'I bet that's it!' My mother sounded pleased to have hit on an answer. 'You're just overtired. You'll feel much better after a good night's sleep.' This was my mother's favourite explanation for any irrational display of emotion ever since I had been a child. I was just tired. I would be better in the morning.

Except this time, I wasn't.

I could understand why they didn't take my distress seriously. I could also understand their determination not to rescue me and let me off the hook. This trip away was a rite of passage, a step towards independence and growing up, and they weren't going to let me fall at the first hurdle. I understand their feelings very well because I went through the same thing with my own elder daughter when she headed off to work as an au pair in New York during her gap year between school and university.

Like me, she experienced a storm of anxiety and homesickness once she arrived. Like my parents, I was determined not to let her give in to it. Also like my parents, I dreaded the nightly phone call she made from New York in which she sobbed out her homesickness over the phone. I dreaded it because I hated to hear her in such distress but also because I knew that there was nothing I could do to save her from it. Pain is part of life. As her parent, I was luckier than my parents were with me – thanks to Paris Hilton.

At eighteen, Polly was a Paris Hilton tragic and Janet (Polly's American host) saw an ad in the paper announcing that Paris was launching a perfume at Macy's. She encouraged Polly to go along. Polly was reluctant, not feeling like doing much of anything, but she allowed herself to be cajoled. Having made her way across town, she waited in line at the department store to get her newly purchased bottle of (disgusting) perfume signed.

'Who shall I sign it to?' said a fragrant Paris.

'Polly.'

Paris looked up. 'You're Australian!' she said, with real pleasure.

'Yes,' replied Polly, surprised that Paris had recognised her accent so easily. Most Americans thought she was English or South African.

'I love Australians!' said Paris, smiling warmly at Polly. 'And I love your outfit!'

By this time Polly was glowing but aware that the line of girls behind her was growing restless. She took back her perfume and indicated she'd better move on.

'See ya, Sexy!' Paris called after her.

That night's phone call was bubbly and excited, and from that moment on Polly loved New York. She even stopped calling us so often. We were her boring old parents again, just as we should be. To this day, I will not countenance a nasty word about Paris Hilton.

Unfortunately, back in 1974, neither my parents nor I were to be rescued so easily.

As I sobbed out my misery in my parent's Melbourne hotel room, I thought they were ashamed of me. Maybe they were, or maybe they just felt as I did when Polly rang in misery thirty years later. I wasn't ashamed of her. How could I be? I knew exactly what she was going through. Maybe it wasn't Andy and Kate who were ashamed of me; maybe it was me who was ashamed of myself. I had been brought up to admire strength and despise weakness, and I felt that I was being weak. I now think I confused weakness with vulnerability, and the two are not the same.

After our unsatisfactory conversation, I gathered my courage (never very robust) and headed back to the hostel. While I was out being an overgrown baby, Di and Lee had met some of the other young people who were staying in the place. They were gathered in someone's room smoking spliffs. I knew that wouldn't help me; my only experience with being stoned had led to a major panic attack (not that I used those words to describe it at the time) and I was exhausted. I left my friends to it and went to bed in the room we shared. There, I sobbed myself to sleep. Some time later I woke to a loud banging on the door. I had been so deeply asleep that my friends' initial quiet knocks had failed to rouse me. They had to wake the whole building to get me to unlock the door. My sense of shame increased.

I persevered with the trip, hating every minute of it, only holding myself together by ringing my parents daily to sob out my misery. I felt unanchored, adrift and irrationally afraid. I didn't know what I was so miserable about. I didn't understand why I couldn't pull myself together and enjoy the trip we had planned for so long. I felt sorry for my friends, who had to drag a wet blanket around with them from place to place. They were kind enough but I was spoiling their fun. If I had been them, I would have been furious. I decided that I would stick the trip out until we got to Victor Harbor and then I would return to Adelaide to fly back to Sydney. I urged Di and Lee to go on to Perth without me. They refused. They would cut their trip short and come home early too. I felt even worse.

Our next hostel was in a small town some fifty miles out of central Melbourne but, for the life of me, I can no longer remember where it was. I remember the hostel was on a semi-rural block with chickens, dogs and many cats, and that I slept on an old feather mattress on an old iron bedstead. It was soft and lumpy and squeaked alarmingly every time I rolled over, but it was also strangely comfortable and – most importantly at that moment – comforting. There was something old-fashioned and homey about the entire place. It was like stepping back in time.

On the drive there, however (I think some friends gave us a lift but, once again, my memory draws a blank – perhaps I was too caught up with my own internalised misery), I suffered a further humiliation. I have never had much spatial intelligence (we can argue later about what kind of intelligences I may actually possess), but for some reason I was charged with reading the map. It took me a while but, looking from the road to the map and back again, I realised something was not quite right.

'I think we might be going in the wrong direction,' I ventured.

'What? Don't be ridiculous!'

'Well, we're not passing any of the places we should be passing if we were going the right way.'

'You're joking!'

'I wish I was. But I think we may have turned right a while back when we should have turned left.'

My companions all turned to glare at me – even our driver, although he only glanced around quickly, thank goodness. Then someone impatiently took the map from me and took over the navigation. It turned out I was right, but it didn't matter; I had proved incompetent even at this simple task.

We did have some good times. We joined Julie and some other school friends in Croydon, an outer suburb 27 kilometres east of Melbourne, where the jazz festival was being held. They were with a gaggle of boys and girls, most of whom we did not know. The festival was fun and it was a relief to stay in a modest but clean motel room rather than the sleazy, slimy hostel in Melbourne. We also got up to some mischief. Some of the boys decided to streak (it *was* the 70s) and we decorated them using my Mary Quant make-up crayons, which, for some absurd reason, made me feel I had at least contributed something. When we parted company, we discovered that Julie and some of the others would be in Adelaide at the same time as us and we gave them the address of our hostel.

I cheered up the further we got from Melbourne, but I also came down with a hideous cold. That's when the rules at youth hostels added to my sense of being cut adrift. Youth hostels kick you out at 9 am and don't let you back in until 5 pm. I took myself off to a GP. He listened to my tale of woe and my chest and gave me a massive dose of intravenous penicillin. The cold dried up in no time.

Our last night was spent at a hostel in the Adelaide Hills; we were due to fly home the next day. We had intended to take a bus to Adelaide from Victor Harbor but had met a young man who offered to drive us instead. Di and Lee were very keen. I suspected Di fancied him. When I saw his car – a weird hybrid between a Mini Moke and a jeep that looked distinctly homemade – my anxiety intensified. No way was I going to get into that car. I was absolutely convinced that we would have a car accident and be killed. But Di and Lee were determined and we had missed the bus. I already felt guilty about spoiling their holiday. As the smallest – and perhaps as an act of understandable revenge on the part of my long-suffering travelling companions – I had to lie on a pile of filthy mattresses in the back (I suspect our driver lived in that car) while they got to sit in the front. Along the way, my companions happily rolled a joint and shared it between them. I, of course, refused.

Not far from our destination, we had the car accident I had prophesied. The car was badly damaged but all of us – even me, lying in the back – were completely unhurt. As we climbed out of the vehicle, Di gave me a look of thunder and hissed, 'Don't! You! Say! A! Word!'

I didn't.

The police arrived. By some miracle – I don't remember how; perhaps the Moke-jeep was still drivable – the car made it to the car park of the police station. There (perhaps because of the appearance of our driver and the mess inside the car), it was searched and our driver's drug stash – cunningly hidden in the glove compartment – was discovered.

Now it was my turn to give my companions a look of thunder. I didn't even smoke dope and I was about to get a criminal record because my friends had persuaded me to accept a lift with a handsome dropkick! It was, however, strangely comforting to be the victim of their behaviour for once, rather than the other way around.

The cops interviewed each of us one by one. We all denied knowing anything about the dope and told the truth about the handsome dropkick offering us a lift after a chance meeting. I doubt they believed us (about the dope, I mean), but I could tell they recognised us for what we were – nice middle-class girls probably not destined for a life of crime. They were two country policemen, no doubt with kids of their own, and, after telling us that they were going to charge our friend (he's no friend of mine, I thought) with possession, they gave us a bit of fatherly advice. They asked us if we were going to university. Yes, we replied, all three of us were. They said that we would probably be offered all sorts of substances at university and – and this was the really lovely part – they gave us their cards and told us that if we ever needed any advice about such things, we were welcome to call them at any time. I have had a really positive view of the police ever since.

By this time, we were very late for our arrival at the hostel. In keeping with all their other rules, youth hostels had very strict admittance times. The police had allowed me to use their phone to tell the hostel staff we'd had a car accident and might be late arriving. They were not sympathetic. Indeed, once everything had been taken care of and we were free to leave the station (I can't remember what happened to our driver; I don't think he was put in the cells), it was long past hostel lockout time.

One of the cops offered to drive us to the hostel – they really were lovely. We arrived, rang the bell, but the staff refused to answer the door. The copper shrugged, went back to his car and turned on his siren – LOUD. It worked. The staff of the hostel relented and gave us the key to our accommodation.

When we unlocked the door we found Julie and half the kids from the Croydon Jazz Festival waiting to meet us. They looked terrified as we opened the door and then very relieved to see it was only us. They had been smoking a spliff while waiting for us to arrive and the sound of that police siren had made them get rid of the stuff in a hurry. I'm not sure how we could have talked our way out of a drug charge a second time.

seven

It had just always been assumed I would finish school and go to university. My father talked about his time at St John's College in Cambridge as some of the best years of his life. My mother had come to bitterly regret her lack of tertiary education.

'Don't do what I did,' she said to her three daughters on a regular basis. 'Don't just get married and have kids. You'll get trapped and regret it. Go to uni, get trained properly for something professional. That way, you will always have choices. Whatever you do, don't do what I did.'

I don't think she ever regretted being married to my father – well, not often and not for long, anyway – but she was bowed down by the boredom and drudgery of looking after four children and taking care of a house. She was not interested in domestic duties and it showed. Our house was always fairly chaotic. I had taken her advice to heart and never had a moment's hesitation about going on to university. I felt confident about it, perhaps because my father had always had a touching (and reassuring) faith in my ability to do whatever it was I wanted, despite very little evidence. Most of my friends were going to uni, too. Julie was going to the University of New England, Becky to Sydney University and Lee to Macquarie.

Not that that should have made any difference to me. Over the long summer holiday between finishing the HSC and starting university – from November 1974 until March 1975 – I separated myself from most of my old friends and they separated themselves from me. Di and Lee couldn't wait to see the back of me after our disastrous holiday, and I didn't really want to see them. They reminded me of my weakness, my failure and my shame. But it was more than that; it was a pattern I had. After I finished primary school, I had wanted to reinvent myself, and it seemed I wanted to do the same after high school too. Most of my friends had become hippies and I was always too down to earth for all that peace, love and dope nonsense. I had no desire to live on a commune or learn African drumming or do a clowning workshop. I remain equally uninterested in all three pursuits to this day.

I had formed a close friendship with Sally, the sister of an ex-boyfriend. Sally and her friends were former private school girls, from Abbotsleigh and PLC, and they hung out with a group of former Barker and Knox boys. I enjoyed spending my time with this group, not least because it was a relief to hang out with people who knew nothing about me. One of them – though not the young man I first paired up with – was to become the most important person in my life.

Sally's friends were not a great advertisement for the posh schools they had attended. I was – if I recall correctly – the only member of the group who was attending university. The rest were working as shop assistants, secretaries, dental nurses, council workers, labourers and bartenders. The boys all rode very large, very noisy motorbikes. I found them all very attractive, not least because, despite being pretty aimless, they were not hippies.

The young man I first hooked up with – I'll call him Ben – was a strange character. A few years older than the rest of us, he lived with his mother and younger brother in a large house. He was very wealthy and owned a part-share in a shop where he worked (as far as I could tell) only when he felt like it. His mother also owned a shop but she worked very long hours. I liked her, though she was rarely around; she was a warm and friendly woman, but she seemed nervous around her eldest son. The large (and usually empty) house included a poolroom with a full-sized pool table, a fully stocked bar, a huge (for the times) TV and a state-of-the-art hi fi system – of course. It was the regular gathering place for my new group of friends. Every time I drove my mother's Morris Marina to Ben's place – having recently got my P-plates – I'd find at least one or two of the group there. Their motorbikes would be parked in the driveway, while Ben's magnificent machine was treated more like an art installation than a vehicle. Complete with customised paint job, his Honda Four stood resplendent in the hallway, parked under the stairs – yes, on the carpet. It was rarely ridden. No matter how much I wheedled and nagged, I could hardly ever persuade

Ben to wheel his bike outside the front door and join the others on a ride.

Ben appeared to hate leaving the house and was largely nocturnal, staying up most of the night and sleeping most of the day. When I could budge him, he preferred to drive his van or commandeer his brother's car. He also owned a vintage sports car (I told you he was rich), a car that looked amazing but broke down every time I was in it. I was dazzled at first by all these glamorous objects and Ben's veneer of troubled sophistication, but not for long.

His was a dark presence. As I write this, I realise that he resembled the sullen but watchful fathers I had known in my childhood.

Ben was not unattractive in an enigmatic kind of way, but his taciturnity gradually became rather boring. All he wanted to do was sit at home and watch TV. The only fun I had was with Ben's most frequent visitor – the most charismatic member of this group of private school misfits – Ralph Dunning. Ralph was a golden boy. He was acknowledged as the best and most daring on a motorbike. He was a skilled surfer, having spent much of his adolescence living on the Gold Coast. He was different from the other private school kids because, while they had been day boys and girls, he had been a boarder – at various schools in both Australia and the UK – since he was six years old. Even by 1970s standards, this was extreme. The others in the group were playing at independence but in reality still lived off their parents (as did I). Ralph was independent and had been for years. He worked for Turramurra Council as the leading groundsman at Turramurra Park. He shared a scungy two-room flat in Wahroonga with Andrew and Murison McCrae. Murison was Sally's boyfriend, while Ralph had been going out with the glamorous Nikki for a number of years. Nikki, fortunately for me, seemed to be more interested in her horse than her boyfriend, so Ralph was often at a loose end. Kicking back at 'the hole' (which was what everyone called the flat Ralph shared with the McCrae brothers) didn't bear thinking about, so most evenings you would find Ralph at Ben's place – which was also where you would find me. While Ben watched telly, Ralph and I talked, argued and got to know one another.

We had, in fact, met before. When Sally turned seventeen, her parents held a small party at their house in Wahroonga. I was invited. I didn't know anyone there except Sally and her brother Chris, my ex-boyfriend, but I was enjoying both the party and Sally's friends. Midway through the party, a loud noise disrupted everything. A large and powerful motorbike was roaring down the driveway.

'It's Nikki and Ralph!' said Sally excitedly.

A young couple entered the room and joined the party. They took their full-face helmets off as they walked in, to reveal two of the most beautiful young faces I have ever seen. Ralph looked like a young Brad Pitt, Nikki like a modern Marilyn Monroe. They sat near me and were both immediately easy-going and friendly. I couldn't help noticing, however, that Ralph's helmet bore a sticker. It said: 'Gair to Dublin, Whitlam to blazes'. I was horrified! It was 1974 and I was a supporter of the Whitlam government. I immediately bristled at this derogatory reference to Whitlam offering Vince Gair, the head of the right-wing Democratic Labor Party, the post of ambassador to Ireland. The job offer was a ploy to end Gair's influence and destroy the DLP altogether. Since the DLP was then (as it is today) a profoundly socially conservative and anti-women party, I was very happy to see the back of Vince Gair. Being me, I immediately took this glamorous bikie on.

'Don't tell me you're a right-wing bikie! Can such a thing be possible?'

'I'm no fan of Whitlam, if that's what you mean.'

And we were off, arguing politics hammer and tongs, oblivious to everyone else around us. The astounding thing was that this young man called Ralph (such a funny name for the 1970s; everyone I knew was called Greg, Craig or Mark) sparked up as I argued with him. He loved the cut and thrust, and he was a worthy opponent. Most boys I knew at that time were either bored with politics, or parroted the arguments their parents had drummed into them, or, worst of all, felt insulted that a girl (*a girl!*) had dared to disagree with them. This guy was different. As I made my case, I could see I was going up in his estimation, not down.

When I started hanging out with Sally's friends again during my first year at university, I was very pleased to reconnect with that now not-so-right-wing bikie. Quite apart from the charisma, the fun, the instinctive respect for and liking of women (not to mention the masculine skills of surfing and daredevilry on a motorbike), Ralph was just as I remembered him. Tall and slender, with blond hair to his shoulders (as I keep reminding you, it was the 70s), he had brilliant blue eyes, a chiselled chin (I tease him about his resemblance to Dudley Do-Right to this day) and a smile that split his face. John McCallum, the producer of *Skippy*, was a friend of Ralph's father and had told Ralph that if he ever wanted to try acting he should give him a call. I occasionally see young men today who look like the young Ralph. One, as I said, was Brad Pitt – in *Thelma and Louise*; the other, more recently, was Chris Hemsworth in *Rush*.

I liked Ralph very much, but I did not think I was in his league. His long-time girlfriend – Nikki, the one who looked like Marilyn Monroe – was stunning. They were a glittering and gorgeous young couple. I was quite pretty in those days, but in comparison to Nikki? No-one would have looked twice. Nevertheless, I was beginning to think about moving on from Ben. He was silent and unpleasant and treated me dismissively. Sometimes he used to complain to me about how his friends used all the stuff in his house carelessly – he had a particular thing about people putting their shod feet on the sofa as they watched TV. On one of the few occasions I persuaded him to have dinner at my house, he did exactly what he had always complained about others doing.

'Hey,' I said to him, meaning to tease rather than accuse, 'what's with the feet? You hate it when people do that at your house.'

'But the sofa at my place is worth thousands!'

I broke up with him soon afterwards at a party but, having treated me like shit while I was his girlfriend, he now became desperate to woo me back. When I arrived home from uni, his van would be parked outside. He would get out, often weeping, and beg me to reconsider. He called me frequently. He gave me an expensive silver necklace by way of a friend; I tried to give it back but he wouldn't accept it. I felt sorry for him but also vaguely repelled. We were both very immature, I suppose. While he had seemed unattainable to me – i.e. treating me like shit – I had found him mysterious and attractive. Now he was sobbing all over me, I felt like the cat who was wooed by the cartoon skunk, Pepé Le Pew. All I wanted was to get away. He persuaded me to go for a drive with him one day and drove far too quickly. He was pulled over by the cops for speeding.

'Any extenuating circumstances?' the cop asked.

'I've just broken up with my girlfriend,' said Ben, pointing at me with a hangdog expression.

Honestly, I could have killed him.

There was one thing I missed about being Ben's girlfriend and that was hanging out with Ralph. Obviously, I was no longer welcome at Ben's place and, even if I had been, I didn't want to go. Ralph solved the problem. Instead of spending every evening at Ben's, he rode his bike a little further down Mona Vale Road and spent it at my place. But we were still only friends, even after the glamorous Nikki broke up with him. I had a short-lived affair with a guy I met at Macquarie University. Richard – such was the incestuous world I was living in – turned out to be the ex-boyfriend of the ex-girlfriend that Ben had always held up to me as a woman who was my superior in all things. I even met her once at a party where Richard's friends played Roxy Music and smoked hash. I tried hash. It put me to sleep. I woke up just after the party had finished. Drugs and I just didn't mix.

After only a couple of months, Richard and I drifted amicably apart. Throughout all this, Ralph had continued to drop by my place every evening after dinner. One day, my mother – who liked Ralph very much – asked me a question: 'Do you think Ralph is interested in you?'

'Oh no,' I answered. 'We're just friends.'

'Are you sure? A boy doesn't come to see a girl every night of the week unless he's interested.'

And that's when it struck me. He did come to see me every night of the week. Perhaps this man I had assumed was unattainable was not out of my reach after all.

That week, Ralph was turning twenty-one, and I saw my chance. On the evening of his birthday he arrived at my place as usual. We went downstairs to watch our favourite TV show (*Within These Walls*, a BBC drama about a women's prison starring Googie Withers, who – as John McCallum's wife – was also an old friend of Ralph's family). When it finished and Ralph got up to leave, I threw caution to the winds.

'You can't go until you've given me a birthday kiss.'

He didn't leave for hours. From that day – 4 November 1975 – until this we have been together.

Our new relationship sent a shockwave through our group of friends. I had nabbed the most attractive man in the group. This did not endear me to some of the other young women. One of them famously predicted our relationship would last six weeks. Nikki was horrified and began stalking us, suddenly turning up wherever we were and weeping on Ralph's shoulder. Before we became a couple, Ralph and I had been talking about renting a share house together with one of our other friends and we decided we would continue with our plan. Although I had pushed my awful weakness and homesickness from the previous year to the back of my mind, I was still keen to prove to myself that I was able to exist independently and moving out of home seemed a good way to do this. Ralph was desperate to escape 'the hole'.

As we checked out possible rental properties, Ben decided to throw a twenty-first birthday party for Ralph and everyone was going. I wanted to go too. I asked Sally (who had remained stalwart) to check with Ben if it was okay for me to come to the party. I asked Ralph to check with him too. I assumed Ben must have been told that Ralph and I were now a couple because he had stopped calling me and no longer turned up at my house unannounced.

I went to the party and it was a disaster. There was a lot of tension in the room, not all of it to do with me. One of the girls in our group had been recently caught flirting with the boy-friend of another. The wronged party spent the evening on one side of Ben's enormous pool table, drunkenly yelling, 'Fat arms! Fat ankles!' at her former friend, who was standing on the other side. It's funny how we always blamed one another and let the bloody blokes off the hook in those days.

The pool table itself was covered in booze. Supertramp and David Bowie's *Young Americans* boomed from Ben's state-of-the-art speakers. His bike stood centre-stage. There were all sorts of people there, some I knew and many that I didn't. I tried to keep my distance from Ralph, but after a while, flush as we were with young love, we signalled to each other and went outside. Mistakenly, we thought we might find some sort of privacy. It soon became obvious that Ben was watching us like a hawk and following us about. Eventually, we ended up sitting on the couch (yep, the one worth thousands of dollars) in the lounge room. Ben came in and he was clearly very drunk. He lunged across the glass coffee table and grabbed me by the wrist.

'It's been fun having you, Jane, but now you leave!'

And with that he flung me across the room. I landed on my hands and knees and stayed that way as I crawled rapidly out of the door. Behind me I heard the sound of glass shattering. Uh-oh! That expensive coffee table.

Pretty soon, Ralph was beside me and we decamped on his motorbike to another friend's unit, behind the shops in Lindfield. Slowly all our friends left the party and – drawn as young people so often are to any kind of drama – they all ended up at the Lindfield unit. There I heard what had happened after I had high-tailed it (well, low-tailed it, more accurately) out of there. Ralph had squared up to Ben but they had both been restrained by other guests. Ralph left and then Ben had thrown everyone out of his house. Ben lost many of his friends that night. We obviously didn't feel like seeing him anymore. His house had been the meeting place and now it couldn't be. I feel very bad about that. The only justification I can offer is that ours wasn't just a fly-by-night relationship motivated by lust and excitement – although there was a fair bit of that. It did turn out to be the love of both our lives.

Not that I had any idea about this at the time. I was dazzled by Ralph's charm, beauty and charisma, but I was only eighteen and had no idea I was now going out with the man I was going to spend the rest of my life with. If I thought ahead at all, I simply presumed that this would be a relationship like all the others I'd had – fun while it lasted. Ralph, to his credit, was both much more mature and much more serious than I was. He had already told his half-brother John, who lived in Queensland, that I was the girl he was going to marry. Wisely he didn't say anything to me about that for years.

eight

Ralph, our friend J.O. (his real name was David, J.O. was a nickname) and I finally found a place to rent. We called it – accurately – the only slum in Killara, a suburb on Sydney's North Shore. The house had many advantages. It had five bedrooms, which we rapidly filled so the weekly rent – divided between seven – came to an extremely affordable nine dollars a week. It was just around the corner from the Greengate hotel and there was a bus to Macquarie Uni from nearby Gordon station. It also had a few disadvantages (hence the low rent). For the first few months it only had an outside toilet and the lounge room, while vast, had only one power point and one tiny high window. There was no phone and this was decades before mobiles, so we had to rely on the public phone in the Greengate. The kitchen was primitive and the stove positively ancient. The landlady lived next door. It had a large, completely overgrown back garden, which we ignored, only ever venturing as far as the dunny. But despite its ugliness and lack of comfort, I was deliriously happy. All my failures and anxieties disappeared in a fog of young love.

To support myself, I worked as a shop assistant at Tony Staunton's pharmacy in Manly on Saturdays and as a check-out chick at the supermarket in Terrey Hills. I was only able to get to my pharmacy job on Saturdays because Ralph had bought an EH Holden for $400; he still used his Honda Four most of the time. The EH was a bomb. When it rained, the floor on the passenger side filled up with water. If Ralph was driving I sat with my feet curled up on the seat while water sloshed from side to side below me. We were lucky it didn't end up killing us. One morning, Ralph backed it out of the driveway and the entire front wheel fell off. Only the night before we'd been driving the EH fast along a deserted Mona Vale Road.

My wonderful feminist mother insisted on giving me an allowance of thirty dollars a week to top up my part-time earnings. Mum did not want me to be financially dependent on Ralph, who was working full time. I am not sure when my mother became overtly feminist. She had felt thwarted and unhappy as a stay-at-home mother and housewife for a long time. She tells a lovely story about being at a dinner in the early 60s and listening to some bloke wax lyrical about how much he venerated women.

'Women aren't the equal of men,' he said. 'No, no, no! They are men's superiors. They are so delicate, beautiful and pure. Not for them the earthy, nasty competitiveness of the workaday world. They are above such venal and petty pursuits. Women are special creatures who deserve veneration and protection from the cut and thrust of ordinary life.' This bloke was really falling in love with his own flowery rhetoric. When he finally ran out of ethereal adjectives to attach to his ideal of womanhood, my quiet, bespectacled mother spoke up.

'If that's true,' she said, 'if women really are so pure and delicate, so special and so above the concerns of everyday life, how come it is always us who get down on our knees to scrub the toilet?'

I think she had always had feminist instincts, but – as for many women of her generation – it was probably the explosion of second-wave feminism that turned those instincts into activism. She joined the Women's Electoral Lobby. She ran a group determined to stop a planned airport in Duffys Forest, on the edge of the Ku-ring-gai National Park. Eventually she formed the Liberal Feminist Network and stood for Liberal Party preselection for the Senate. Given the LNP's sharp turn to the right not long afterwards, the fact that she wasn't selected was probably a good thing. In the long run, her feminism took her to university and into a career she loved as a relationships counsellor. But that was in the future. At this stage, her feminism made her very wary of her eldest daughter being financially dependent on a man, even a man of whom she was already very fond.

My father, unlike many of the men of his generation, was very supportive of Kate's desire to expand her horizons. My dad genuinely liked women and treated them just as he would anyone else. He was one of the first to begin promoting women into management positions (something that was to prove a little complicated when he became managing director of World Series Cricket, but more about that later). To Dad, women were neither on a pedestal nor to be despised. We were to be taken on our merits like any other person. This was a pretty revolutionary attitude at the time. I suspect it still is. His ability to see women as people was of enormous importance to his daughters.

* * *

Despite living in (relative) poverty, I was feeling good. I was in love and, despite my shameful homesickness of the year before, I had proved that I could be independent. I was also enjoying being at uni. I was the lucky recipient of a free university education, thanks to the Whitlam government – though there was a slight downside to this, at least for me. As I have said, like many women of her generation, my mother had not had the chance to go to university. A natural intellectual and now a feminist, she felt this lack keenly. When she saw her chance, she grabbed it.

While I was studying for the HSC, so was my mother; she was doing the mature-age matriculation course at what was then called North Sydney Tech. Motivated as only people who know they are getting a second chance can be, she far outperformed me in the exams. She also decided to do arts at Macquarie Uni. Yes, thanks to Gough Whitlam, I went to uni with my mother. Very occasionally, we did the same courses, though we always tried to arrange it so that we did not do them at the same time.

One of the reasons I was so keen to do second-year English in my first year was to get a bit of a jump on my mother. Unfortunately, this backfired because I wasn't really up to it and my marks were pretty lacklustre – unlike, of course, hers. In the face of such unfair competition, I did the only thing I could. I took the attitude that P's get degrees and did only what I needed to pass. I threw my energies into the extracurricular activities that were so much on offer at university campuses in the 1970s. But, I have to be honest, my mother even helped me to do that.

Having done okay in ancient history for the HSC, I took a course on Pericles in my first semester. I hated it, university ancient history being all about the veracity of sources and evidence. I couldn't give a toss about that; all I cared about were the stories and we got none of those. I managed to scrape a pass and decided to steer clear of ancient history subjects from then on. I got more than the credit points, though, because one day a young man came into our lecture and announced that they were looking for people to try out for a planned Ancient History Revue. I was dying to put my hand up and volunteer to audition but shyness and anxiety stopped me. A few days later, as my mother and I were walking through the uni car park, I saw the young man who had come into the lecture and pointed him out to my mother.

'Look,' I said, 'that's the guy who's organising the Ancient History Revue.' I had told her how much I wanted to be in it but how I hadn't felt able to say so.

'Well, now's your chance – grab him!'

'I can't.' I still felt terrified.

My mother, conscious perhaps of how often fear had stopped her doing things, was not about to let the moment pass. To my horror, she bustled after him.

'Young man!'

Oh God! Could anything be more embarrassing?

'Young man! Yes, you!'

He stopped and she caught up to him. I was still hanging back, mortified.

'You're the fellow who is organising that revue?'

He acknowledged that he was.

My mother then pointed to me. 'My daughter is interested in trying out for it.'

Far from having to try out, I found I was immediately cast in a series of plum roles, including a parody of Anne Deveson called (what else) Anne Devastating. Anne Devastating opened the Ancient History Revue at the beginning of time, interviewing a somewhat donnish Primal Man (the student playing the part eventually became a don in ancient history).

After struggling for a while with this pivotal part, I finally found my way by playing Anne with a Mae West voice. I had a moment where I walked slowly around Mr Primal Man (as Anne politely but suggestively referred to him) saying, 'Virile, virile, virile and virile.' It became a bit of a catchphrase. A few years after I had left Macquarie, I was standing at a crowded bar in the city when someone behind me muttered, 'Virile, virile, virile and virile!' I swung around but no-one owned up. I did feel a little bit famous when that happened.

That first Ancient History Revue in 1975 was a smash hit. So in 1976 we did it again.

I played a host of parts in both revues. A pregnant vestal virgin – who died having her balloon stomach popped; Gertie – an upper-class-twit time traveller; the Queen of Sodom and Gomorrah (who sang a rewrite of 'The Lady is a Tramp'; 'Love Mesopotamia, it's cold and it's damp'); the heroine of a silent spaghetti western called Polystyrene, and various other bizarre characters. Ralph – despite not actually being at uni – was cast as Machismo the Mighty in that same spaghetti western. There remains a print of this film, as we discovered at Ralph's fiftieth birthday party when a friend from those days played it for us. It was even worse than we remembered.

I loved being in those revues and I made all my lasting uni friends from the ranks of the other players, for which – like Ralph, my feminism and my feistiness – I have to thank my mother.

I was very close to my mother when I was young. I think we have a very similar kind of brain. We could spend hours analysing ourselves and the people around us because we were both driven by an intense curiosity about what makes people tick. I valued her judgment and opinion more than anyone's at that time in my life. This closeness gave me many benefits but it may also have inadvertently caused me some trouble. I remember saying to a therapist some years later, as I struggled with an anxiety neurosis, that I wanted to *be* my mother. I did sometimes feel that I operated in her shadow and having her outperform me at university probably didn't help. I think it took me longer than it should have to find out where I stopped and my mother started. Mind you, I don't think this is an uncommon struggle for young women, particularly if you are lucky enough – as I was (and am) – to have a wise and warm female parent.

The downside of strong loving mothering is that it can take longer for the child to emerge as a separate individual. The upside of lousy parenting may be the opposite. Certainly Ralph was appallingly badly parented, but – unlike me – he was a grown-up from an early age. Perhaps my overwhelming homesickness of the year before was to do with the fact that away from my parents, and particularly my mother, I didn't feel like a whole person at all. Given that my eldest had a similar reaction to me when she went to New York, perhaps I have unwittingly passed on the same legacy to her.

Mind you, it was easy to admire my mother. Some years later, while I was in therapy and learning a great deal about myself, I began to get a clearer idea of how my parents had unwittingly fucked me up. That's what therapy is for, in a way. Anyway, jumped-up little convert to self-awareness that I was, I took myself off to see my mother with a list of all her shortcomings. She was, of course, a relationships counsellor herself by this time. She sat patiently and listened to me as I listed my complaints. Even to my own ears, many of them sounded a little lame, but I persevered. I had expected her to protest, to deny, to fight back, maybe even get upset. She did nothing of the sort. When I got to the end of my (not very long) list, I paused.

'Is that it?' asked my mother. 'Have you finished?'

'Well . . . um . . . yes. I . . . yes.' This interview was not going the way I had anticipated.

'Good. Well, you should thank me for all of those failures and shortcomings, because they are your opportunities for growth. Would you like another cup of tea?'

How can you not admire and want to emulate a woman like that? Indeed, when my own daughters come to me, as they inevitably will, with their list of my own failures and shortcomings, I am going to give them exactly the same answer their grandmother gave me.

* * *

I have to thank both my parents for their progressive attitudes. Even for the fast-changing 1970s, they were way ahead of their time. Unexceptional now, it was still rather new and shocking to live together out of wedlock in the mid-1970s. The fact that Kate and Andy were so relaxed about it that they gave me an allowance so I could be independent of my higher-earning boyfriend was extraordinary. A friend at uni, Brigid, came from a very Catholic family. Her mother, like a lot of women at that time, was beginning to see the world rather differently. Brigid's mum worked for a Catholic boys' school (I can't remember in what capacity, I don't think she was a teacher) and had decided to arrange a debate about marriage versus what was still called 'living in sin'. I was the only person they knew who was doing such a thing so she asked me if I would represent that side of the argument. Coward as I may have been about drugs and getting caught doing the wrong thing, I did not lack courage when it came to defending ideas. I agreed.

It *was* somewhat confronting for a nineteen-year-old to front up to a Catholic boys' school to argue for the new morality against a priest in front of the senior students. But I need not have feared. As it turned out, I had a couple of advantages, none of them to do with my (not very advanced) debating skills. I was not celibate, so I had some idea what I was talking about, and I *was* talking to adolescent boys. The debate was decided by a vote. I won by a landslide.

I did not think of myself as a representative of alternative lifestyles. I was really very straight and conventional. Ralph and I might not have been officially married and we might have got around on a large and noisy motorbike, but we were monogamous, gainfully employed and – apart from on the road – law-abiding. Nonetheless, according to some, I was the living example of a scarlet woman.

One afternoon, I came home from uni to find I had forgotten my house key and was locked out. Fortunately, our landlady lived next door. She was an elderly Lebanese lady who was confined to a wheelchair. She lived with her carer, a small, thin, spiky woman with a perpetually cross expression. I knocked on the door and it was answered by Miss Spiky (I am convinced she was a Miss). When she saw who it was, she gave me one of the blackest looks I have ever received. Undaunted, I explained my dilemma and asked if I could borrow the spare key to let myself in.

'No,' was the short answer, followed rapidly by the door closing – none too gently – in my face.

I had no idea what I had done to offend this woman, to whom I had never spoken before, until it dawned on me that she thought I was a scarlet woman – a whore, living unmarried and unchaperoned with – at that time – two men. It was an unexpected but not unpleasant feeling to be seen as a woman of ill repute. I was walking away feeling a little more glamorous than usual when the door behind me was suddenly flung open and my name was called. The landlady was on the verandah in her wheelchair, smiling and signalling to me to return. Behind her was Miss Spiky, still glowering furiously at me. I walked back to the beaming landlady. She did not speak much English but she thrust the spare key into my hand with what were obviously apologies and some expressive gestures aimed at Miss Spiky. I got the gist, accepted the key, thanked my landlady profusely and, as I was leaving, could not resist a triumphant glance at her carer.

Once I had let myself into my house, I returned next door, knocked again and handed the key back to a simmering but silent Miss Spiky. She took the key between the tips of her thumb and forefinger as if my presumed immorality could infect her like germs. I wasn't insulted or hurt. I thought it was hilarious and I retained a permanent soft spot for our landlady.

* * *

We had a lot of fun at 9 Bruce Avenue, Killara, the first year we lived there. We threw a lot of parties. I remember a dark mark that ran along the length of the long central hallway after one major bash. We wondered what it was for a moment and then realised it was the mark made by everyone's shoes as they stood chatting in the hall propped up by one foot behind them. It was the sort of house where that kind of thing didn't matter at all. But, as old housemates moved out and new ones moved in, I started to feel less happy. As is the way with house-sharing, some people are easy to live with and some are hard. At the end of the first year, there seemed to be more people in the house who were driving me nuts than otherwise and, to be completely honest, I felt I needed some space from Ralph. I still loved him and I didn't want to end the relationship, but we had moved in together only a few weeks after we had become involved and I wasn't yet twenty. It had all become a bit intense. I needed some breathing space, so I used a particularly difficult housemate as an excuse (the poor guy was eventually diagnosed with schizophrenia) and moved back home. Ralph, as always, was understanding, patient and gave me the space I needed.

As I have said previously, Ralph was a grown-up – the first grown-up I had ever gone out with. Thank goodness he stuck by me through what would turn out to be my prolonged adolescence. He was grown up because, unlike my sheltered childhood, his had been the opposite.

Ralph's father was a military man. Alan flew ninety-nine bombing missions over Germany and rose from wireless operator to squadron leader in the RAF during the Second World War.

At war's end he went on to become a senior military policeman in first the British sector of Berlin and then in Northern Ireland. He met Ralph's mother, Doreen, at a ball in Northern Ireland. He attended as the representative of the Queen. Doreen was a wealthy young widow at that time, with two small sons, Ralph's half-brothers John and Robert. Alan was a dashing and devastatingly handsome single man (complete with pencil-thin moustache and military hat worn at a rakish angle) on the lookout for a wife. Poor Doreen never stood a chance.

It was only after they were married that Doreen discovered the truth about her husband. The reason Alan had remained single for so long (he was well into his forties when he married) was that he was primarily a gay man. Indeed, Ralph is not Ralph's real name. It is a nickname he was given in his teens. He was happy to adopt this alias because he knew that he had been named after his father's long-time American lover, Harold Molton.

Before the war, Alan was a Broadway actor in New York and he and Harold had lived together on Lexington Avenue for years. When Harold died, not long after Alan had married Doreen, he left his very considerable fortune to Ralph's father.

Doreen was also very wealthy – her first husband had owned quarries – so Alan was now able to leave the air force (taking with him a generous annuity) and move his family to Jamaica, where he bought a banana plantation. Ralph (or Harold as he then was) was born in Belfast and was a toddler when they moved. His sister Rosslyn was born in Jamaica. Alan had wanted a son and heir, but he didn't like the reality of children at all. He was also a bit of a fraud – and not only when it came to his sexuality. Squadron Leader Dunning spoke with the modulated accent of an upper-class Englishman. He was punctilious about all the markers of what appeared to be his class, including, of course, sending children off to boarding school at a very early age. The trouble is, Alan wasn't really that posh at all.

Ralph and I went on holiday to England before we were married and went to visit Alan's brother Percy and Percy's wife Joan. They lived, to my surprise, in a perfectly respectable but very ordinary terrace house in Southend-on-Sea (Sarffend to residents) in Essex. When we pulled up outside, a little man who looked just like Alan came bouncing out of the front door and down the garden path, beaming. He held out his hand in welcome.

''Ello, 'Arold!' he said enthusiastically. ''Ow are ya?'

All Alan and Doreen's children were sent away to boarding school in the UK at the age of six. At first, they didn't come home for holidays because Jamaica was so far away, but even when Alan and Doreen returned to live in England, the children continued to board. When they did go home, Alan was a strict disciplinarian. Ralph remembers that the first day home from school, Alan would call them all into his study one by one and give them one cut of the cane for every spelling mistake they'd made in their letters home. At every family meal, Alan sat with a cane by his side, ready to thump anyone who spoke with their mouth full or put their elbows on the table. Maybe he was afraid that, without eternal vigilance, they would betray their inferior breeding. Whatever the reason, Alan dominated everything.

Ralph recalls that the only person in their house who was ever allowed to be angry was their father.

From what Ralph has told me, I think Alan was also an abusive husband. I don't mean that he hit Doreen, but he certainly continued to have affairs with men and made little effort to hide them. He also dominated and frightened his wife. He successfully separated her (as abusive husbands always do) from her friends and her family. Ralph and his siblings were brought up believing that they had been rejected by their mother's family because she had married an Englishman. As we discovered many decades later, after Alan's death, nothing could have been further from the truth. Doreen's brother Bunny had never given up hope of seeing his sister again and – when he died – gave his own children the task of seeking out their long-lost cousins. Ralph and two of his siblings (his older brother Robert died at fifty) then discovered a whole new side to their family and learnt just how comprehensively Alan had lied to them all.

After a decade or so of marriage, Doreen began to get very sick. She had blood clots, apparently, and her doctors advised her to seek a warmer climate. Alan considered moving the family to Africa but the Mau Mau Uprising put him off that idea. Instead, they came to Australia and settled on the Gold Coast, where Ralph and his brothers were sent to board at the Dickensian (according to Ralph's description) Southport School. Tragically, the move to a warmer climate came too late and, within a couple of months of their arrival in Australia, Doreen died, aged just forty-six. Ralph was eleven at the time and his sister Rosslyn was nine. Life had not been great for the four children up to that point, but once their mother died it got a lot worse. Alan was poleaxed by grief and guilt. He also had no idea what to do with four children. From this time on, they very rarely came home, being either at boarding school during term time or working on holiday farms during vacations. Rosslyn was sent away to America for a year because while boys were hard, Alan had no idea at all about girls. Alan also set about losing all of his money. By the time I met him, he'd virtually blown the lot and lived in a very modest flat in Newport on Sydney's northern beaches.

Ralph had the sort of childhood that either makes you or breaks you. It made him. To Alan's credit, he was honest with his kids about his sexuality and I think that made a big difference to how they were able to deal with their peculiar background. A very wise counsellor once said to me that you are only as sick as your biggest secret. Ralph also felt loved by his father, even when they weren't getting along. Maybe that's why Ralph not only survived his childhood but learnt a great deal from it – not least what sort of father he definitely did not want to be. I was (and still am) beyond fortunate that he set his sights on me. I have always wondered if he partly did so because my outspoken nature really, *really* annoyed his father.

* * *

But all that was either in the past or in the future. To return to the mid-70s, I continued to enjoy university and in my third year began to get slightly better marks. I felt much more confident about myself than I had done when I started. Indeed, I think I probably became a little cocky. I was the star of the Ancient History Revues, my marks had improved, I had lots of interesting friends and I had a very glamorous boyfriend who rode a great big motorbike rather quickly and very noisily. Oddly, given I was at uni during the Whitlam years and for the cataclysm that was the Dismissal, I wasn't terribly interested in student politics. I had been a great supporter of Whitlam early on, handing out how-to-vote leaflets for Labor in 1972 (before I was old enough to vote myself) in the pouring rain on election day. Indeed, Ralph and I had bonded while arguing over politics. But by 1975, I felt very disillusioned. I was angry with Whitlam for having been great at policy but lousy at politics. What was the use of having visionary ideas if you couldn't stay in power to implement them? I was also (and again, this is odd) much more conservative then than I am now. I was still very much under the influence of my small-'l' liberal parents. My social conscience has not changed, however. I had massive arguments with Ralph's dad, for example, about racism and sexism, both of which he practised with an evangelical zeal.

Perhaps I was having too much fun to worry about politics. If I thought about that frightened, homesick, weepy failure of a few years previously, I quickly dismissed it. My misery on that trip with Lee and Di had been an aberration. Maybe I had been sickening for that cold I came down with. Yes, that must be it; that must have been why I felt so terrible. I even remember telling one of my mother's uni friends (the mature-age students all hung out together) that I knew exactly who I was. Perhaps I should have paid more attention to her reply.

'How wonderful to be so young and yet so sure.'

nine

As it had in that motel room in the middle of the night, halfway between Melbourne and Sydney, it came upon me suddenly. I was driving to uni as usual one morning when I began to feel desperate – my stomach fell to my knees and I was fighting tears. I could find no reason why I felt this way, but I felt unable to go to my classes as usual. I did a U-turn and drove home. I got inside the door and I descended into a level of misery I had never felt before. My homesickness had nothing on this. I was permanently dizzy and terrified. All I could bear to do was watch TV, read and sew. *Sew!* I had never liked sewing before in my life. I went through all my clothes and repaired them obsessively – every small tear, split seam, lost button and dropped hem. It soothed me somehow. It felt like I was doing something while it demanded nothing of me. The worst thing was that I had no idea why I felt so afraid. My mother forced me to go out with her; to the shops, to the post office, to pick up my brother and sisters. I trailed along behind her, weeping. My poor bewildered parents had no more idea why I had suddenly fallen apart than I did. I suppose I had what is called a nervous breakdown. As I had the first time, I felt ashamed, as if I was letting them down.

Looking back, I think I had serious problems with identity. I don't think I had a clue who I was or what I wanted. But I was brought up in a family that was by nature very definite, very emphatic. Not knowing was not an option. We were expected to have opinions and points of view and to be able to back them up. This was very valuable and I learnt great skills by arguing my point of view around our family dinner table, but the down-side – for me, anyway – was that rather than appear uncertain I took on the identity and desires of others and convinced myself they were what *I* wanted. I can see writing this that both times I fell apart just when something I thought I had been anticipating with enthusiasm was about to become a reality. Last time, it had been my trip around Australia that I had been planning with delight. This time, it was my first foray into the world of work that I had been looking forward to – or so I told myself. Just as everything seemed to be going really well, my psyche put a spanner in the works.

Even before I finished uni, I had a junior marketing job lined up. Having followed my mother into tertiary education, I was now to follow in my father's footsteps. The job I had been offered was in a subsidiary of Reckitts, where my father was now managing director. Given I had a not-very-impressive English literature degree, I was very lucky to be offered any kind of job at all, but I don't think working for the same company my father did helped my sense of understanding where I stopped and my parents began. Maybe my weepy hopelessness was a kind of rebellion against the proactive, take-charge style of both my parents? I don't know. It was a way of establishing some kind of boundary, and mental illness is quite powerful. You can't apply rational arguments to mental illness. You can't argue your way through someone's depression and anxiety. My parents were brilliant debaters. No-one could put an argument better than they could. Maybe I collapsed into irrationality as a defence, as a way of separating me and my desires from them and theirs.

Eventually, I dragged myself back to uni. I was so close to the end of my degree I had to make the effort and graduate. I survived thanks to the student counsellor.

Seeing that counsellor was the first time I reached out and asked for help. I did it out of desperation. I didn't want to talk to my parents about my strange misery – not because they weren't supportive, but because I was ashamed. The overwhelming feeling I had was that I didn't want to be a burden. I didn't want to talk to Ralph – not because he wasn't supportive, but because he didn't know what to do any more than I did. It was a huge relief to talk to someone I didn't feel I had to protect from my own weakness and craziness. It was also a free service for students and that made me feel it was silly not to take advantage of it. When we insist on charging a fee for services like this I can't help wondering how many people then miss out on something that might really help them.

The counsellor, Julie, was a warm and friendly woman in her late thirties. She had a daughter aged around six or seven who was often sitting on the floor in the waiting room drawing if her mother had appointments after 3 pm. I knew she was Julie's daughter because the girl looked exactly like her mother – rosy, round and cheerful. I remember feeling envious of that six-year-old. No decisions to make, no independence demanded, no directions to decide on. What bliss it must be.

'I wonder if I am feeling anxious about going into the workforce.' I was venturing my own diagnosis.

'No, I don't think so.' Julie was quite adamant. 'You sounded so enthusiastic when you told me about the job and your ambitions for the future.'

What neither of us realised at the time is that I always sound enthusiastic and energetic. It is my family's style. Even today, when people tell me they love my 'passion', I'm surprised – particularly when the comment is made in reference to something I don't actually feel all that passionate about.

'I think your anxiety is a perfectly understandable reaction to your recent health problems,' Julie continued. I could see she was pleased to have found such a reasonable explanation.

A few months before my collapse, I had been diagnosed with a tapeworm. How I had got such a thing in 1970s Australia I cannot imagine. I can only think that at some restaurant or other I had eaten some meat that had been sourced illegally, from outside the usual abattoir system. Anyone who has ever had a tapeworm (not many people in Australia, I suspect) will know how awful, mysterious and embarrassing the symptoms are.

It was (and is) so rare that my GP had no idea what the symptoms indicated and it was only pathology that eventually identified my problem. The cure was pretty horrible too, involving taking medication that kills the parasite and then a purgative so that you excrete the whole disgusting thing. You have to catch the result too, so pathology can make sure you have excreted the head! (Who would work in pathology?) It was a thoroughly unpleasant and humiliating experience from start to finish. Julie's theory was that I had experienced this as a violation and was having a delayed anxiety reaction. It was comforting at the time to believe her, but – with the benefit of hindsight – I now know that while the tapeworm did not help, my anxiety was about much more than that.

For a few months, my anxiety and depression ebbed and flowed. After the first intense two weeks I was able to function again, but I still felt dizzy and ill at ease. Then, one otherwise ordinary Saturday night, Ralph and I went to my friend Lee's twenty-first (yes, the same Lee I had travelled around Australia with while I struggled with what I then thought was homesickness). As we drove home I idly looked at the lit windows of the houses we passed. I began to imagine, as I often did, what kind of lives people might be living in those lit rooms – a pastime I had previously enjoyed. Suddenly my mind was filled with violent thoughts. They rushed into my mind as if a floodgate had opened somewhere. They weren't violent fantasies with me as victim; they were thoughts of what I might do to others – specifically, that night, the poor, unsuspecting people living in those lit rooms. The shock of this was overwhelming. What was wrong with me? Why was I thinking such terrible things? Was there some dark, pathological part of me that actually wanted to commit murder? Simply thinking such thoughts made me fear I might act on them. Would I be able to control that part of me? I suddenly felt like Golum, battling with my worst self.

All that weekend, I suffered from recurring disturbing thoughts and began to wonder if I was about to become the sort of violent nutcase who creates headlines. My anxiety remained at fever-pitch all through the following week, and the next, and the one after that. The intrusive thoughts haunted me wherever I went. If I stood on a train platform, I felt that at any moment I might experience an irresistible urge either to push someone or throw myself under an oncoming train. I hated knives and had horrible fantasies about them. I hated edges, open windows, boiling kettles. Driving was a nightmare as I was terrified I might run someone over. I kept thinking that there was nothing to stop me. It was horrible and I began to believe that I was a seriously deranged and dangerous person. I confided in Ralph, sure that he would despise and disown me. He did not. He comforted me just by reacting sensibly and telling me this was all in my mind and that I would never actually do any of the things I had begun to fear so much. It probably helped that I was all of 155 centimetres tall and forty-five kilos. It was hard to imagine me as a murderous fiend. Even in the grip of my terror I had enough sanity left to see that.

Yet still the thoughts dogged me, going around and around in my head, nauseating and horrifying me, week after week, month after month. I could be distracted from them by friends and social occasions, even a good movie, TV program or book, but whenever my brain was idle the thoughts came rushing back. However, now that my anxiety was actually fixed on something – however horrible and unacceptable – I found I could function a little better. I passed my university exams, handed in my final essays and began my new job.

There was also a funny side to my misery. I didn't only have thoughts about killing people or hurting them in some way – if I sat in a very pompous business meeting I'd feel as if I was only just restraining myself from yelling 'FUCK!' very loudly, and that thought horrified me just as much as the thoughts of murder and mayhem. It was as if I was suffering from a kind of silent version of Tourette syndrome. It seemed I wanted to disrupt and disturb, while being equally desperate to stop myself. It was the same in planes or in any quiet but well-populated place. I would suddenly be gripped by a desire (and an equal and opposite resistance) to do something completely inappropriate. I developed a permanent tension in my wrists that manifested as pins and needles. I think it had to do with constantly restraining myself. A restrained and repressed rebellion? It seems almost obvious now, but it was utterly bewildering to me at the time. I had no insight into my condition at all. All I wanted was for the thoughts to GO AWAY!

Then things came to a sort of head. My new job was as a lowly marketing trainee for a frozen bread dough company. Its headquarters were in Girraween, a long way from where I lived in Terrey Hills. I had bought a second-hand Mini and drove myself from the hinterland of Sydney's northern beaches to the far western suburbs each morning and back again each evening. Along the way, I was almost paralysed with fear every time I drove past a pedestrian. The same words looped through my head: 'There is nothing to stop me. There is nothing to stop me.' One day, I so frightened myself with the intensity of my violent thoughts that I pulled over near a public phone box and called Ralph in floods of tears. Uncomplainingly, he left his own work (he was a sales rep for Cadbury Schweppes by this time) and picked me up. I called in sick and decided I had better see a psychiatrist. (I could no longer see Julie at Macquarie Uni now that I wasn't a student.)

The only psychiatrist I knew was a friend of my parents and he was a Freudian. He practised in a Catholic psychiatric hospital that was more or less on my way home. One evening a week I'd drive to that gloomy edifice. For the uninitiated (me), Catholic iconography of weeping Madonnas and graphically crucified Messiahs is very morbid and did not help my anxiety and depression. I developed a fear of being locked up in a place like that.

Being a Freudian, the psychiatrist would listen to my lurid imaginings in complete silence, which I found neither comforting nor helpful. The only action he took was to prescribe me antidepressants. I took one, hated how it made me feel, and threw the rest in the bin. Perhaps some small part of me was not completely insane. The only comforting thing this psychiatrist said to me was that if I thought I was bad, he had another patient who had to stop and check that he hadn't actually run someone over every time he drove over a bump in the road.

It was the first time I had heard there could be other people like me.

What I yearned for was some understanding of what I was going through, but it took me ten long years to discover that I suffered from an obsessive anxiety neurosis. My version of it was a mild form (I'd hate to have had a serious version) of OCD (obsessive compulsive disorder) because I did not also suffer from physical compulsions. The guy who had to stop every time he drove over a bump had the full catastrophe. Now I can see that OCD runs in the Caro family. Both my father and grandfather are determined to the point of obsession. I have a distant cousin who has an obsession about cleanliness and germs. My sister is a hypochondriac and many in my family are quite phobic. Both my father and sister pathologically fear dogs and are generally uncomfortable around animals, although my father is very fond of cats. As far as I know, I am the only member of my family in which the OCD manifested as obsessive violent thoughts. At least, that is how my neurosis began.

I saw that Freudian for six months and I gained neither insight nor peace of mind. He was also horrendously expensive and I was earning very little. I gave up on therapy, at least for the time being.

The thoughts remained as a constant invisible tic, though, and I began to believe that I would never escape my mental torment. I began to see it as something akin to a sixth finger; a deformity that I would simply have to live with. No matter how philosophical I tried to be, however, the obsessional thoughts retained the power to upset me. Although on one level I could see that day after day, month after month, year after year, I did not act on my thoughts and so it was likely I never would, fear of the possibility of disaster – any minute now – still gripped me. Even when I later found a psychiatrist – a behaviourist this time – who was willing to give me some actual facts about my condition, including that it was the nature of the condition that sufferers never did what they feared, I still feared it. I suppose if rational explanations could cure mental illnesses there would be no mental illness. And yet, despite my anxiety, I functioned. I only had that one day off from work; otherwise, I kept going.

I comforted myself in the oddest ways. I found the idea of my own insignificance deeply reassuring. I remember thinking that no matter what happened, or what I did, the sun would keep coming up in the morning and going down at night, people would continue to go about their business as usual. Sometimes, at my lowest, I would reassure myself with the thought that my love of reading would stand me in good stead if I ever did end up in prison. I had a poem on my wall in my bedroom that I'd cut out of a magazine while I was at school when I was trying to convince myself I could be a hippy (I failed). It was the 'Desiderata'. Now, in the night, I would look at its words and feel immeasurably better.

Go placidly amid the noise and the haste, and remember what peace there may be in silence.

I set myself the task of learning it off by heart and doing so calmed me.

You are a child of the universe no less than the trees and the stars; you have a right to be here.

And, the most comforting line to me of all:

And whether or not it is clear to you, no doubt the universe is unfolding as it should.

I liked how that reminded me that I had very little power in the greater scheme of things and whatever I feared was miniscule by comparison. Perhaps I recognised that my fantasies were rather grandiose (what did I think I was about to become – Ted Bundy?) and that I did not really have the power to wreak the havoc I feared.

I did wonder if I would be able to look after children responsibly, and the idea that I might not be able to trust myself as a parent was awful. I saw myself once again as inadequate, weak and pathetic. I wondered why I had turned out so badly. I began to believe that I was just a bit of a mistake, badly wired, a lemon, a human version of a Friday car. I saw myself as the sort of person who should probably be returned to the factory as faulty. I was frightened I might end up in a mental hospital. This wasn't the most positive place from which to begin my brilliant career because, paradoxically, I was still ambitious. I still wanted to achieve something, to make my mark, to make a difference. To put it bluntly, at twenty-one, only a year out of university, I was convinced that I was and always would be a failure. I couldn't for the life of me see why everyone around me couldn't see it too, but they couldn't. My parents, friends and, most crucially, Ralph continued to see me as they always had. And the way they saw me was mostly positive. I knew that, but I also felt that if they could get inside my head, they would quickly change their minds.

ten

The job for the bread dough company only lasted a few months; things not being very rosy in the world of frozen baked goods. Very kindly, however, they gave me time to look for another job and I found one in an advertising agency as a junior dogsbody. Officially my position carried the title assistant account executive. Lowly and underpaid as it was, it was the kind of job people with much better track records than mine would have killed for. Indeed, you may be wondering how a young woman with a very ordinary degree in English literature and no work experience bar that of shop assistant or sales promotion girl managed to waltz so easily from one promising job to another. Part of the reason may be timing. I graduated in 1977, when there was not just full employment but a labour shortage. Moreover, only 10 per cent of the population had any kind of university degree, ordinary or otherwise. (These days it's 30 per cent.)

Degree or no degree, though, the major reason I was able to begin my brilliant career so relatively easily was due to my father. He was the MD of the multinational that owned the frozen bread dough company – although they hired me against his wishes. (I only took that job because it was offered to me. I had no idea what direction I should take. I was like a dandelion spore, carried by whichever wind was blowing at the time.) Andy had been awarded the title of Ad Man of the Year in the early 1970s and that helped me with the ad agency job.

I had struggled as a marketing officer at the dough company and now I struggled at the ad agency. I am sure my obsessive thoughts and anxiety didn't help, but I don't think they were the major reason I found the world of work so difficult. The first problem was that I had very little to do. The second was that when I was given a task I mostly fucked it up.

This is how being an assistant AE in an ad agency in the late 1970s felt to me. My boss, the group account director, would ask me to ask a question of the head of another department – usually, in those days, the head of print production. (This was long before email, remember; one of the reasons there were so many assistant-type jobs in those days was the need for someone to scurry around bearing messages.)

'Ask Peter why the herny hern of the squiddidely pop isn't here yet.'

Desperate to please, I would hurry across the office to the fearsome print production manager and repeat the question syllable by syllable. I couldn't do it word for word because I was often not sure where one word stopped and another one started.

No matter how politely I put the question, however, it always seemed to cause an explosion.

'But he hasn't given me the verialities of the synapolobops! I can't do anything without the verialities of the synapolobops – any fool should know that! Ask fucking Steven when I can expect those.'

And so I'd scurry back, ears ringing and feeling like a fool. When I repeated this response to my boss I would get yelled at again.

The more hopeless and bewildered I felt, the more people yelled at me. The more people yelled at me, the more hopeless I felt and the more mistakes I made. My worst-ever mistake (I am surprised I wasn't fired) was when I had to dispatch an urgent parcel for one of our biggest clients – Cathay Pacific. It had something to do with a touring Chinese opera company they were sponsoring and was URGENT! URGENT! URGENT! Somehow – sheer nerves, probably – I managed to transpose the street number on the parcel and it failed to arrive on time. When the evidence of my error (my handwriting was on the parcel) was shaken in my face, I was rendered mute for hours.

I hated that job and quickly became convinced that administration and organisation (which is what junior account service largely consists of) were not for me. As I said, I was just taking whatever came my way. I did not know what I was good at or what I might like. I hadn't been a particularly successful uni student (apart from as a sex bomb in the Ancient History Revues). I had been a hopeless marketing assistant (not being able to add up) and now I was proving to be an incompetent ad agency shit-kicker! Where had the smarty-pants who had got into Opportunity Class gone? Not to mention the fact that I was spending every idle moment terrified I was about to kill someone. Mind you, if I had killed my permanently red-faced, head-slapping screamer of a boss, I suspect I could have pleaded justifiable homicide; I wasn't the only staff member he bullied into incoherence.

I hated that job but I gritted my teeth and was determined to stick it out for at least twelve months. I may have been hopeless at everything, but I was smart enough to recognise that a CV of two short-term jobs straight out of uni was probably not a great way to start. And though I hated that job there were moments that were almost bearable. The first was when I was given the chance to oversee a photographic shoot of a poster campaign for Cathay Pacific. It involved shooting a Cathay stewardess with a surf lifesaver (symbolising Sydney) and an Aboriginal man (symbolising Darwin). The lifesaver was easy, but it was the young (and beautiful) Aboriginal man who most interested me. He was from a remote part of the Northern Territory and was very shy. He'd never been to Sydney – or any major city – before. I did my best to put him at ease. I have no idea if I succeeded, but he looked bloody marvellous in the photographs.

The campaign was shot by a German photographer. He and his assistant – also German – were flying around the world taking shots of 'typical' inhabitants in every Cathay destination alongside various female cabin staff. It is the sort of job that used to be quite common in advertising but I suspect rarely happens anymore. The Cathay stewardess was uninterested in the whole process, though the four of us did have a hilarious dinner where she got a bit pissed and told me and the Germans exactly what she thought of *gweilos*. We stink, are very hairy, and have huge noses and enormous breasts, apparently.

During the actual shoot days I had little to do but be on hand just in case. Consequently I spent most of my time with the hairdresser – Max Pinnell – and the make-up guy. I got on really well with both of them. I got on with them so well, in fact, that Max did my hair for a few years in his home over his kitchen sink. We lost contact in the early 1980s, when he moved to New York and did some work with fashion photographer Herb Ritts. Max is now one of the most successful and famous hairdressers in the world. I quite like telling people I was one of his earliest customers.

The job became more bearable when I got a new boss. He was an American and (what a relief) both softly spoken and supportive. He actually took time to explain things to me, which made everything much better. Even more encouragingly, he stopped by my desk one day and told me that he thought I showed some promise as a writer. When I had first arrived, I had been given a week or two in the creative department during my 'orientation'. To keep me occupied, I had been given some ad briefs to work on (brief is advertising speak for the jobs that clients give to writers and art directors). When I showed my work to the creative director I had been told – very bluntly – that I obviously had no talent in that direction. I was crushed, as I had been nursing quiet hopes. Now my new boss asked me to write the company newsletter. At last, I had something to do which, whether or not I was any good at it, at least I understood.

But I still hated that job and I hated the way the agency was run and I hated most of the people who worked there. It was hierarchical and cliquey. Everyone was trying to be cool. You were either in or you were out and I was totally out. I had gained weight since leaving uni so I was a pushy fat girl with too much to say and too little talent. I knew that was what they thought of me no matter how pithy or engaging my newsletter.

The agency was at the top of Foveaux Street in Surry Hills and I remember dragging myself up the steep climb from Central Station to my office every morning. It was a very sleazy part of town at that time and at lunchtime I would sit with the few friends I had made in the park at the top of the street. We were the most poorly paid people in the place, so we could rarely afford to go to the Dolphin or the Clock with everyone else. I had a rather creepy experience in that park. It was often filled with homeless people, many of whom, I am sure, were mentally ill. I think there may have been a hostel nearby. There was a particular man who seemed to develop a bit of an obsession with me (perhaps he recognised a kindred spirit?). He would stare at me as I sat with my friends to eat lunch. He would follow me as we walked back to work, muttering to himself. He frightened me.

I had another unsettling experience. I'd left work early to pick up my car, which was being serviced. I was standing on the platform at Central, waiting for the next train. I suppose it was about four in the afternoon; I had to pick up the car before five.

Suddenly, a young but rather large woman grabbed me by the arm. She was holding me fast with both hands.

'Does the next train go to St Leonards?' she asked in a very high-pitched and peculiar-sounding voice.

Always obliging, I looked up at the train schedule above us. 'No. It only goes as far as North Sydney.' I had to raise my voice a little because that very train was now approaching the station. My information seemed to upset the woman. She tightened her grip on my arms and began to moan and mutter in real distress. Then her face changed completely and she began to pull me towards the edge of the platform and the oncoming train.

I don't know about you, but whenever things like this happen to me, I am always so completely taken by surprise that I almost cooperate. I went along with it for a moment, then I began to pull back a little against this woman's seeming maniacal determination to cast me under the wheels of the train. As we got closer to the edge, another woman, watching us, politely got out of our way, even moving her bag so that my assailant could have a clearer trajectory towards the train tracks. It was such a weird situation it appeared to be happening in slow motion.

Anyway, I obviously did not end up under the train. I managed to slow her down enough so that I was able to step onto the train (I was going to North Sydney) and free my arms. I saw the strange woman glowering at me as the doors closed and the train pulled away. The woman who had moved out of our way was also on the train.

'Did you know that woman?'

'No, I have never seen her before in my life.' I looked down at my arms. They were red and quite sore where she had been gripping them.

It was deeply unsettling to have an encounter with just the sort of person I feared I might turn into. I began to wonder if there was something about me that attracted weirdos. Did they recognise something in me? Was it simply the sleazy end of town in which I worked that made such encounters more likely? Or was it that I was a young woman at that time and young women are often seen as both vulnerable and desirable? Maybe it was all of the above. In any case, I was glad to get out of there.

When the year was up, I found myself another job; my father's glory was still working its magic. In fact, he was now really famous, having left Reckitts and become the managing director of Kerry Packer's fledgling World Series Cricket. I remember being transfixed in the street when a bus went past me bearing the message in large letters: ANDREW CARO, YOUR WSC SIDES WOULD BE MORE POPULAR IF YOU USED SOME OF OURS. It was an ad promoting a new phenomenon – paid advertising on the side of buses. It is quite something to suddenly see your dad's name rushing towards you on a busy city street. I felt very proud of him. My only regret was that I was turning out to be such a disappointment.

I felt even more pride on the first night of the second series of WSC. I went to the game (the first cricket game ever played under lights in Sydney) after work and I will never forget the sound of the roar of the crowd as I approached the SCG. Despite the success of the ad campaign that Dad had commissioned from

Mojo – 'C'mon Aussie C'mon' – he had been nervous about how many people might attend. Clearly, it was a great success. Once inside the ground, I had to find my parents. Dad, true to his belief in merit, had employed two senior female executives at WSC: Margaret Harrop was the marketing manager and Irene Cave the PR manager. Women had never been allowed into the members' stand at the SCG before but, thanks to Margaret and Irene, the powers that be had to soften their stance because WSC had offices there.

There was also a VIP room where women were allowed, and I went there first, but I couldn't find Andy and Kate.

'They're in the WSC office,' someone told me, so I made my way up the stairs; I knew that, as a woman, I was only allowed to walk up the stairs and across the bar in order to get from one side of the stand to the other. As I climbed the stairs, a friend of my father's waylaid me, eager to chat about the huge crowd and great success of the night. (Such was the jam of people trying to get through the gates earlier in the day, Kerry Packer had told the attendants to stop taking tickets and just let everyone in.) I had stopped to talk to him when suddenly a little man in a grey coat appeared beside me, hopping from foot to foot angrily.

'You're not allowed to stand here!'

I turned to look at him.

'You're not allowed to stand on the stairs.'

'What?'

'Ladies are only allowed to walk up the stairs and across the bar. They must remain in motion at all times!' The man was apoplectic.

I was proud of my father's career success, of course. I was (and am) even more proud of the fact that his commitment to hiring and promoting talented women integrated the Sydney members' stand in 1978.

Thanks to my father's reflected glory, my next job was another good opportunity. I was back in the world of marketing, this time as a marketing officer (another junior shit-kicker position) for Lever & Kitchen. I would even have two brands of my own to manage – Lux and Softly. I was to be immersed in the world of laundry detergents!

My new offices were about as far away from my previous workplace at the seedy end of Foveaux Street as you could get and still be in the CBD. The Lever & Kitchen fabrics group was ensconced on the ninth floor of Unilever House. Unilever House was one of the first all-glass skyscrapers in Sydney and sat opposite the Opera House – directly opposite – between the Botanic Gardens and the harbour. (It was eventually torn down and replaced by the Toaster.)

Unilever House was a lovely place to work, even though its 1950s, all-mod-cons, *Mad Men*-esque, wood-veneer glory was already looking very dated. The disadvantage of being the first of anything was also beginning to tell. The technology was not quite up to the building design. Beneath the splendid glass windows framing the extraordinary view were metal windowsills. When they heated up in the sun you could give yourself a third-degree burn if you carelessly rested an elbow or leant back too far on your chair. And when the weather turned bad and the wind dashed rain against the windows, they leaked and the metal windowsills were lined with plastic cups to catch the drips. Many a pile of papers was ruined by a sudden squall.

The fabrics group (our responsibilities were the detergents that washed fabrics) was much kinder to me than my previous employers. I did at last feel like part of a team. But it took a while.

'We'd like to offer you the position, but you have one hurdle to overcome.' My new boss was never one to mince words.

'Great!' I was pleased to get the job. 'But what's the hurdle?' I was not pleased such a thing existed.

'There's one member of our team who does not want us to hire you.'

This was a blow. I'd been quite excited just a few moments ago and now I felt like I'd been slapped.

'The fabrics group secretary does not want to work for a woman. She says she is opposed to women in management.'

'Oh.'

'We've told her that's not reasonable and that we will be offering you the job – but it's only fair to warn you that she is much more important to us than you are, so if you can't get along, it'll be you who goes.'

Well, that knocked the wind out of my sails.

In the late 1970s it was still common for female clerical staff to refuse to work for a woman. Not that the secretary was working for me; I was the lowliest link in the chain of command. But I was the first female marketing officer the fabrics group had ever had. The two other marketing officers who joined the company at the same time – in households (cleaning products) and personals (soaps and shampoos) – were both blokes.

I set out to win the secretary over. Not only did I say 'please' and 'thank you' if she ever did anything for me, but I offered to help her with her own work when I had time. The strategy worked and we became friends. It did gall me to see the guys – even the ones as junior as I was – drop typing on her desk without so much as a by-your-leave, but it was a lesson well learnt: it stands you in very good stead to treat everyone with respect and ask for help politely rather than demand it as your due. I think women in the workplace then feared that women in management (even just potential management like me) would treat them the way the men did. There was no way they'd accept that from a woman. I think that turned out to be a long-term advantage for women of my generation. We became easy to work with – not because we were nicer but because we had no choice. I still believe women who are described as 'bitches' in the workplace or have the reputation of being difficult to work with are probably just women who behave too much like men.

Apart from the fact that it was a well-managed workplace in a glorious setting, my new job had another advantage: there were a few tasks I was actually good at.

Everyone, from the highest to the low, would go to the meetings at which the ad agencies presented the latest creative work. We – as the client – sat on one side of the desk and the agency representatives – usually from the account service and creative departments – sat on the other. On our side we sat strictly in order of seniority. The head of the fabrics group,

Peter England (who went on to worldwide glory in Unilever), took the top seat, followed by the three product managers. I took the seat at the bottom of the table. Peter always asked me for my opinion first. I loved anything funny or surprising and my enthusiasm caused the agency people – particularly the creatives – to beam at me. I was picking the work they liked best. This approval was an entirely new workplace experience. Peter, of course, being more sensible, quickly shut me down and usually picked an execution that wouldn't do us much good but certainly wouldn't do us much harm. But my comments amused him. I had the feeling that, despite his stern demeanour, he saw something in me.

The other area of the job I was good at was market research. I was fascinated by the lives and attitudes of consumers. In research debrief meetings my genuine interest and curiosity led me to ask sensible and intelligent questions. I also attended some training courses run by a market researcher Unilever worked with regularly. His name was Hugh Mackay. I remember he began one of the sessions by saying that the next generation of consumers would never have known a home without a TV. I didn't like to tell him that I had never lived in a house without one.

I also attended the annual in-house residential training course for potential leaders. Like all such courses, it was a lot of fun and I also learnt a great deal. What was really interesting, though, was a remark made to me by the trainer. He told me that the year I attended was the first time there were an equal number of women and men on the course, and he'd been running the course for almost a decade. Prior to 1978, there were at most one or two female participants out of twenty. Something was changing. Maybe there were a few more executives like my father, prepared to hire women on their merits.

It was about bloody time they changed too. It wasn't much fun being a woman in the workplace up until that time. It wasn't that much fun afterwards either, but it did very slowly get better. The floor I worked on consisted of a series of offices of various sizes depending on the importance of the occupants. The offices were arranged around the sides of the building. They had windows, views and doors you could close, and their occupants' names were embossed on the door in brass. These occupants were virtually all male. There were only two female managers. One, the research manager, was single and regarded as very odd. The product manager was married but childless and she was regarded as very scary.

The centre of the floor was open plan, crammed with desks occupied by women, most of them married with children. They'd rush in from the train at 8.30 am looking harried. They'd sit down at their desk and crunch sales numbers with their adding machines (this was long before calculators or computers) until 12.30. Then they'd dash off to the shops and buy the evening's groceries, returning with plastic bags of meat and vegetables they'd put in the office fridge. Sometimes they queued up at the bank or the post office to pay bills. At 1.15, they were back at their desks crunching the endless columns of numbers again. At 4.30, they rushed for their train, heading home to cook dinner for their families and put a few loads of washing on.

Nothing about their lives looked like any fun. They just worked – paid and unpaid – from the minute they got up in the morning until the minute they went to bed at night. Is it any wonder that women in the workplace began to demand more?

Being good with the agencies and the market researchers was a great improvement, and going on the various training courses was interesting and useful, but this represented only a small part of my role. Most of my time was taken up with wrangling the nightmares that were FUF, SUF and TUF.

FUF, SUF and TUF stood for first updated forecast, second updated forecast and third updated forecast, and they had to be done for both volume (anticipated amount of boxes sold) and value (anticipated amount of money earned). Worse, every line on the lengthy and complicated form had to balance both horizontally and vertically. Mine never, ever did, even with the help of an adding machine. I can remember erasing incorrect numbers so many times from the dreaded 'white sheets' (that's what we called them before they were filled in) I rubbed holes in the paper. Despite my inability to add up (a problem that continues to this day), wrestling with FUF, SUF and TUF did lead me to anticipate the Global Financial Crisis – although my timing was out by at least a few decades. Let me explain.

The numbers in FUF (the first updated forecast), even when they added up, were completely imaginary. We weren't putting in the numbers we realistically expected to make in either sales or profit for each of the four quarters of the year; we were putting in the numbers that would add up (or so they told me) to a preordained, politically acceptable number. The numbers in

SUF (the second updated forecast) were slightly more realistic because we had the actual sales and earnings for the first quarter. Surprise, surprise, they were always lower than the original forecast. So what did we do? We simply inflated the next three quarters so we would still make the required totals. By the time we did TUF (the third updated forecast), it was perfectly clear we would not make the sales or profit we had forecast. What we did then was simply cut the price of our products and sell them into retailers furiously to make our volume targets and cancel the last quarter's advertising and research so we could make the profit required. In other words, we milked our brands so that our big bosses (whom we never saw) wouldn't lose face and ruin their chances for promotion.

Even I could see this was not sustainable and that one day the whole thing would come tumbling down. I saw it as a corporate game of hot potato. Everyone knew the sales and profit figures were not reflective of the real situation, but everyone hoped they'd have been promoted to Europe or the US or Canada long before those particular chickens came home to roost.

Despite FUF, SUF and TUF, I stayed at Lever & Kitchen for eighteen months. I gained some confidence. Like my last boss at the ad agency, my bosses and colleagues at L&K identified my strengths as words and communications and my weaknesses as numeracy and any kind of organisation. They encouraged me to think that maybe I could write after all and I started to imagine going back into advertising as a writer. There was just one problem. There were almost no female writers in advertising agencies at that time and virtually no natural pathway for them to find such a job. But once again, my father's fame in the world of advertising and marketing was to come to my rescue.

eleven

As my confidence grew a little – at least I was good at two of the things I did at L&K – I revisited the idea of being a copywriter. These days, I'd tell a young woman (or man) to go to AWARD School (AWARD is the Australasian Writers and Art Directors Association), but it didn't exist back then. There were plans to start such a school and it opened its doors in 1980. Having taught in AWARD School over the years and seen the standard of its students – chosen by competitive entry – I am grateful that I snuck into the industry just before it began. I'm not sure how I would have gone if I had been forced to compete with so many talented people.

As it became clear that marketing wasn't for me either, I put out some feelers. Once again, my father's contacts helped and I found a couple of people in creative departments who were prepared to help me. They set me tasks and assignments (much like AWARD School) and then gave me feedback. One guy wanted to hire me but the job fell through. I got my hopes up a few more times for no result. Nevertheless, thanks to the assignments, I did manage to build up a collection of scripts and ideas. Then I met a woman at an industry function who, when I told her my dream of becoming a copywriter, offered to send my amateur portfolio to a friend of hers. His name was Bryce Courtenay and he was the creative director of George Patterson, the largest advertising agency in Australia at that time.

I got my hopes up again – Patts were big enough to take on trainees – but his feedback, when it came, was not encouraging. He set me yet another set of problems to solve with a short deadline. Sulky about another disappointment and sick of all the different opinions I was getting, I ignored his new briefs. I assumed that if I did nothing he'd forget about me and it was obvious I didn't have much hope of becoming a copywriter anyway. I started to think my choices were dwindling down to having kids (yikes) or working in a sandwich shop.

Bryce was not as easily discouraged as I was. When his deadline had passed I received an urgent call from the woman I had met (I still had not actually met Bryce) telling me he had called and asked where my work was. Aware that this was a great compliment, I sat up all night and worked on his briefs. I got them to him the next day. This time his feedback was much more positive and he told me that I had talent and that what I needed to do was 'look for a very small job in a very big agency'. Not his, sadly.

No matter; he gave me just the kick up the bum I needed. I got wind of a junior copywriter's position at the agency then called USP Needham (it is now DDB). This entailed more briefs that I had to solve and much toing and froing. I was on tenterhooks for weeks. To get this close to a job and to miss out yet again would have been very hard to bear. To my relief, I was eventually offered the position.

Beside myself with delight (and terror), I went to L&K the next day all set to resign. I had been moved from the fabrics group to the household group by this time and my new boss, John Clarke, was a lovely man with a wry wit. Less ambitious than Peter England, I think he might have liked to be a copywriter himself. Before I had a chance to give John my letter of resignation, he told me that L&K had decided I was more suited to working as an advertising creative than in marketing and so they had negotiated a junior copywriter's position for me at the advertising agency that Unilever then owned: SSC&B Lintas.

Frankly, his news completely floored me. From being a girl with no obvious talent or direction (not to mention a mental illness) contemplating life as a sandwich hand (either paid or unpaid), I had now been offered not one but two much coveted, rare-as-hen's-teeth junior copywriter positions!

It was bizarre to go from failure to even such relatively minor success almost overnight and I was moved by the kindness of my employers at L&K. However, overwhelmed though I was, I still realised that it was probably better to take the job I had got under my own steam rather than the one where I had been foisted on a creative director. I chose the job at USP and at the beginning of 1980 I took up the position. John Clarke wrote the following perceptive message on my farewell card: 'You may find blank sheets even harder to fill than white sheets' (a reference to the dreaded FUF, SUF and TUF). He would have made a good copywriter.

* * *

Despite my unexpected taste of success, I was still in the grip of my obsessional neurosis. It didn't stop me functioning – or even succeeding – but it haunted me. I had found another psychiatrist; I suppose my GP must have referred me. He was a behaviourist and much more helpful than the Freudian. He was warm and gentle in his responses to me and he was willing to give me hard information. He also began to subtly challenge my view of myself.

'I notice you are always beautifully dressed,' he said one day. 'Your clothes are always well coordinated and the colours go together very well.'

I was pleased with his observation. I love clothes (I still do) and I enjoy putting colours, cuts and proportions together in a way that I think suits me. However, I realised that he was trying to suggest that, far from being lazy, careless and slapdash, I might actually be a bit of a perfectionist. I denied it at the time, but little by little he did begin to chip away at my rather relentlessly negative view of myself.

Soon after I began seeing him, he asked me to write down every violent thought or fantasy I had in a small notebook. I did so, although I was careful to keep it hidden. God knows what people would have thought if they'd come across my lurid imaginings – probably, quite accurately, that I was a bit nuts.

Within days of beginning to record them, my obsessive thoughts began to recede. By simply getting them out of my head and onto paper I was able to reduce their power. Was I about to be cured? Not so fast. As the violent thoughts began to recede I read an article about agoraphobia – the fear of leaving the house – and within the time it took to read its 800-odd words, I replaced one fear with another. My fear of doing violence to someone was replaced by a fear that, any minute now, I would have a ferocious panic attack and be condemned to live within four walls forever. It seemed I needed my obsessive fears and was not about to let them go. I guess in the weird world of mental illness, moving from a fear of harming others to a fear of harming myself (literally locking myself up) is a step forward, albeit a gloomy one.

Needless to say, just as I never actually hurt anyone, so I failed to succumb to agoraphobia, although I did have a couple of nasty panic attacks. My psychiatrist told me that this kind of panic was physical and I could only take myself so far emotionally. What he meant was that I couldn't make myself become agoraphobic just by fearing it. I didn't believe him, of course.

I had also decided to take my weight in hand. Through a combination of diet and exercise I managed to whittle myself down to forty-five kilos. (Don't get too alarmed; I'm only 155 centimetres tall, so I was slim but not skeletal.) I only kept myself at that weight, however, with vigilance. I ate one meal a day – usually in the evening. I ate no breakfast and only a tub of low-fat yoghurt and a piece of fruit for lunch. As watching the clock is not of great importance for creative people, I was also able to hop on the bus at lunchtime and go to the newly opened John Valentine's Fitness Centre in Crows Nest three times a week and work out. The gym only had one change room so they ran men's days and women's days. Women could come on the men's days; we just had to change in an office. That suited me because the men's aerobics classes were harder and my obsessive tendencies had latched onto exercise with a vengeance. I don't think this unhealthy fixation on controlling diet and exercise is unusual. I watch with interest (and some concern) the obsession some people display on Facebook about how much they eat and how much they work out. Excessive health on the outside, as I know only too well, can sometimes indicate a lack of emotional and psychological health within. It certainly did for me.

I think my successful weight loss gave me a sense of some control. My mother worried about it. I think she was concerned I might develop anorexia and, given my mental state, who could blame her? I never did develop anorexia, however, though I did have an eating disorder – restricted eating, they call it – and, as a result, I ruined my metabolism forever. I find it almost impossible to lose weight these days, thanks to my obsessive vigilance in the 1980s. It was the era of Jane Fonda and 'going for the burn'. What a child of my times I was.

* * *

Teetering on the brink of nervous collapse or not, life went on. Ralph and I had bought our first place together, a very rundown one-bedroom apartment in an old 1940s red-brick block on Blues Point Road in McMahons Point. Once we'd spent three months doing it up, I was able to walk to work from McMahons Point to the top of Walker Street in North Sydney. This I managed to accomplish every morning and every evening, despite my fear that I would suddenly be stricken with the screaming heebie-jeebies and have to flee back to the safety of my little apartment and lock myself away in it forever. Even at the time I could see that this new neurosis of mine had its absurd side. I was also aware that, from the outside, I was looking pretty good for a twenty-three-year-old. I had the job I wanted, a man who loved me and a foot in the housing market. However, my good fortune just made me beat myself up about my inability to 'pull myself together'. As anyone who has ever struggled with their mental health will understand, it wasn't life, it was my own wonky mind I found impossible to control.

Nevertheless, things were improving. I made a much better copywriter than I did assistant account executive. It looked as if I might at last have found a niche for my rather odd self. This made sense when I looked at some of the other people I was working with. Quite a few of them were a little odd themselves. Maybe this was due to the way we made a living – writing TV ads for Ronald McDonald and the Hamburglar in the morning, finding new ways to communicate 'crunch' at midday or composing radio ads for the latest soap on Channel 10 (*Sons and Daughters*, I think) or print ads for 2GB News Talk 87 (as it was then called) in the afternoon. Despite – or maybe because of – my high anxiety, I liked the variety, the pace and the pressure. I responded well to urgent deadlines.

I did so well writing ads for 2GB that I became friendly with its manager, a young Nigel Milan. He was a real gift for a young copywriter who was trying to make her way. I remember him ringing me up to make a comment on an ad I had presented to him, then stopping himself, saying, 'Come on, Nigel, why pay a dog if you are going to tell it how to wag its tail?' I never found out what his concerns were because he then apologised and hung up. Frankly, I didn't even mind being called a dog if it meant my ad could go through unchanged. Nigel and his then-wife, Lindy, became friends. We were entertained at their house and they came to our funny little flat. It did feel as if I might be growing up – on the outside, anyway.

At USP I was put to work with an equally young and untried art director and, although I liked her, we did not work particularly well together. When TV took over from print as the dominant media for advertising, art directors (visual people) and copywriters (word people) were teamed up. Most of my career, I have been paired with an art director, and I still prefer to work this way; two heads are better than one. That said, I am not a fan of the brainstorm. More than two heads are a pain in the arse because it becomes a competition rather than a collaboration. I have always found collaboration to be much more creative than competition.

For really new and original ideas to emerge you need (well, I do, anyway) a completely fear-free environment. I need to feel respected by my colleague before I will risk suggesting something out of the box. This was the problem between my first art director and me. We were competing with one another to prove who was the best. Neither of us was confident enough to let the other shine. I think this is a perennial problem with young creatives. It is usual to put two juniors together, two middleweights together and two seniors together. It's also usual to put two women together and two men together. Honestly, for people with the word 'creative' on their business card, creative directors show precious little of it. If anyone had ever made me a creative director (and they should have), I would have paired each junior with a senior. The junior would challenge and stretch the older creative, and the senior would teach the junior while hopefully being confident enough to let them shine.

Chris and I were locked in the usual fight for dominance and, to my relief but also shame, I won. I could see the writing on the wall when my creative director (a genial Yank who rarely emerged from his office) turned up in my cubicle one day to tell me that he really liked my work and that he was giving me a chance to work on my first new business pitch. It was for Drum tobacco (I know, I can hear the howls of horror from here, but bear with me) and he wanted me to work with one of the senior art directors – all of whom, I hasten to add, were blokes. Anyway, I was thrilled to be offered the assignment (at that stage of my career I'd have advertised weapons of mass destruction if I'd been asked) and also aware that Chris had been sidelined. I felt some guilt about this, but not enough to make me turn down the opportunity. The CD left my cubicle to be quickly replaced by the senior art director who was to be my creative partner on this important pitch.

'No offence,' said this bloke as he lowered his leather-clad posterior onto my spare chair, 'it's no reflection on the quality of your work or anything, but I don't want to work on this pitch with you. I don't think you're the right person for it.'

I was devastated. I had learnt, however, that when you get hit in the face in the workplace, the best thing to do is keep your mouth shut.

'It's just,' he said, after an uncomfortably long pause, 'that this is for Drum tobacco, which is a very male product, and so I think I should work on it with . . . um . . . well . . . with another bloke.'

'Hang on,' I said, regaining the power of speech, 'you and Fred have just finished a campaign for Olay skincare. How come you can think like a woman but I can't think like a man?'

Even under his year-round tan, I could see he had gone a little pale.

'Well, um, maybe it's my problem, but I still don't want to work with you on it.'

I lost my opportunity. Poor Chris, however, lost her job. In the long run, there was no downside to me losing the opportunity to pitch for Drum tobacco. I was quietly pleased when the agency failed to win the account and I have also been able to put my hand on my heart ever since and say that I have never advertised cigarettes – or weapons of mass destruction, for that matter.

twelve

Other things happened to me while I was cutting my teeth as a copywriter. The first was that I became pregnant and had an abortion.

For reasons I no longer recall, I had stopped getting my period, so my GP took me off the pill and said Ralph and I should use condoms and spermicide for a month to 'give my body a rest'. Not such good advice as it turned out. The very first time we took the doctor's advice, the condom tore. These days, I'd simply have popped into the chemist the next day for a dose of the morning-after pill. In those days, I had to wait and see if disaster had struck and think about what I would do if I had conceived.

Disaster had struck. We were pregnant. I didn't have a moment's hesitation and nor did Ralph. I could not go through with the pregnancy. It felt as if it had happened to my body and not to me. This was not because of my anxiety or obsessive neurosis. That didn't help, certainly, but I'd be lying if I hid behind that as an excuse. If I'd wanted that baby, I'd have gone ahead and had it, mental illness or not. I simply did not want it. My life was finally looking up. I was focused on my career. I was not ready to walk away from it. You can judge me and call it a 'lifestyle choice' if you like, but I have no regrets.

I booked a termination as quickly as I could and that was the end of that. Did I feel any grief? Did I feel guilty or ashamed? No, and I never have. We had been responsible. I had been following doctor's orders. I would much rather have not become pregnant, but as I had, it had to be dealt with. When I woke up from the anaesthetic and realised I wasn't pregnant anymore all I felt was overwhelming relief. I could go back to my real life.

Many years later, I was scheduled to appear on Richard Glover's 'Monday Political Forum'. It is a weekly segment airing as part of his *Drive* program on ABC Radio 702 in Sydney. I was booked to debate the issues of the day with former New South Wales Liberal Opposition leader John Brogden and the Anglican Archbishop of Sydney, the Reverend Peter Jensen. Tony Abbott, then the federal health minister in the Howard government, was in the middle of a scandal surrounding his son, who had been born to a girlfriend and adopted out. (It later transpired that the adopted child was not Abbott's son, but that information was not known by anyone at the time.) Abbott had been a very high-profile opponent of abortion all his life and, as health minister, had recently tried to get the abortion drug RU486 excluded from the Australian market. He had failed, largely due to cross-party voting by the women in parliament. I knew, therefore, that abortion was likely to be on our list of topics for discussion, particularly considering the presence of Archbishop Jensen. When I opened Richard's email listing our topics, sure enough, abortion led the list. I immediately wondered if I was going to have to talk about my own experiences.

That evening in the studio, when the discussion about abortion started, Jensen was unequivocal in his condemnation. Brogden was less definite but still negative about it as an option. When Richard asked for my opinion, I began by talking about the giant female silence around the topic and how it was a rare sexually active woman who hadn't wondered with white knuckles whether she would be faced with having to make a decision that wasn't abstract and theoretical (as it was to the men discussing the topic with me) but real, visceral and life-changing.

When asked to respond to my remarks, Brogden shifted a little in his position. Jensen did not move an inch. Abortion was wrong, it was murder, and so on and so forth.

Glover turned back to me and I knew I could not live with myself if I did not break the female silence I had named. I told them I had a fairly typical maternal history for a woman of my age (I was in my forties by then, I think). I'd had two children, one miscarriage and an abortion. There was a deathly hush as I explained that abortions weren't something that happened to some nasty promiscuous bunch of not-very-nice women, but to all sorts of women for all sorts of reasons. Indeed, I said, it wasn't that the men discussing the topic with me didn't know anyone who'd had an abortion, it was just that if women knew you had very negative views on the subject, they simply wouldn't tell you about it. I was also very clear that I did not regret my decision at all. 'How could I?' I said. 'If I'd had that child, I would not have had the two much-loved and wanted daughters that I have now.'

The conversation moved on (I think we talked about the Iraq War) and Glover finished the show by asking us what our favourite recipes from the 1970s were. I chose apricot chicken – the one made with sachets of French onion soup and tinned apricots and sour cream.

Apricot chicken notwithstanding, when I left the studio I was terrified. I wondered if I would get death threats, be picketed or shunned. I walked back to my car waiting for someone to throw something at me – if not a rotten tomato, then at least an insult. Nothing happened. On my way home I got a few text messages from friends who'd been listening. They were all very supportive, and many told me about their own abortions (confirming my point rather nicely). But they were my friends; surely it would be different with strangers?

That night I had to attend a P&C meeting at my daughter's high school. It was a secular public school, thank goodness, but even so, many parents had very conservative views about life and many very religious families sent their kids to the school – as is their right. It is often the more conservative parents who populate P&Cs. As I arrived, I felt very nervous.

The P&C president greeted me with a wide smile. 'Hi, Jane,' she said. 'I heard you earlier on Richard Glover; loved that bit about the apricot chicken!'

And that was it. The sum total of the response. Abortion is normal. It's simply not an issue for most people.

While we are on the subject of abortion, I found myself at a very prestigious International Women's Day lunch some time in the late 1990s. It was in honour of the wife of one of the senior executives at Saatchi & Saatchi, the agency for which I was then working. The woman was a sculptor (not a very famous one) and she had put together an exhibition to celebrate women's bodies for IWD. It involved plaster casts of well-known women's naked bodies. Her husband was a very important and influential man, so the people who attended the exhibition mattered. They included an international guest – a famous author and thinker whose name would be very familiar to you. I found him utterly repellent. He arrived at the opening of the exhibition surrounded by a bevy of pretty young women. He was middle-aged at that time and corpulent. On his tie – and this was International Women's Day, remember – he had pinned Polaroids of young women in various stages of undress. The gleeful look on his face reminded me of a naughty boy trying to upset his teacher. I did my best to ignore him, but I found myself seated near him at lunch. He began spouting the most predictable sexist nonsense in the same naughty-boy fashion. I can't remember now exactly what was said, but it was the usual sniggering stuff that insecure men say about women's bodies. I suppose I should have expected it, given the subject of the exhibition we had all just attended, but it was depressing hearing this stuff at a supposedly feminist gathering on International Women's Day. Unable to bear it any longer, I took him on.

'You may be world renowned for the originality of your thinking, but you are an incredibly conventional thinker about women.'

This remark caused hilarity at the table and had the effect of shutting the so-called great man up. (And, yes, I am very proud of that.)

What my remark also did was alert one of the pretty women in his entourage to my presence and she engaged me in conversation. She was quite young and had a lovely Irish accent. She was also much more interesting than her boss. As the lunch wore on and more wine was consumed, she began to confide in me. It turned out she was pregnant and was in a complete quandary about what to do. I had no idea who she was pregnant to; I was relieved to find out later it was her boyfriend back in Ireland and not her repellent boss. As we talked, she told me that she desperately did not want to keep the baby but she was terrified that to terminate the pregnancy was a terrible sin. She didn't think she would go to hell, necessarily – I am not sure how religious she was – but all that early indoctrination by the Irish church about women, sexuality and sin had done its work. She felt crippling shame that she would even think of having an abortion. I told her about my own experience and why I felt no guilt, no shame and no regret.

A week or so later, I received a letter from her. I have treasured it ever since. It read in part:

Being able to talk to you and hear of your experience made me realise that making the decision to terminate my pregnancy wasn't as selfish an act as I had first believed . . . You helped me diminish many of my fears and resolve certain dilemmas I was facing.

I suspect it was the memory of this experience that led me to speak openly about my abortion on radio while debating an archbishop. That young, frightened Irishwoman showed me how damaging the great female silence on abortion can be to flesh-and-blood women leading real and complicated lives. She also told me in that letter that, apart from her boyfriend, I was the only person she had dared to talk to about the situation. I continue to write and speak openly about having had an abortion, as I am doing again here. I hope it passes on a little courage. Whether it does or not, I do know this for sure: silence merely passes on shame.

* * *

Back in 1981, as I worked away at the briefs I was allocated, I found a different kind of silence oppressive. I needed background noise while I worked. This was long before there were any desktop computers or iPods, so I had a little transistor radio. I used to tune it to the ABC and my favourite program was a precursor to *Life Matters* called *Offspring*. Once a week, they had a regular guest, Terry Colling, who ran the Marriage Guidance Council of New South Wales at that time. Every week, he would discuss a different aspect of relationships, covering not just marriage but kids, grandparents, extended families even workplace relationships and friendships. I found everything he had to say sensible, clear and wise. One morning, the radio host asked Colling if only people with relationship problems could seek counselling from Marriage Guidance. No, said Colling, anyone who thought they could benefit from counselling was welcome.

I didn't hesitate. I rang the nearest office – over the highway in Milsons Point – and took the first available appointment.

I arrived at the converted terrace house at the appointed hour, filled in the required forms and then waited for my randomly assigned counsellor. The woman who greeted me in the reception area was tall, in her forties by the look of her and very attractive. She had a wide, warm smile and the faintest trace of a foreign accent. She introduced herself as Jytte.

From the first, I felt much more at ease with her and the common-sense approach that counsellors take than I did with all the storied psychiatrists I had previously consulted. We both talked – not just me. She listened with compassion and empathy. She could be quite tough and confronting when she needed to be, but when I left her office at the end of our weekly hour together, not only did I feel better but I had learnt something.

For the first few weeks I was her client (counsellors don't call the people they work with patients), I would often just sit and cry. It was a relief to be able to just let myself go in her supportive and non-judgmental presence. Slowly, however, we began to do some real work. I remember arriving one day fresh from a bruising encounter on a shoot for a TV commercial

I had written. When Jytte asked me how I was, I launched into a full explanation of what had just occurred.

'There was a discussion about a particular shot and I felt – I did write the bloody thing, after all, and it is *my* idea – that what they wanted to do was wrong. I said so. The agency producer disagreed with me. I listened to him but I made the point again that the direction being suggested was not in keeping with the concept – *my concept*! Eventually I won the argument. Then this man, this supposed colleague . . .' I was working myself up all over again '. . . called me aside and publicly tore strips off me for daring to stand up for my idea – which, by the way, I thought was my job! I was so astonished and humiliated by his behaviour I felt close to tears and, of course, he noticed and then he said, "Oh, for God's sake, and now you're overreacting again. You are so overemotional!" '

I got so upset just telling Jytte the story I felt close to tears all over again.

She stopped me. 'Hang on; this overreacting, overemotional thing – do you think he was right?'

'People are always saying it to me so I guess he must be. Other people don't seem to get as het up as I do.' I was feeling really bad now and a couple of tears fell.

Jytte passed me the ever-present box of tissues. 'Really?' She sounded sceptical.

I took the tissues.

'Tell me something,' she said. 'How much reaction is enough? How much is too much? And who decides?'

I gaped at her. My tears stopped. When she put it like that, I could see what absurd criticisms 'overemotional' and 'overreacting' really were.

'Well?'

'You mean I don't have to accept his judgment of me?'

'That's exactly what I mean. Next time someone tries to close you down like that – and if my clients are any guide, it happens to women a lot – just ask them that question. It shuts them up fast.'

I was experiencing a successful therapeutic relationship. I trusted her and knew she was not judging me. She didn't think I was crazy but nor did she spend much time on my neurosis. She focused on all the other dysfunctional ways in which I interacted with the world and it turned out that there were many of those.

Thanks to Jytte's warmth and intelligent understanding, I learnt about boundaries – where I stopped and other people started. I learnt to think about who really owned a problem in any conflict. For example, if Ralph wanted me to do something in a certain way and got annoyed when I didn't, even though it didn't bother me, then that was actually his problem. He could do it himself or put up with the way I did it. I didn't have to change anything just because someone else wanted me to. This was a revelation to me. Just because someone was blaming me for something didn't automatically mean that it was my fault or even my problem. I could choose whether I wanted to do something about it or not. I could also choose how I reacted or whether I needed to react at all. I learnt that other people's sadness or anger was just that – theirs – and that I did not need to take it on, to take responsibility for it or try to fix it. I learnt that I was entitled to my feelings just as other people were entitled to theirs. My feelings didn't have to be sane or reasonable for me to be entitled to them; what I felt was legitimate just because I felt it.

I have remembered so much of what she taught me. I told her that I was being selfish about something in a session and she interrupted me again.

'You know what it really means when someone calls you selfish, don't you?'

'No.'

'It means, "Don't you be selfish, let *me* be selfish." It's just another criticism women hear all the time, usually when they dare to put their own needs first. Don't buy that one either.'

I also learnt I was only answerable for my actions, not my thoughts or my emotions. It was not my responsibility to keep everyone else happy and peaceful; it was only my responsibility to take care of my own emotional state in an adult and self-responsible way. Enormous bricks of guilt toppled off my shoulders every enlightening week.

These are lessons I have never forgotten. They have become to me like driving a car, so automatic that I'd have trouble describing to you how I do it. The lessons learnt then have given me an understanding about emotions (EQ, if you like) that serves me well to this day.

* * *

Not all of the consequences of my new self-awareness were positive; at least, not in the short term. As I began to change, so my relationship with Ralph began to change too. Such was my excitement at my new discoveries that I tried to share it all with him and was a bit bewildered when he responded by trying to shut me down. In hindsight, I can imagine how irritating my enthusiasm must have been. There are few people more annoying than the newly self-aware. However, some of our new difficulties were more serious. As I changed the way I responded to events and to other people, including Ralph, the power balance in our relationship began to shift. If we were to stay together, he was going to have to give up a little power in the relationship to make room for me.

I remember trying to tell him what had happened in my session with Jytte that day. I can't remember what revelation I was waxing lyrical about – maybe it was the lesson I'd learnt about overreacting or what selfish really means. Whatever it was, I was bubbling over about it. I was getting ready for bed in our little flat in McMahons Point. I turned around to look at Ralph, hoping for some comment or confirmation about what I was saying. He was already in bed and, as I looked at him, I could see I was talking to a brick wall. His face was blank but the way he was turned away from me looked defensive.

'Can you shut up?' he said. 'I'm tired. I want to go to sleep.'

It was like being doused with a bucket of cold water. I was so excited by what I was learning, I wanted to share it, but all he could hear was that I was changing, and that made him (understandably) afraid.

Our conflict grew and I began to worry that our seven-year relationship might be about to blow apart. I remember a furious fight one night in the car. I was trying to get Ralph to acknowledge that we had a problem.

'But I don't have a problem!' He was now often exasperated with me.

'You are in a relationship with me. This means that if I have a problem, you have a problem.'

Fortunately, Jytte was a relationship counsellor, and she suggested we come to some sessions as a couple. To his eternal credit and my eternal gratitude, Ralph agreed. The first session was tense to start with, as Jytte asked us both to describe how we felt about our relationship. Ralph was resistant and defensive at first. Then, quite suddenly, he dropped his guard. He burst into tears.

'I don't understand,' he said. 'I don't understand why it's all going wrong and what she wants!'

I know this sounds awful, but as soon as he broke down I knew we would be okay. It was what I had wanted from him (I know, that sounds worse). I wanted him to trust me enough to reveal his vulnerability as I was revealing mine. I didn't want him to change in any way except to let me in more; to let me see him when he felt weak, inadequate and vulnerable as well as when he felt strong, joyful and in charge. I didn't want him to be the strong one and me to be the weak one. That didn't seem real to me. We both needed to be weak sometimes and strong sometimes – to be ourselves with one another and not to pretend, if this was to be a relationship that was going to last. When he cried, he let me in.

It was all we needed. With a dispassionate and skilled third party, we were able to work through our conflict and renegotiate the balance of our relationship. Thirty-three years later, I remain evangelistic about couples counselling – all counselling, in fact. When I need help, I ask for it.

I was so fascinated by what I was learning – neurotic anxiety notwithstanding – that after my six months of therapy with Jytte were up (that was the maximum Marriage Guidance allowed) I trained as a group leader with the Institute of Group Leaders. I became a volunteer telephone counsellor with Telefriend for a while (Lifeline rejected me because I didn't believe in their god). Eventually, I began to co-run groups for Marriage Guidance in the evenings, after work. I ran communication and self-assertion groups, self-awareness groups, separates groups (for people who were either leaving a relationship or had been left), and one group for children of separated parents, which really tested my mettle. I learnt more from leading those groups than the participants did from attending them, I am sure. Slowly, painfully, I was starting to develop some understanding of myself.

On the first night of any group we sat around in a circle and introduced ourselves by saying our names and telling the group a little about our lives. Often this resulted in someone asking me how a writer in an ad agency could also be a group leader. My answer was always, 'When I get a brief from a client in my day job, they have information that they want me to communicate to an audience in a way that the audience can hear it. When I come here, my job is also to give you information in a way that you can hear it. The two jobs are the same.'

And they were.

I now realise that my anxiety neurosis, although I longed to be free of it at the time, was a gift. One of the other things I learnt in therapy is that people only change when it gets too uncomfortable to stay the same. I think that is what my anxiety was trying to do for me. In many ways, despite how crazy it seemed, it was the healthiest part of me. My anxiety, I believe, came from a part of me that knew I needed to change. It was nipping at my heels, pushing me to reach out, to search for the skills I needed and the understandings about myself and life in general that I lacked. I am glad I didn't ignore my anxiety. I am grateful it was so intense that I could not just turn my face away from it. I sought help. I got help. I learnt things that stand me in good stead to this day. I would urge anyone struggling with any kind of misery to do the same.

thirteen

After two and a half years at USP, I knew that if I wanted to progress as a copywriter, I had to move to a different agency. In advertising, there are the well-respected creative agencies that are often smaller, flexible and locally owned, and the large, boring, much more profitable multinationals. (The latter often buy the former.) USP was one of the latter. Its work rarely appeared in award shows (no industry on earth gives itself as many awards as advertising) and it was not prestigious to work there. I met another junior copywriter at a party. The hostess introduced us, thinking we'd have things in common. Scott worked for one of those locally owned, creative hot shops; when he discovered that I was at USP, he quickly found a reason to walk away. I felt the slap and it stung.

I was doing well at USP. I had my own accounts. I had made some TV commercials that were well liked in the agency. The ad I was proudest of was written for a Toltoys product – Pipsquirt, a pen that squirted water. (Advertising has always been a weird way to earn a living.) I wrote a Bugsy Malone-style script where kids played bored office workers who livened up their day by squirting one another with the pen. It was fun and funny and, if I do say so myself, well-written. It also gave rise to my first-ever moment of taking a moral stand in the workplace.

One of the office characters was a 'secretary filing her nails' and we cast a lovely ten-year-old with (I'd guess) a West Indian background. She had fabulous funky hair and a cheeky manner that was perfect for the character. When I showed the Polaroids (old-school technology) of the cast to the account director (the agency person who managed the client relationship), he nodded at all the shots of the children we'd cast until we got to the secretary.

'I don't think the client will approve her. Do you have an alternative?'

I smelt racism.

'Why won't he approve her? She's perfect.'

'I just don't think he will.'

'Why? Because she's black?'

'Yeah. He won't want to run the risk.'

'Well, if the client is going to reject a child because she is black, he is going to have to tell me that directly to my face. I am not prepared to offer an alternative. If he's a racist, he'll have to own up to it.'

We presented the shots of the cast and the client approved all of them enthusiastically. He wasn't the least bit bothered by the girl we'd cast as the secretary. She went on to do a terrific job in the commercial.

The only conclusion I could draw was that it wasn't the client who was racist – it was the account director. That encounter taught me that it is less risky than you'd think to speak out against discrimination. If you refuse to allow people to get away with it, even a shit-kicking junior copywriter with no clout can make a difference.

I was now working with a much more sympathetic art director. She was more experienced than I was and so we supported one another rather than competing. Working with Eleni (she was Greek with the coolest hair I had ever seen) was fun, but I was restless. Maybe my confidence was growing, partly because I was gaining some respect in the workplace, but also because of the work I was doing with Jytte. I wanted to move on. I wanted to work with clients who were more likely to approve the riskier work that might win awards and so build my career.

The way creatives get ahead is to win awards – which may be why there are so many award shows. It is also how agencies build their reputations and sell themselves to potential clients. There is always a conflict between ads that sell lots of product and those that win awards. They are not necessarily different, of course, but back in the days when consumers had a much more restricted choice of media than they do now, a large media budget could make a lousy ad very successful. By playing the bloody thing over and over and over, advertisers could literally bore (in both senses of the word) their way into consumers' heads.

I was also sick of being treated like a junior at USP. It has been my experience throughout my working life that if I ever wanted to progress, I had to move on to another employer. I don't know if this is about being a woman in the workplace or simply the nature of advertising. Agencies are often not very good at promoting from within.

I went about finding a job in a more creative agency in a way that I now realise was very naive. I simply picked up the latest AWARD annuals and noted the credits for the featured ads that I admired the most. I then made a list of the creative directors to whom I wanted to show my portfolio and rang them up. Yep, cold-called them, just like that. I suspect they thought I was very ballsy. I wasn't. I was just wet behind the ears.

For whatever reason, most of the people I called agreed to see my 'book' (my creative portfolio). When I showed them my work, most were encouraging, but didn't have room in their agency for a writer with only two and a half years' experience. I rang Peter Carey (yes, *the* Peter Carey) at his agency McSpedden Carey. He was both kind and encouraging, but it was the same old story. That's the trouble with small, creative agencies. They are, well, small.

Lionel Hunt is not a name that many people outside of the ad industry would be familiar with, but within it – certainly in the 1970s, 80s and 90s – Lionel was Martin Scorsese, Clint Eastwood and George Clooney all rolled into one. In the late 70s, he and art director Gordon Trembath started an agency called the Campaign Palace. It began with principles about the kind of advertising it wanted to produce; creative, risky, attention-getting. It believed in the campaignable idea (hence its name) and argued that a strong creative idea was the only way to get the most out of a limited advertising budget. The work the Palace (as it became known) produced lived up to its ideals and it quickly became internationally famous. Everyone in every creative department in the land (and quite a few in other lands, particularly the UK) wanted to work there.

The 1970s and 80s were the heyday of TV advertising in Australia. If you put an ad on TV, sales went up, so budgets were big. You could reach 80 per cent of the population between 8 and 10 pm by running your ad on the three commercial stations. As a result of this power, two schools of advertising arose. The British-influenced school of creativity favoured subtlety and wit; it was often literate and intelligent. In Australia, this style was epitomised by the Palace and was the advertising that most creative people admired and so was the kind that won most of the awards. The second school was more influenced by American advertising and so was brash and populist but also more uniquely Australian. This type of advertising was epitomised by an agency that opened around the same time as Hunt and Trembath started the Palace. The two creatives behind it were called Alan Johnson and Alan Morris. They called their agency Mojo. Clients loved what Mojo was doing. Their ads sold product by the pallet load. Creatives also admired their work. The two Alans specialised in jingles, sung by Jo in his very distinctive Aussie voice – but not as many people aspired to work there. Mo and Jo had a great style, but it was *their* style. You had more of a chance to develop your own voice at the Palace. I admired the work done by the Campaign Palace because it was the sort of witty, literate, thoughtful work I wanted to do myself. I was also under no delusion that I was remotely musical – remember the piccolo?

There was something else about the two rival agencies. Mojo started in Sydney and was very Sydney in its style and, frankly, its blokeyness. The Campaign Palace began in Melbourne and reflected the more intellectual and understated style of that city. Ads that older readers may remember from these agencies include 'One day you're going to get caught' for Rio underwear, the 'I'm wearing No Knickers' for Holeproof No Knickers and the 'Get Wrecked' radio campaign for Great Keppel Island from the Campaign Palace. Mojo were winning accolades for 'C'mon Aussie C'mon' for World Series Cricket with my dad as the client (you can see why he was so much more famous than I was), 'You Ought to be Congratulated' for Meadow Lea and 'I feel like a Tooheys' for the beer brewery.

All I knew was that the ads I admired the most in the 1979, 1980 and 1981 AWARD annuals were written by Lionel Hunt. So, just as I had with all the other creative directors whose work I enjoyed, I rang the Palace office in Sydney (I was so out of the loop I didn't realise Lionel was based in Melbourne) and asked to speak to him. My ignorance worked in my favour. Lionel happened to be at the Sydney agency that day and so the receptionist assumed I must be someone who knew him and put me straight through.

'Hello, is that Lionel Hunt?'

'It is.'

'Oh . . . hi . . . um . . . my name's Jane Caro and I'm a junior copywriter at USP Needham and . . . um . . . I'd like to show you my book.'

'Sure, can you be here by five?'

Just to put this into perspective, this was the advertising equivalent of getting put straight through to Martin Scorsese and asking if you can show him your screenplay! God knows what Lionel thought, but it has been my experience that people who are really good at their craft are always generous with young people.

I was pleased with the speed at which I had gained an appointment, but when I told a couple of people at USP that I had an interview with Lionel Hunt at 5 pm that afternoon, they freaked out. That's when I realised I had achieved something special and it immediately made me nervous.

I turned up at Boronia House in Mosman on the dot of five. Boronia House, then the premises of the Sydney Palace, was (and is) a gracious old mansion surrounded by gardens, set back from busy Military Road. The reception area perfectly combined the old and the new, and the walls were lined with framed examples of the agency's equally elegant, refined and tasteful work. Frankly, I would have killed to work in such an environment.

I didn't have to wait long before I was ushered in to meet the great man. He was charming but no-nonsense and wasted little time on social niceties. He flicked through my book quickly – which was worrying – then he looked at me.

'This is the best young book I've seen in ages,' he said. 'But I can't hire you here yet' (I loved that 'yet') 'because you're still only half cooked. Is there anything else I can do to help you, though?'

'Well, I've heard there's a job going at Forbes Macfie Hansen . . .'

'Derek Hansen is a great friend of mine; I'd be happy to put in a good word for you.'

'Um . . . thanks!' I was still giddy with pleasure over that 'best young book I've seen in ages' remark.

Lionel called Derek Hansen, and within a day or two I was hired as a writer at a small, creative locally owned agency with lots of shiny advertising awards displayed in its foyer. I couldn't believe my luck. Nor could many of my colleagues.

The reason there was a job going at FMH was that the previous junior creative team was off to London to work for Abbott Mead Vickers. It was another agency spoken of in hushed tones at the time. I was to replace the writer and Derek Hansen (the creative director) had hired a rather more experienced art director from JWT to partner with me.

'He's good,' Derek told me, 'but he's picked up some bad habits which I'll need to train him out of.'

My new partner could not join FMH straight away, as he had to work out his notice at JWT, so I sat in the office with the departing creative team, Scott Whybin and Grahame Smith. Both of them were lovely to me, so I refrained from telling Scott that we had actually met before – he was the one who had walked away from me at that party. He clearly had no recollection and I decided to leave it that way. However, I did nurse a secret satisfaction that the young writer he had dismissed so completely was now about to succeed him in the job he had thought so special.

I did what I could to help out on briefs, but what I seemed to spend most of my time doing was fielding phone calls for Scott. Scott Whybin was in his mid-twenties at that time. A Newcastle boy originally, his confidence plus his good looks were a powerful combination. I liked Scott but I wasn't remotely attracted to him. It seems I was more or less alone in this. Scott persuaded me to answer all his incoming calls (remember this is 1983, long before mobile phones) and they were almost all from young women. I was instructed to pass on messages and soon became aware that there were some women he would talk to and some he wouldn't.

Scott was receiving so many phone calls because the 1983 AWARD night was around the corner and every girl in town (well, in advertising, anyway) wanted to be his date. I was looking forward to going. It would be the first-ever advertising award ceremony I had attended.

I remember it as a glittering and glamorous occasion. I have been to many AWARD nights since; I have even been lucky enough to get up onto the stage and accept a couple of gongs now and then, and in 1997 I was the chair of judges – but not one of those occasions comes close to that AWARD night in 1983. First, I was sitting at the FMH table, next to Scott Whybin, the lucky girl he had finally deigned to bring as his date and Grahame Smith. Scott and Grahame were off to work at AMV, so the great and the good kept dropping by to congratulate them and I had the considerable thrill of being introduced as their replacement. Second, the event was held at the Sydney Town Hall and every table seemed full to bursting with beautiful people in drop-dead gorgeous clothing. Later in the evening, I found myself dancing with Fred Schepisi, who had recently made *The Devil's Playground* or *The Chant of Jimmie Blacksmith*, or both. He started out as an art director. He flirted with me outrageously. My hard work at the gym and my borderline eating disorder were clearly doing their thing. I held him at bay but thoroughly enjoyed the flattering attention I was receiving.

Soon after the heady experience of my first awards night, Scott and Grahame headed off to greater glory and my new art director – the oddly named Rocky Ranallo (his real name was Michael) – finally took his seat at the desk opposite mine. Where I had been indifferent to handsome Scott, Rocky was another story, with his courteous manner and wide smile. I have always been a sucker for a smile; Ralph has one of the best I have ever seen, but Rocky ran a close second. Indeed, there were many similarities between Rocky and Ralph. They both went by nicknames. They were both warm and genuinely liked women as people, a rarity among men in the 1980s. They were both smart, creative and good-looking. Even more weirdly, we soon discovered that they had both gone out with the same girl a couple of years apart. Rocky was an alumnus of Belmore Boys High School in Sydney's south-west while Ralph went to Barker College on the Upper North Shore, yet somehow they had both met and romanced the same girl from St Ives! No matter how big we may think Sydney is, it's really a very small place.

The minute I laid eyes on Rocky, I sensed the danger. This was a young man it would be very easy to fall for. I could see other girls in the office doing exactly that and Rocky was not averse to a little extracurricular activity – this, despite the fact that he had a live-in girlfriend (whom I met and liked). I did not want to fall for my art director. First, I could see it was a mug's game. Second, I loved Ralph and I knew he was completely trustworthy and grown up in a way that the boyish Rocky was not – yet. Third, Rocky had shown absolutely no interest in me romantically. But most important of all, I knew that a fling with Rocky would mean the end of my job. I needed to make a professional success of this partnership.

I was in my mid-twenties at this time and as I look back on the young woman I was then, I am proud of her common sense. I did not let my heart rule my head. Once again, I think this was a legacy of my anxiety and the lessons it had taught me. Lots of young women starting out back then (we were still a novelty in positions with career prospects) – and, no doubt, quite a few today – were not so fortunate (I admit that is an odd thing to say about someone who had an obsessive neurosis). I saw young women have romances with the smart, charismatic men that populated advertising agencies in those days and I saw what happened to their careers. Once they were discarded, their presence in the same workplace became an embarrassment, and if one had to go, it was the girl who did. When I give advice to young women who want to get into ad agencies I tell them never to sleep with anyone they work with unless they intend to marry them. After you have had an affair or even just a fling, it affects your career from then on, because people move a lot between agencies and if you go for a job at a place where an ex-lover works, nine times out of ten he'll sidle up to the bloke doing the hiring and say something along these lines: 'Mate, she's great, but, you know . . . there's a bit of history, and, well, mate . . . it'd be a bit difficult . . .'

I thought about the problem of charismatic Rocky for a few days. I liked him very much and quickly came to respect his talent as an art director. It was hard to talk myself out of my attraction. Then he told me that he was the youngest in his family with two older sisters. This gave me the clue I needed as to how to handle the relationship. I was the oldest sister in my family and I knew the role well. He knew how to be a younger brother. Despite the fact that he was three years older than me, that was how I approached him. It worked; my initial attraction faded and we became friends. We are still friends today.

fourteen

That first year at FMH was one of the happiest I ever spent in a workplace. After spending so long trying to find work that suited me, it seemed copywriting was something I was quite good at. Rocky and I got on well and began producing work we were proud of. Despite the awful reputation advertising has, copywriters and art directors do strive to do work that informs, surprises and entertains as well as sells the client's product or message – and sometimes we succeed. That's why you occasionally see an ad you like.

I was also very lucky at FMH to get some real old-fashioned training, the sort of on-the-job apprenticeship that I don't think happens much anymore. I was working for Derek Hansen, who is now a successful novelist. (It's interesting how many of the people I knew in advertising have gone on to be successful filmmakers, artists and writers. Advertising has always been a haven for creative people; it's an industry where they can get some training and experience while also making a reasonable living.) Although his literary career was still ahead of him, my new boss was already regarded as a writer's writer. Derek cared about crafting copy properly and he wanted me to care about it too.

It was a hard school. If I was between briefs, I didn't get to goof around playing pool with the blokes. I was set the task of writing out – by hand – the copy from the ads that had won copy awards. It may sound like a waste of time, and it certainly often felt that way, but it wasn't. Copying those ads word for word taught me how to structure a piece of writing and how to make the flow of words and ideas fluid and logical. Derek used to describe good writing as being like building a brick wall. If the foundations weren't right, the whole thing would topple; thus, each brick (word) had to be placed perfectly.

Derek was a harsh taskmaster. I came to dread taking my copy in to him. He liked the ideas Rocky and I came up with – getting the concepts through was not the hard part – but FMH was largely a print agency and we were expected to write a lot of copy. Derek allowed no clichés, no lazy sentences, no unsound structure. He would not let me use predictable joining words, for example – words such as 'if', 'and', 'but' or 'so'. In desperation, I pinned a list of alternative words above my desk, such as 'hence', 'therefore' or 'despite'. Even 'moreover' got a few runs – as it probably does in this book.

I began taking my copy to Dean, one of the senior writers in the creative department, before I had to front Derek. Dean was tough too, but he occasionally gave me a gold star. Nevertheless (notice that joining word?), when I took the copy to Derek, back it would come covered in bold red pen slashes and comments that were not designed to spare my feelings. For that first year, I didn't really mind (well, I did, but I also knew that I was learning a great deal), and it helped that Rocky and I were starting to get some industry accolades.

It is one of my regrets that, with the fall in the power of newspapers, newspaper advertising has also collapsed. A well-designed, well-written double-page spread in a broadsheet newspaper was the sort of communication that could stop people in their tracks and get them talking. It was big, it was dominant and it was confident. Even if you didn't get to do a DPS – they were rare and much sought after – the sheer size of broadsheets meant there was room for great photographs and plenty of words. Print ads were not as easily ignored as online ads are today. They also borrowed a sense of urgency and newsiness from the media in which they appeared.

Back in the 1970s, to promote the importance and value of newspaper advertising, all the newspapers in the country joined together to create newspaper-only advertising awards called the Caxtons. (Well, the *West Australian* sometimes participated and sometimes didn't.) The Caxton Awards for newspaper advertising were unique, as they were combined with a two-day conference held in a different exotic Australian location every year.

The Caxton committee, headed for many years by Bryce Courtenay and then by Ray Black, would invite exceptional speakers from Australia and all over the world to attend. Many – but not all of them – were from the advertising industry. I first met Annabel Crabb at a Caxtons conference, and reconnected with my old schoolgirl crush, Bill Leak, at another. Most of the gifted and the famous came not only because they were attracted by the exotic location, but because of the reputation the Caxtons had gained internationally. It was not just that these were credible advertising awards well worth winning or that the speakers at the two-day conference were invariably of a high calibre and enlightening – it was also that the weekend was known for hard-core fun. Put a bunch of highly competitive, witty and creative people together in a fabulous location where the booze (and other substances) flows freely and you have a recipe for – yes, the occasional disaster – but mostly a bloody great time.

One of the highlights of the Caxtons was the talent quest that followed the awards on the Saturday night. I know, it sounds ghastly – but believe me, it wasn't. It was often obscene, anarchic and hilarious. I'm not sure that in today's more puritanical and risk-averse society anyone actually gets to have fun like that anymore. Highlights of the Caxton talent quest included a couple of bemused Japanese tourists on Hamilton Island being taught Australian slang by experts. They were treated respectfully and the joke was on us but it was both audacious and side-splittingly funny. There was the Caxton celebrity vomit-tasting in the Barossa, where a group of us tasted disgusting-looking slush (it was cold chunky soup) in massive tasting glasses and by its smell, colour, flavour and character tried to identify which famous ad person's 'vomit' it was. (Quite a few people had to leave the room.) There was the back- , sac- and crack-shaving challenge, and I remember some guys doing astonishing things with a bucket of squid. There were songs, dance acts, jokes and stories that were all booed, applauded and cheered by an exuberant and (ahem) uninhibited crowd.

One year, the bus driver who had brought us to the venue won the coveted Caxton Talent Quest Lemon simply for wholeheartedly entering into the spirit of the thing. Yes, it was often offensive, usually sexist and only occasionally clever – but my god, it was fun. I always entered but never won. I did win the Chadwick Chalice once. Named after Susie Chadwick – who was celebrated as the absolute master of the brilliant one-liner – the chalice was awarded for the wittiest line of the weekend. Her winning bon mot was to skewer a man who was rather too quick to find fault by saying, 'He whined like a stuck diff.' My winning line wasn't nearly so elegant: 'I'll flirt with you old blokes in a minute, but I have to go to the loo first.' (I was actually heading to the loo and their table was in the way. Oh well, it amused them.) Some of the winning lines were unprintable but – unlike mine – they were also clever.

'Your horizontal hold is interfering with my vertical hold' – a complaint to hotel staff about a dodgy TV picture while the Chalice winner was watching porn.

'How do you tell a female parrot fish from a male parrot fish?' asked the guide on a tour of the Barrier Reef. 'One of them smells like fish,' came the answer.

You get the picture. I know; juvenile, silly, naughty – but I loved it. It is the best thing about advertising. It is one of the last industries on earth that doesn't take itself too seriously. It is also where I learnt not to take myself too seriously.

I attended my first Caxtons in 1984, because Rocky and I had a finalist. It was a small newspaper ad for the Maritime Services Board showcasing their recent dredging of Newcastle Harbour. The brief was quite tight and hard to crack. Given their limited budget, we had to work with the photo we were given, which was of one of those enormous cargo ships in the harbour. To turn it into an ad, we needed a strong headline. I remember Rocky and I pinned the photo up on our wall and sat staring at it for hours, trying to come up with the right set of words. Finally, I said, 'It's amazing what you can get out of Newcastle Harbour if you dig deep enough,' and we'd cracked our ad. (I was never naturally witty. If I have developed a modicum of wit, it has been something I have had to learn. I doubt there is any better way to learn it than by having to come up with pithy headlines for what are mostly dull messages day after day, and that was what I now did for a living.)

The Caxton finalists in each category were prominently displayed at the conference venue. This gave delegates a chance to see the work, argue about its quality and pick their favourites. I looked at our little ad up on the wall with the other finalists and tried to convince myself (as finalists do everywhere in every kind of awards) that just to be nominated was enough. It wasn't though. I wanted to win that award badly. It was daunting for a new copywriter like me to see my ad up there and hear it being judged by my peers.

Awards were given in all sorts of categories and, sometimes, if the judges didn't think any of the finalists worthy of a Caxton, they would simply announce that no Caxton was awarded in the category. That was the fate of the finalists in the three or four categories before the one our little ad was competing in. (The categories, by the way, were decided according to factors such as size and type of media – it wasn't fair to have a small-space ad compete against a DPS, for example – and there were specialist awards for copywriting, art direction, best photograph, typography, illustration and so forth.) I broke into a sweat when our category was announced. The three or four finalists were duly shown and the chair of judges took the microphone.

'And a Caxton has been awarded in this category . . .' Applause greeted these words; people hated it when there was no winner at all. The man paused, took a breath. 'And the Caxton goes to "Newcastle Harbour" – client Maritime Services Board of New South Wales, agency FMH, writer Jane Caro, art director Rocky Ranallo.'

And my head exploded! I stood up and grabbed Rocky's arm so we could go up to collect the gong.

He wouldn't come with me. 'It's yours,' he said. 'All I did was set the type.'

It wasn't true, of course, but it was generous.

* * *

It's funny about getting what you want. The few times that a dream has come true in my life, the aftermath has never been as I expected. I had put my heart and soul into becoming an award-winning copywriter – and I had achieved it, much more quickly than I had thought possible. But now I would have to keep achieving it. One award was not enough. Shit. Doing it once had been hard enough. How was I ever going to pull off another fluke like that one?

Not long after Rocky and I won the Caxton, just when I thought we were working together really well, a new creative director was appointed at another agency, DDB. His task was to re-create the glory days of this once-great shop. Doyle Dane Bernbach is legendary in advertising. The agency even scored a mention in an episode of *Mad Men*, when Peggy and Don are seen poring over Bill Bernbach's famous negative-sell campaign that launched the VW Bug into the American market in the 1960s. Bernbach's witty, understated approach revolutionised advertising and he and his agency were lauded. By the 1980s, however, DDB had become another big, boring multinational. The new CD's brief was to bring it back to life. He immediately began hiring people from all over the place, including FMH. One of the people he hired was Rocky. Despite my pathetic little Caxton, he did not hire me. I didn't blame Rocky for grasping the brass ring. We were both young and ambitious. He got a chance, I didn't.

The loss of many of the best creatives in the department knocked FMH for six. There had always been some conflict between the three partners, Keith Forbes, Malcolm Macfie (architect of the famous 'It's Time' campaign) and, of course, Derek (his most famous ad was 'Who wants to be a millionaire?' which launched Lindemans Ben Ean moselle). Keith was a rather old-fashioned ad guy. He once asked me to wear a frock to a new business pitch. I politely refused. Derek and Malcolm were both larger-than-life personalities and there were often fireworks. When there is conflict at the top, the whole organisation begins to shatter.

I would never have believed that the place which had been such a joy to work in could become such a disaster within eighteen months, but that is what happened. We stopped having fun, people became very bad-tempered, the standard of the work declined and the staff often shuddered at their desks as Derek and Malcolm raged at each other behind closed doors. Worse, I didn't have the support of a creative partner. I had to weather the storms on my own. I began to wonder about getting another job.

I don't have a clear a memory about how I went about finding a new position this time. I have never found a job in the traditional fashion. I have never, for example, seen an ad in a newspaper or online, written an application, had an interview and been successful. Jobs in creative departments are generally not advertised in that way. The usual method is to be headhunted – or, rather, the usual way *if you are a man* is to be headhunted.

I have lost count of the number of times I have sat opposite a male art director (often less senior and less awarded than I am) and watched them receive yet another phone call from a (usually female) headhunter inviting them to apply for a job. In my thirty-five years in the advertising business, enjoying a fair level of success, I have been rung about a job by a headhunter once, and that was a couple of years ago, long after I had started my own business. It was for a very interesting job but not in an ad agency. I have never been headhunted for a job in an ad agency. A headhunter in the ad business told me that whenever she sent a list of possible candidates for jobs in creative departments, it would often come back with a note that said 'no women'. Admittedly, this was a long time ago and maybe things have changed. I hope so anyway.

The practical aspect of this for me as I gained experience in the competitive and male-dominated world of advertising was that I had to find my own jobs. I can't have been that unemployable, because I always did. Nevertheless, as I watched those phone calls come in for the blokes, I felt downhearted. It seemed that however hard I tried, I was always seen as a riskier proposition than the bloke sitting opposite me. As I became more experienced I realised that *I* was not the problem, but when I was young and hungry, I took what felt like a rejection to heart. Now I know there is a logical reason why female job candidates are a less-attractive proposition for headhunters: women are paid less than men. In advertising they are (or were, anyway) often paid a lot less than men. Headhunters are paid a percentage of the final negotiated salary. If women are paid less and, in big jobs, often far less, then it is in the headhunter's interest to push men over women. As for the CDs who quietly banned women? That was just misogyny, pure and simple. There's still a lot of that about.

To get another job, therefore, I had no option but to take my portfolio out and about. As is so often the case, there were a couple of precipitating events that got me angry enough to pick up the phone.

The first was in a meeting – as usual, it was all blokes and me – and we were trying to solve a problem. As we talked, I had what seemed to me a sensible idea. I piped up with my suggestion. There was a deathly hush. Then one of the senior men opened his mouth and suggested – virtually word for word – what I had just said. The idea was suddenly greeted with great enthusiasm. I felt as if I didn't exist.

The second was when a strong campaign I had written was sold down the river by more senior creatives. Alan Morden (my then art director) and I had written a campaign for a manufacturer of a wide range of high-quality, expensive electronic goods. They didn't want to promote one product in particular, but wanted to tell people about their commitment to quality in general. Alan and I had written TV commercials that showed one of their products being put together on an assembly line. A voiceover said, 'We make the best [whatever it was] . . .' Then a great big smasher (like the ones that crush cars in wrecking yards) came into the shot and completely obliterated the just-completed object, leaving it in shattered pieces. The voiceover continued '. . . or we don't make it.'

I went into the meeting to present this campaign full of confidence. I thought it was simple, dramatic and completely on brief. Unfortunately, I was forced to compete with a more senior creative who had written a campaign using Dr Spock from *Star Trek* as a presenter. At the time, Peter Allen was in the midst of his long-running campaign spruiking the products of National Panasonic (a direct competitor with our client). I had quietly christened this predictable campaign 'Peter Allen with ears'. For reasons known only to them, management decided to push this lousy work over ours to the client. They were using our campaign to sell against – as meeting fodder. I was incensed and decided to throw caution to the wind. I fought for our work and I almost won the day. I could see the client was swayed by my arguments.

'I think the idea that you would rather destroy a faulty product than sell it is single-minded about your commitment to quality. That is the only thing the ad is about. No-one will fail to get the message. And that was your brief.'

The client looked at his minions. 'She has a point. It is exactly what we asked for.'

'But Dr Spock is a popular character and very well-associated with high-tech blah, blah, blah.' Management was not giving an inch. This really pissed me off. We could have sold this work if they'd swung behind it. I couldn't understand why they didn't. I still don't understand it.

In the end, senior management have more power than wet-behind-the-ears copywriters and our campaign lost. As I left the meeting and headed back to my office, one of my bosses came up behind me.

'Don't you ever do that to me in a client meeting again!' he hissed at me furiously.

All right, I thought to myself, equally furiously, I won't. I went straight back to my desk and began looking for a job.

After a few phone calls and a couple of interviews, I found myself where I had always wanted to be. I was offered a copywriter's position at the Campaign Palace in Sydney.

Another dream had come true.

Uh-oh.

fifteen

It was 1985. I was twenty-eight years old and newly married. Ralph and I had tied the knot in my parents' garden at the end of 1984. We'd been living together for nine years when my parents announced they'd decided to sell their house in Pymble. It was the perfect place for a secular wedding – indeed, Ann and her husband Bill had been married in my parents' garden just the year before.

'If Mum and Dad are going to sell Pymble,' I said to Ralph as we drove home from lunch with them one day, 'maybe we should get married before they do.'

You've got to admit, that is one incredibly romantic proposal. I remember a friend asking me many years later why I thought Ralph and I had stayed together for so long. I answered, 'Because I don't have a romantic bone in my body.' By this I meant that we stared reality in the face as a couple, we didn't romanticise our relationship. And the way I proposed to Ralph confirms it. Bless his heart, he was unfazed. He said yes.

Of course, being me, no sooner had the date been set and everything planned than I started to get anxious – at least it was about something real this time. I hadn't really wanted to get married, but – after seeing Ann's wedding the year before – I did fancy the party, the presents and the dress. I secretly worried that getting married might stuff everything up. People kept warning me that couples who married after living together for years often broke up soon after the ceremony. I needn't have worried. In our case the opposite happened. After the ceremony and the public celebration, I felt even more committed to Ralph. We were married. It was serious.

I was also the proud new co-owner (or, more accurately, co-mortgagor) of an actual house in Naremburn. Ralph and I had sold the one-bedroom flat in McMahons Point and upgraded to a two-bedroom semi with (tiny) garden. That flat – which we had loved living in – remains the only bad real-estate investment we ever made. We sold it right in the middle of the short-lived end of negative gearing and the value of flats like ours plummeted. Frankly, we could have just dug a hole and shovelled $30,000 into it when we calculated the money we'd spent renovating and the interest we'd paid on our mortgage.

Despite financial setbacks, from the outside, I was doing well. On the inside, I remained an anxious and neurotic mess. Every day, I wondered if I would be able to leave the house and, as I travelled to work, whether I was about to have a panic attack that would send me fleeing to the safety of whichever four walls I was currently helping to pay off. I had a fear of fear, and while I was aware of how silly that was, it seemed impossible to shake. That's the problem with mental illness – it doesn't make sense, so applying sense does not help. As with my previous obsessive fear of doing something violent, the hysterical, humiliating and debilitating collapse I feared never actually eventuated, but that had no effect whatsoever on the fact that I continued to fear it. I remember the sense of being unanchored I experienced when outdoors. I found beautiful, cloudless skies oppressive, as if they were bearing down on me, as if the vastness of the blue was strangely hostile. I felt – I don't know – exposed, unprotected and vulnerable. I had an unpleasant awareness of the limitless space behind the benign blue. I even pictured gravity suddenly switching off and imagined (horribly) what it might feel like to fly off into vast space. I would sit beneath a beach umbrella, not just to protect myself from the sun, but to stop myself flying into space. It was nuts and I knew it, but that just made me more afraid. I feared my fear, as I said, and I also feared collapsing into madness. I went outdoors every single day because that was how I proved to myself that I hadn't – as yet – gone completely barmy.

The skills and insight I had learnt from Jytte were helping me in all sorts of ways in my everyday life but they had not (yet) made a dint on my craziness. Looking back, I think everything I learnt had a cumulative effect, but it was slow and my neurosis was not done with me yet. The work I had done on myself was good, but there remained more to do.

Yet while I obsessively feared such fantasies and phantoms, I was still able to take risks in my professional life and function under considerable pressure. My neurosis seemed unconnected with ordinary, everyday reality. It appeared to occupy a different part of my psyche. The good thing about pressure at work was that it distracted me, but whether at work or play, my fears were always there. They ebbed and flowed; sometimes it felt like they were about to engulf me, sometimes they were just sloshing around my ankles. Looking back, I sometimes wonder if corralling my anxiety and focusing it on phantasms was my way of managing it – though none of this was conscious, of course. Maybe there was method to my madness and it was better to fear shadows than allow myself to fear the risks I was taking in my real life.

Exercise helped and so did strictly controlling what I ate. I still went to the gym three days a week. It helped work off some of the anxiety and – like functioning effectively at work – gave me an illusion of control. I might not be able to control my wayward mind but I could control my body. I was slender and fit. I hadn't yet consciously realised that control was one of the issues I was struggling with. I felt out of control. What I didn't understand was that the opposite was true; I was actually controlling myself too rigidly. That is why from the outside everything looked terrific, but on the inside not so much. When I see the obsession many young women (and increasingly young men) have about exercise and diet, I often wonder if some of them are also trying to put some order into a life that feels increasingly out of control. Maybe the plump are also the sane.

* * *

Meanwhile, just five years after I had finally nabbed a job as a junior copywriter, I found myself the delighted but terrified possessor of a position at the hottest ad agency in Australia.

The Palace had become a much bigger business in the two years since my interview with Lionel Hunt and they had moved from the gracious old mansion in Mosman to a rabbit warren of connected terrace houses at the top of Burton Street in Darlinghurst. In my new job, I was ensconced in an office next door to the ladies (convenient but a clear indication of my place in the pecking order) to await my new art director. Jack Vaughan and Bob Isherwood (the two creative directors at the Sydney Palace) liked the look of a female art director and instructed me to meet her for lunch. It was entirely up to me, I was told, whether they hired her or not.

I arrived at the designated restaurant first and positioned myself so I could watch as people entered, wondering which of the women who came in might be the person I was waiting to meet. A beautiful, tall and shapely young woman with long brown and gold-flecked hair entered and looked around the room. She looked like a young Jane Fonda. Oh God, I thought, I hope it isn't her.

She walked towards me. 'Hi, I'm Lynne.'

It was even worse than I thought. She had the deepest, sexiest voice I had ever heard – think love child of Lauren Bacall and James Earl Jones. I would pale into insignificance next to this exquisite creature. No doubt she was incredibly talented too.

'I'm Jane.'

'Do you smoke?'

'Huh? Um . . .' This was not the opening gambit I had expected. 'Er . . . no, I don't.'

'Good.' Lynne took her seat. 'I couldn't possibly work with anyone who smoked.'

I had, of course, thought I was interviewing her. Silly of me.

Soon Lynne and I were sitting opposite one another in the office next to the ladies. We were both determined to impress and were prepared to work hard at it. And I genuinely liked Lynne – once I had got over how intimidatingly beautiful she was. Like me, her inside was nothing like her outside. She was unselfconscious about her appearance and was actually rather serious-minded and insecure. Like a great many art directors, she was also a bit of a control freak. She found it difficult to come to decisions quickly and took great care over everything. This made us quite a good team because I tend to be quick and decisive but also careless. We balanced each other nicely.

We were also watched closely by our new employers. We were the first all-female team employed at the Palace and – as we found out later – we had been neck and neck with another team: Mara Marich and Sarah Barclay. Eventually, they were hired by the Melbourne Palace and went on to glory in the US. Unlike blokes hired at such an agency, we had a lot to prove and we knew it. Our bosses had taken a risk on us. The pressure was enormous and it showed. Our first brief took us nine long weeks to crack. It was for a pesticide company that was selling termite protection. It is quite a challenge to spend nine weeks thinking about termite protection. I still know almost all there is to know about the life cycle of the common Australian termite. We took concept after concept to Bob and Jack, only to have them rejected.

Bob Isherwood is one of the most successful advertising art directors Australia ever produced. By the end of his career, he was creative director of the world (I quietly called him God) for Saatchi & Saatchi. He was to prove instrumental in my career. In 1985, he was famous in Australia for the beautiful and hypnotic campaign that had launched *Harper's Bazaar* magazine into the country featuring the famous Erté letters brought to life by dancers. It is still one of the ads I love most and it was also hugely successful. The first issue of the magazine sold out in a few days. Bob was an Aussie, but he lived and worked in the UK for many years and was very much part of that explosion of working-class talent that characterised London in the Swinging Sixties. He knew people like David Bailey and told me a fabulous story about a young Charlie Watts. (Yes, *that* Charlie Watts, the one from the Stones.) Charlie and Bob looked a bit alike. They both have that slender, slightly arty aesthetic. Apparently – and I have no idea if this story is true or not – Watts started out as a graphic designer, or commercial artist, as they were often called in those days. He also played jazz in the evenings. He then got a gig as a drummer with a new rock-and-roll band. Quite quickly, the band started to experience a bit of success, even though they mostly did covers. The demands of rock-and-roll began to impinge on Charlie's day job at an ad agency. Eventually he went to his boss to resign so he could concentrate on the Rolling Stones.

'Charlie,' said his boss (according to my boss), 'I urge you to think carefully about this. You've got a good job here and frankly I think you are pretty talented. You could have a good, steady career in advertising. Don't waste your time with rock-and-roll.'

Jack Vaughan is still regarded as one of the finest advertising writers in the history of the business. In 1985 he was famous for his long copy ads and for a witty and imaginative TVC (TV commercial) for Holeproof Computer Socks. It featured Isaac Newton eating his apple at the patent office after discovering computer socks never fall down. Jack was a gentle and courteous man, but he had very high standards that he was determined we would reach.

Finally, at the end of those nine long weeks, Lynne and I took a layout in to the two men with our fingers crossed. We were very pleased with what we had done and seriously thought we couldn't do anything better. The idea had come to us thanks to a piece of advice Jack had given us a week or so earlier. 'Find one strong fact,' he said, 'and the ad will write itself.' That's why I know so damn much about bloody termites. The fact we found was a statistic. The visual was of a (huge) ordinary match with its wooden stem being devoured by termites. The headline read: 'Your house is nine times more likely to be eaten than burnt down'.

Jack and Bob loved it and the relief and excitement we felt was enormous – not least because we wouldn't have to spend another day dragging termite ideas from the depths of our brains.

Then, as happens so often in advertising – I'd go so far as to say nine times out of ten – the client rejected the ad. Not because they didn't like it but because they'd decided to spend their marketing budget on another product. Frustrating bloody game, writing ads.

* * *

Both Lynne and I had gone to work at the Palace with high expectations. This was going to be nirvana in comparison to other agencies we had worked for.

In the event, it was a terrific ad agency, but it was not nirvana. It was subject to all the frustrations and roadblocks that bedevil any organisation that tries to marry art and commerce. There were compensations – we were surrounded by smart and talented people (Rocky had joined the Palace just after I had; the new, improved DDB hadn't worked out so well) – but the Palace wasn't a happy place either. There was a level of tension I hadn't expected and a struggle was going on for the heart and soul of the place. It was the usual battle: would creative reign supreme, or would business realities win out?

Bob Isherwood was the first victim of this battle of priorities. While there were two creative directors, the balance of authority rested with the creative department. This had worked fine until quite recently. What had changed was the appointment of a new and very glamorous CEO.

The CEO was smart, very well connected and dynamic. The problem was he wanted to call the shots. He wanted to swing the balance of power away from creative. Bob had to go. It was very painful to watch and I think it damaged the place for a few years. Eventually, it turned out to be the best break Bob ever had. He left to be creative director at Saatchi Australia. When Saatchi worldwide split into two after founders Maurice and Charles Saatchi marched out with the British Airways account to start M&C Saatchi, Bob was suddenly the most senior creative director at Saatchi anywhere in the world. That's when he got his chance to become God.

But that was in the future. He was devastated to be moved on and felt betrayed by Jack. It also fundamentally shifted the power from the creative department to account service. I still think it was a mistake. But, a bit like me, from the outside the Palace Sydney looked like it was going gangbusters. Thanks almost entirely to the new CEO, business was coming in at a rate of knots.

As the business grew and changed, the tensions grew and changed too. This had the usual effect on the creative department. We began to compete with one another and were rated according to our ability to win awards. In this, Lynne and I proved less successful. Partly it was down to luck – we did good work but for one reason or another it didn't get made – and partly it was due to the tension itself. I know a lot of people believe fear breeds results, but I have found that I produce my best and most creative work when I feel relaxed and am having fun. I wasn't having much fun.

The agency's perceived success contributed to the problem. All sorts of clients wanted to say their agency was the Palace, but they didn't actually want to make the kind of ads that had created its reputation. To keep your job in the agency everyone wanted to work at, you had to win awards, but if clients wouldn't approve the work that could win them . . . well, you see the problem. This conflict increased the pressure on everyone and behaviour began to reflect that. I was as guilty as anyone. My anxiety about doing the creative work Jack wanted was compounded by the frustration of seeing the work approved by him knocked back by clients.

One of my strengths is that I am fairly plain speaking – what you see is what you get. I am spontaneous in my responses, both positive and negative. My greatest strength, however, is also my greatest weakness. In other words, when an ad we had sweated blood over got rejected, I didn't always react well. I was not alone in this. One morning, while climbing the stairs to my office, I heard another writer tearing strips off an account service guy who had returned from a client meeting to tell him an ad had been rejected. The two blokes were having an argument about the rights and wrongs of the client's decision but all I heard reverberating around the stairwell was: 'I don't give a shit about your opinion. You're just the monkey that carries the bags!' I promise you that however frustrated or anxious I felt when receiving yet another knockback, I have never in my life said such a thing to another human being.

That afternoon we were all called in to a departmental meeting. Jack told us that the rest of the agency (read account service) were complaining about how difficult we were to work with. Then he turned and looked at me.

'Jane, you are the person they have complained about the most.'

I was completely gobsmacked. I knew that I stood up strongly for the work – Lynne and I wouldn't present an ad we didn't believe in – but I had never personally insulted anyone. I said as much and repeated the insult I had heard delivered that morning as an example of behaviour I had never indulged in. It was a remark that had genuinely shocked me.

My response was greeted with silence. I felt close to tears. I knew perfectly well that the rest of my colleagues were understandably relieved they were not the focus of complaints and were unlikely to speak up in my support.

'It's because she's a woman, Jack.' It was a man's voice, coming from the back of the room.

Everyone turned to look – it was Rocky – and suddenly what had been a disastrous moment for me became the opposite. Everyone began to mutter in agreement. I had been singled out because while the account service people – both male and female – could accept being insulted by male creatives, they held female creatives to a different standard. We were expected to be nice and defer. I am quite a nice person (I was once introduced to an audience as 'the nicest person in advertising') but I have never been one to defer.

The longer I have been an advertising creative or a writer of any kind, the more I have noticed that it is only creative men who are cut any slack for bad behaviour. I have watched them insult others (see above), indulge in physical fights in the workplace, punch holes in walls, destroy expensive equipment, throw tantrums, scream abuse at underlings and return to the office dead drunk every single afternoon and still be treated with indulgent respect by their colleagues and management – to the extent of getting promotions and pay rises.

I remember one well-respected and talented team who occupied the office next door to me in an agency I worked at later in my career. The pair often fell out with each other. One day there was a kerfuffle in the hall outside my door. I went to see what was going on. There were these two adult males squaring up to each other, dukes raised! They had to be forcibly restrained – not by me, fortunately.

At another agency, I remember being told that after a drunken party on the premises the night before, staff arrived to find a photocopied photo of the office junior's genitals on their desk. A senior creative bloke had persuaded this very drunk young woman to take off her knickers and sit on the photocopier. This behaviour was generally regarded by the staff, the perpetrator and the rest of the industry as a 'joke'. I doubt very much that it was seen that way by the young woman in question.

I have been in meetings – with clients – where male creatives have been so drunk they can hardly string a sentence together. I've watched them disappear from shoots they were meant to be supervising, miss meetings and simply not show up. I've seen them hurl phones across crowded offices. I have watched junior staff being bullied, screamed at, insulted and humiliated to the point of tears. I have lost count of the number of sobbing young women I have scraped off the floor of the ladies because they have just been threatened and intimidated by much more senior men. I now think there are some blokes in positions of power who get a physical charge out of making pretty young women cry.

No-one was fired for any of this behaviour or, as far as I know, even reprimanded. It was seen as proof of creative temperament, of genius, and was indulged. Boys will be boys, you see.

I have watched as equally talented female creatives were fired for being 'difficult' (occasionally disagreeing with the boss or a client), for immaturity (returning late from lunch) and for no apparent reason at all.

Thanks to Rocky (if I had claimed my gender was the reason I was being singled out for harsh criticism, I'd have been seen as making excuses), I managed to survive the meeting with my job and (most of) my morale intact. Nevertheless, I stood up for my work a little less, which meant the more edgy stuff stood less chance of getting approved and made. That meant Lynne and I were less well represented than the others in the department in that year's award shows. Gender bias is so insidious its effects ripple through everything you do and creates an invisible drag that holds you back in ways you may not even notice. Being less represented in the awards meant our cards were marked. The feedback Lynne and I received that year was that we were the most professional team the Palace had ever had. This was not meant in a good way. The agency didn't want professional; they wanted brilliant. We were damned if we did and damned if we didn't. If, like the blokes, we stood up for our work and tried to force it through, we were seen as unacceptably difficult to work with. If we accepted rejection and feedback graciously, our work suffered and we were seen as not as talented as the blokes.

sixteen

By this time, I was twenty-nine and my biological clock was ticking. Ralph and I decided to stop using contraception. Well, more accurately, I had persuaded Ralph that we should stop using contraception. I hadn't thought about having children much – always assuming that I would, but a long time in the future. Then, quite suddenly, I felt a real urgency about time. I suppose it was my looming thirtieth birthday, but it was probably also the birth of Ann's daughter – my niece Alice – that made the idea of a baby seem possible.

The actress Claudia Karvan says she decided to have children because she knew it would make everything more difficult and I know exactly what she means. When I thought about not having children, I realised that all that would happen with my life was that I'd get more of what I already had; more work, more money, more travel etc. It sounds great, but I just felt weary when I imagined that kind of future. I wanted a spanner in the works (I even started writing a book called exactly that when my first child was a baby; I never finished it). I think at least part of the urge to have children – unconsciously, once again – was to test myself, to take a real risk, an actual leap into the dark. If that was my intention, I certainly got my wish, and then some.

Given what had happened the one time a condom had broken, I fully expected that by going off the pill I would get pregnant immediately. If there is a god (which I doubt very much), she has a wicked sense of humour. Nothing happened for six months. Being a fertile female is a pain. I had spent about fifteen years being deathly afraid that I would get pregnant and now I was afraid I wouldn't. For years, the arrival of my period had been greeted with relief; now it was greeted with disappointment – to the point of tears.

After six long months, my period failed to arrive. We got our hopes up, I peed on a stick and the longed-for pink lines appeared. I went to my GP and he confirmed it: we were officially pregnant! Jubilant, I announced the good news to the world.

You may be wondering what a neurotic basket case like me was doing deciding to have children. Wasn't I afraid I might do something awful? Or that I would find myself succumbing to agoraphobia and so end up locking us both inside the house? Why on earth would someone with my psychological and emotional problems have kids? And, of course, I obsessively asked myself all those questions and frequently woke up in a cold sweat in the middle of the night to torture myself with catastrophic imaginings. But I had decided that my anxiety was an abnormality – a deformity – something I would simply have to live with. And, as usual with contradictory, complex me, I wanted to have children as much as I feared having them. I used to wonder what it must be like to be as other people appeared to be, able to make simple clear decisions about what they did or didn't want. I now suspect there are actually very few people like that.

I asked my GP to refer me to an obstetrician. My only requirement was that she be a woman who had had children. There were only two who fitted that description at that time in Sydney. Dr Sue Fleming was in Annandale and I rang her office to make my initial appointment.

Receptionist: Your name?

Me: Jane Caro.

Receptionist: What school did you go to?

Gosh, I thought, they are thorough! I wonder why they need to know that?

Me: Forest High.

Receptionist: Jane! It's Rosie Cook here!

Rosie had lived up the road from me when we lived in Frenchs Forest and had gone to Forest High with me. The fact that she was Sue Fleming's nurse was a good omen, or so I thought. Sadly, I didn't make it to my first appointment. My next phone call to Rosie Cook was because I was bleeding. She put me through to Sue immediately. It was a Friday. Dr Fleming told me to stay flat on my back with my legs raised and to have an ultrasound on the Monday.

'Unfortunately,' she said, 'you might be having a miscarriage.'

I felt icy with dread.

I did what I was told and stayed flat on my back all weekend, but the blood leaked out of me steadily. If I hadn't known I was pregnant I would just have thought I was having a rather late, rather heavy period.

On Monday morning I headed for the ultrasound appointment with my mother, who came with me because Ralph could not.

The woman performing the ultrasound seemed to take a very long time about it (not that I'd actually ever had an ultrasound before) and dug her wand roughly and repeatedly into my pathetically flat stomach.

'Well,' she said, 'I can't find anything.' She searched for a heartbeat again, and there was another agonisingly long pause. 'Are you sure you were pregnant?'

The remark went through me like a knife. Was I sure? Had I just made this whole thing up? Was I as crazy as that? But I had peed on a stick and a GP had confirmed the pregnancy . . . or maybe he'd just gone along with what I'd told him. Perhaps I was even nuttier than I thought? That ultrasound technician's remark added a layer of humiliation to my grief. I suddenly felt like a fool. I went to the loo and emptied my uncomfortably full bladder (anyone who has had an abdominal ultrasound will know how good that feels). I left the appointment fighting back tears. I had wanted that baby.

Life went back to normal, sort of. I had to go through the dispiriting and strangely humiliating experience of telling everyone I was no longer pregnant. I felt like a failure. People were nice about it, of course, but all they had to confirm my pregnancy was my word and I was still fighting my own doubts about that, thanks to the ultrasound lady. I felt like a fraud for being upset.

'Never mind,' people said, 'you'll get pregnant again.'

But I did mind. How did they know if I'd get pregnant again and whether, if I did, it would stick?

Some people even told me that it was for the best and that miscarriages were nature's way of preparing your womb for the proper pregnancy. That made me feel my grief was somehow illegitimate. Funny, isn't it? Women are meant to feel devastated by an abortion but philosophical when they have a miscarriage.

Three months later, we were pregnant again, but this time I wasn't jubilant. I was wary. Beyond immediate family, Ralph and I kept the news to ourselves. This was not easy, especially when I went to a shoot for a commercial Lynne and I had written and the make-up artist and producer were pregnant (they were a couple) and due at almost the same time as I was. They were bubbling over with excitement about the baby and their future. I said nothing.

After twelve weeks, I finally felt confident enough to make my pregnancy public. The baby was due in early June so I told Jack I would be leaving the Palace at the end of April. There was no such thing as parental leave back then, paid or unpaid.

It seems odd to me now that women like me just passively accepted that we'd have to give up work once we had children. There were few alternatives. Despite all the brave talk of women's lib in the 1970s and the huge strides women had taken in education and – yes – the workplace by the 1980s, once you got pregnant it was like sliding right back to the 1950s and my mother's situation. It became secret women's business. Men were more involved than my father had been in pregnancy and childbirth – including participation in prenatal classes and at the birth – but child-rearing? Still women's work. The price of children on your career and income, both current and for the rest of your life? Still paid entirely by women. Looked at like that, it is arguable that men only gave ground on the things that benefited them – it is entirely due to feminism that fathers today have a much closer relationship with their children than they used to – but no ground on the things that might actually cost them anything.

Of course, I was too busy contemplating my own next move to worry about things like that at the time. I had no real plan about what I would do after I had the baby. I suppose I thought I'd spend a year or two at home, then find childcare and go back into the fray. Bwahhahahahhaha!

I was (still a little nervously) happy to be pregnant but I was sorry it meant I had to give up work. I never considered that I could somehow hold on to my job and have a baby. Partly this was the demanding nature of being a copywriter and partly it was that Ralph had just been promoted into a job where he had started to travel a lot. Somebody had to be home with the baby, at least at first, and the only practical person to do that was me. I wasn't thrilled about it, but I couldn't see any other realistic alternative.

* * *

In the early days of my pregnancy, I started driving to the office for the first time. It helped me to cope with my overwhelming feeling of tiredness at the end of the day. Across the road in Burton Street at that time there was a small mechanics workshop. My car was due for a service and I booked it in. I dropped it off in the morning and crossed the road to work. That afternoon I walked back across that road to pick it up. The guy who handed me the keys inclined his head towards the elegant green and black terrace I had just left.

'You work in there, do you?'

'Yes.'

He leant a bit closer to me and lowered his voice. 'What is it?'

'It's an ad agency.'

His expression cleared. 'Ah! We've been trying to work out what it was. We thought it was some kind of high-class brothel. The most beautiful women in the world work in there.'

I thought this was hilarious. However, the mechanic was right: the women I worked with were very attractive (the men, not so much). This was no accident, of course. A new account director hired an assistant on her merit, and rumour had it that he had received an earful from management because she was dumpy and plain. He was told that the clients expected glamour when they came to the agency and looking good was part of the job description – for female employees only, of course. To his credit, the account director defended his hire and the woman kept her job. She was terrific.

Glamorous or not, the Palace suffered the ups and downs that bedevil such a volatile industry. Not long before Christmas, we lost a major account and suddenly rumours were flying around the agency about who would lose their jobs. When an account is lost in advertising, overheads must be cut and the only overheads an agency really has are its people. I was pregnant, noticeably so by now. I was pretty sure I'd get the chop. After all, I had already told them I would be leaving in April. I prepared myself for what I assumed was the inevitable. I had my strategy planned, thanks to some wise advice from my father. I would ask to be interviewed on my own and try to negotiate the best possible deal for myself.

Then an all-staff memo landed on everyone's desk. It ticked us all off for spreading rumours, unequivocally stated that no-one would be fired, except perhaps the idiot who had started the rumour – if they could ever find out who that was. I relaxed. I would be able to work out my notice as I had planned.

That Friday at lunchtime I lay down on the couch in the office to take a short nap. Driving to and from work was only helping so much. Lynne was out somewhere and I took advantage of her absence to sleep. I woke to see Jack poking his head around the door. It didn't matter that I was pregnant or that I was entitled to have a break over lunch, I immediately felt both muddle-headed and guilty. I sat up quickly.

'Where's Lynne?' he asked.

'Gone out for lunch. She should be back soon.'

'When she comes back, could you both pop down to my office?'

'Sure.' I was unsuspecting. After all, hadn't there been that memo denying that any staff were going to lose their jobs?

I thought that maybe he was going to give us a brief. That was unusual for a Friday afternoon, but not unheard of.

Lynne returned from lunch and we went down to Jack's office.

'I'm afraid I have some bad news.'

Oh no! What was my strategy for dealing with this? I was to ask to be retrenched separately.

'Can we do this separately?' I said, starting to stand up.

Jack dropped his head into his hands. 'I can't do this twice!' he said.

Feeling sorry for him, I sat back down, and Lynne and I were duly informed that we were no longer employed at the Palace and that we were to clear out our desks and leave the premises immediately. It was awful and made us feel as if we were criminals and had actually done something wrong.

Once the interview had finished and Lynne and I were leaving Jack's office, I couldn't resist a parting shot.

'You do realise –' I turned to look at Jack as I reached the door '– that you have just fired the only staff member who cannot get another job?'

He had the grace to look even more stricken.

I felt terrible for Lynne. If I had not been pregnant, would we have been let go? My situation had made her more vulnerable. She was good about it, but she wouldn't have been human if the thought hadn't also crossed her mind.

We weren't the only staff members who lost their jobs that day. Six of us were cut adrift. When Lynne and I went to see the accountant to pick up our final pay, she confided that the cheques were generous and that Jack had fought hard to get us a decent payout. That, at least, was some comfort, but I still felt miserable. I was going to leave the advertising career that I had worked so hard to establish with no farewell, no card with witty remarks from well-wishers, nothing. I just skulked out of my brilliant career feeling rejected and humiliated.

When I got home, I discovered that Ralph was having the exact opposite experience. While I was paid $10,000 to leave (given my salary, my payout was generous), he had been offered $50,000 to stay in his job as part of a golden-handcuffs scheme. Oh well, it meant we could pay off our mortgage.

* * *

The first few days of unemployment were not too bad. It was a weekend much like any other, except I had to go through the dreary task of telling everyone I had been fired. Monday morning, however, was tough. Ralph got up and went off to a workplace where his contribution was valued and sought after. I got up and stared at an empty diary. I kept busy by exercising. I went to prenatal exercise classes at a nearby gym. I swam three or four times a week. I was fitter than I have ever been. Even though I had started eating breakfast now that I was pregnant (I knew one meal a day was not really enough), my top pregnancy weight was fifty-five kilos. I'd kill to get within cooee of that weight today. I even went for a couple of job interviews, but knew there wasn't much point to it. As I had said to Jack, nobody would hire a pregnant woman.

The time passed. I spent a lot of it with Ann and her new daughter Alice as they recovered from the trauma of her difficult birth. Ann had had a perfectly ordinary pregnancy and, given that my mother had popped out four children with relatively little difficulty, none of us had any reason to expect anything out of the ordinary. My sister, being the most academically inclined of all of us and working for a famous and venerable publishing house at the time, read every single book on the topic of birth she could lay her hands on. If words on a page can prepare you for childbirth, she was prepared.

Prepared or not, her daughter's birth was horrendous. Well into the labour – in second stage – the baby's umbilical cord prolapsed. This means that the umbilical cord (providing the baby with oxygen) precedes the baby into the vagina. When this happens, many babies die or suffer brain damage because their oxygen supply is cut off. Ann's obstetrician knew his stuff, but saving Alice meant Ann had to suffer nothing short of torture. He had to cut the baby out of her – fast – using only local anaesthetic. To give you an idea of what this meant, Ann had over fifty-five stitches.

Alice arrived in the world blue and silent. Telling the story of the birth afterwards, Ann told me about the midwife saying calmly but urgently, over and over, 'Come on, come on,' while thumping Alice rhythmically on the back. This was the sound of the medical staff trying to get Ann's newborn to breathe. This small detail was to prove very important to me.

Alice did breathe and there were no ill-effects other than that she is left-handed, which is sometimes attributed to birth trauma. Ann survived too but received no counselling or support. All she was told was that the doctor had pulled off a miracle and that it was rare for babies to survive such a birth. Understandably, her obstetrician expected to be congratulated for his skill, but he was also the person who had inflicted terrible injury on my sister, no matter the reason. Maybe nobody really knew how to deal with this situation and so Ann's appalling experience was not discussed. Unsurprisingly, it took Ann five years to pluck up the courage to have a second child.

My experience was an echo of my own mother's; I was also a young pregnant woman whose sister had just come through a horrendous birth experience. It didn't put me off, however. I just didn't think anything bad would happen to me – apart from going mad and locking myself inside the house or killing someone, of course. Maybe I am right about the method to my madness. The fantastical things I feared (that never actually happened) distracted me from fearing things that were much more likely.

I made it past thirty weeks, and I remember someone telling me to pack a bag to take to the hospital. I thought they were nuts. I had ten weeks to go; aeons of time. When I was thirty-four weeks, we went to a Thai restaurant with some friends. While I was sitting there, eating pad Thai and drinking (damn it) water, I suddenly felt a gush of warm fluid between my legs. Had I peed my pants? I went to the ladies. I had read an article just a few days previously that described what were called 'the waters' as odourless and colourless. On examination, the fluid clearly wasn't pee – and it was odourless and colourless. I went back into the restaurant.

'We have to go,' I said to Ralph.

'But I'm still eating . . .'

'No, we have to go. I think my waters have broken.'

'Don't be silly! Are you sure it's not . . .?'

'NO! I AM NOT SURE ABOUT ANYTHING, BUT WE HAVE TO GO!'

I rang poor Sue Fleming again (I can see why so few women with children go into obstetrics) and she told me to go straight to King George V maternity hospital in Camperdown. I had no idea what to take with me and regretted that lack of a packed bag. I arrived, was admitted and told my hind waters had developed a leak. I was to stay in hospital, in bed with my feet up, to try to hold the baby in and prevent a premature labour. I was given an injection of steroids to speed the baby's lung development and then told to stay put. I had to pee in a potty on the bed but did beg for special dispensation to go to the loo to shit. It was granted reluctantly.

For a week I stayed prone. I passed the time watching TV, reading and generally being bored out of my skull. At least once a day I had to spend forty minutes (I kid you not, forty minutes) rubbing a monitor across my belly so it could record the baby's heartbeat while the baby was both active and resting. I will never forget the whooshy, mushy rhythmic sound of my baby's beating heart as I counted down those forty interminable minutes. The nurses said they could tell what sex my baby was from the heartrate on the printout, but I didn't want to know. I wanted to meet my child for the first time when he or she arrived. I would only create a fantasy baby if I knew its gender.

As it was, whenever I tried to imagine the child in my womb it was faceless – a sort of generic baby. I thought this was as it should be. I still think so. It meant that when I met my child for the first time I didn't have to let go of the fantasy before I could embrace the reality. And I knew just how much of a hold fantasy could have over me.

After a week or so of enforced bed rest, a registrar came into my room.

'Your liquor has grown a culture. Your womb is no longer sterile so we will have to induce labour immediately.'

There is a whole new language you learn when you are in hospital for any length of time. I had wanted the tedium to end, but not like this. I was only just thirty-five weeks pregnant.

They took me to the labour ward and set up the drip. Ralph and my sister Ann (my support person) arrived. Then we waited for something to happen.

Despite the weirdness of the situation, my memories of giving birth to Polly are good. I remember the three of us – Ralph, Ann and I – in hysterics because Ann had brought a book with her (typical) on how to help in a labour. One of its instructions was that birth support people should offer lots of 'verbal analgesia'. Ann and Ralph took this literally. They proceeded to perform a double act, singing the various names of analgesics to me as the lyrics of various tunes: 'Panadol, Panadol, Panadol, aspirin, aspirin, as-pi-rin . . .' You get the picture. It sounds lame now but it was hilarious at the time. I was hyped up on nitrous oxide. What their excuse was for laughing so hard I still don't know.

Despite the hilarity, it was a drawn-out process – it took a long time for the medication (oxytocin) to kick in. When labour did finally start, it was slow. I became very tired. After God knows how many hours, I was still only three centimetres dilated and could hardly lift my head from the pillow. Ann, always no-nonsense, always authoritative and also very conscious of her own horrible experience only eighteen months before, demanded an epidural. It was duly administered (you don't say no to Ann) and I remember the bliss of the pain receding to the end of what felt like a long corridor. I actually slept for about thirty minutes, and when I woke, I was ten centimetres dilated and ready for second stage. God bless that epidural. I will be forever grateful.

Sue Fleming arrived, dressed in a very glamorous white linen suit.

'For God's sake,' I said to her, 'put your gown on – I'd hate to wreck that.'

Epidural or no epidural, I pushed Polly out on my own. It was hard work, it took forty minutes – and the consequences of hard pushing for that long are with me still – but, thanks to that epidural, it didn't hurt.

After such a long, drawn-out and slow process, she arrived, as babies do, in a sudden gush.

'What is it? What is it?' I didn't know whether she was a boy or a girl. They held her up to show me, but the umbilical cord dangled down between her legs.

'I can't see, I can't see!'

'It's a girl!' they said and passed her to me.

I was completely bowled over by her the minute I saw her. She wasn't anybody I had expected or imagined. She was completely, utterly, from that very first moment, herself.

seventeen

We called her Polly Catherine. It was 5 May 1988, and she was five weeks premature, but she was big and healthy at two and a half kilos (five and a half pounds), and her APGAR was eight (out of ten) at birth and five minutes later it went up to nine. She was in such good condition that there was no need to put her in a humidicrib. Instead, she was taken to a special care nursery so they could keep an eye on her.

I was taken to the public ward because there were no private rooms available. That was fine with me, though I was a little sad that – unlike all the other new mothers in the beds lining the walls – I did not have my daughter next to me. But I was exhausted, not having slept for a good thirty-six hours, so once I had said goodbye to Ralph, Ann and my parents, who had popped in to meet their newest grandchild, I pulled the curtains around my bed, rolled over and closed my eyes.

The noise was unbelievable. Not only was there always a baby crying, but there were nurses wheeling squeaky trolleys up and down the aisles, banging them against the end of my bed more often than not. There were visitors stomping in and out and laughing uproariously. Someone, I swear, dropped what sounded like a full drawer of cutlery right next to my bed, causing me to jump out of my skin! Not only was the public maternity ward all hard surfaces and tumult, but it was positioned at the front of the hospital, just above the traffic lights on busy Missenden Road. The trucks slowing on the red light with their air brakes and then accelerating slowly through the gears on the green sounded as if they were driving past the end of my bed.

After half an hour of this cacophony, I opened my eyes and sat up in bed. Sleep was impossible and I began to feel miserable. Where I had been euphoric now I was almost weepy. It was an adrenalin dump, I suppose. I tried to read but I was too jumpy to concentrate. Eventually, I got up out of bed, put on my dressing gown and took myself off to the nursery. If I had to be awake, at least I could spend the time with my new daughter.

I spent a few hours beside her crib, but there wasn't very much for me to do. I felt superfluous and it was not how I had expected to feel. After my waters breaking prematurely, a week in hospital and the excitement of labour and birth, I had not expected the aftermath to be so anticlimactic. I could not sleep, but nor was there anything much I could do while awake. What I was desperate to do – bursting to do – was talk about the birth. Talk it through, discuss it, dissect it, analyse it and begin to integrate it. But no-one had any interest in listening to me. And fair enough; they were busy and I was not ill. My child was premature but in good condition. There was no need to pay attention to me.

At last, unable to think of anything else to do, I went back to the ward. I'd decided it was the place they put women to punish them for having children, but there was nowhere else for me to go and nothing else for me to do. As I walked towards my bed the sister in charge waylaid me.

'Ah, there you are!' she said in a tone that implied I had been deliberately difficult in deciding to visit my new baby. 'We're going to move you. A private room has just become available.'

What a bloody relief! Perhaps now I could get some sleep. I was delighted.

'Well,' said the sister, her voice heavy with sarcasm, 'it seems you *can* smile.'

That wiped the smile right off my face. In fact, I almost burst into tears. I'd just given birth to a premature baby. I wasn't allowed to have her by my side. I hadn't slept for almost forty hours and this woman still appeared to feel it was my job to make her feel better. Some people should not go into nursing.

Nevertheless, I was fortunate. I was a private patient, so I could escape. Most of the new mothers in the ward did not have that option. I hope they have improved public maternity wards since 1988. At the very least, I hope they have soundproofed them. Labour is called labour for a reason. It is bloody hard work even if you have a natural and uncomplicated delivery.

Women need quiet and rest after their efforts, not deafening surroundings and, at best, grudging care.

I shared my new room with a young woman who had given birth to what seemed to me a huge and incredibly hairy son. All the full-term babies looked huge to me. Polly was just the right size for a newborn, I thought, and I felt quietly sorry for all the other women with their gargantuan children. No doubt my love for my new daughter (and my hormones) were making me blind. My new roommate loved having the telly on from first thing in the morning until last thing at night. She didn't even turn it off when her part of the room was full to bursting with her many visitors but, after the public ward, my new situation was blissful. I simply asked my roommate to turn the volume down a little and, when she obliged, rolled over and fell asleep.

I woke to find Polly being wheeled into the room in one of those perspex cribs hospitals use for newborns (do they still?). She was doing so well there was no need to keep her in the special nursery anymore. This was wonderful news, although I had also woken to discover that my milk had come in. This is a horror that mere words cannot describe, but I will try. My breasts had turned into two hot rockmelons overnight. The skin on them was stretched taut by the sheer volume of milk. The bed was swimming in sticky breast milk, thanks to the rubber sheet that protected the mattress. I was also now expected to get on with the business of learning to breastfeed. The misery of the burning boulders on my chest was indeed an incentive to give it a try, so the two of us did our best. Polly manfully attempted to latch on to an absurdly stretched and flattened nipple and I manfully attempted to help her, while wincing. The pain of it brought tears to my eyes.

You think that after you have a baby the pain will stop, but each new experience brings more with it. Engorged breasts rank right up there with labour, as far as I am concerned, particularly as they come with no offer of pain relief. Every movement was painful and I had to support my breasts with my hands if I needed to roll over. Still, Polly and I tried to do what I had always assumed came naturally. Eventually, exhausted by the manhandling and fuss, she fell asleep on my chest and I lay very, very still and stared at her – painful breasts forgotten for the moment. It was incredible to see her face, so relaxed and at peace on my body. She was so trusting and helpless. Despite my ongoing neurosis, I knew as I watched her breathing and felt the warmth of her against my skin that I would kill anyone who tried to hurt her. Mother love is ferocious. I felt a kind of wonder. Who cared about the Campaign Palace or my shredded career?

That afternoon, while Ralph was visiting, another nurse appeared at my bedside.

'We've done some tests and I am afraid Polly's bilirubin is too high. It is causing jaundice, which is quite common in premature babies.'

'Is it dangerous?'

'It could damage her liver, but not if it's treated with ultraviolet light. It means we'll have to take her back to the special care nursery.'

The nurse turned towards Polly in her perspex crib and began to wheel her towards the door. I burst into tears.

Ralph was embarrassed by my display of emotion. 'Don't be silly, Jane!' he said. 'They have to put her under the lights, for her own good.'

'Oh no,' said the nurse kindly (some of them are suited to their profession), 'most new mothers get upset when I have to take their babies away. In fact, I'd be worried about her if she wasn't.'

Bless that nurse, whoever she was; it is so important when you first enter the new country that is motherhood to be told that your instinctive reactions are normal and reasonable and that you are not crazy. It is very easy to make new mothers feel bad because everything is so intense and so unexpected. It is a real kindness to reassure vulnerable young women that they are fine and are behaving just as they should.

It seemed to me that every time I got my hands on my new daughter, and began to get to know her and feel easy around her, somebody came and took her away. I felt bereft. Given I had only known her for a day or two, my reactions seemed extreme and confusing even to me. I also felt a kind of shame that I alone of all the women on that floor did not have my baby with me. I felt the lesser for it. What was lacking in me that I wasn't able to give birth as easily as all the others?

Polly looked hilarious under those lights. The bilirubin made her very sleepy so she lay on her back naked except for a nappy. But because the ultraviolet light can damage their eyes, babies wear protective dark glasses. This made Polly look exactly like a baby on her summer holiday and it made me laugh. I also had to learn how to express breast milk so that she could be tube-fed while she was under the lights. This was a skill that would soon stand me in very good stead.

I spent most of the next few days sitting by her bed working a breast pump. While doing so, I got to know some of the other mothers of babies who were spending time in the nursery, at least by sight. There was one young woman who wore a very beautiful and exotic dressing gown – it was silk and embroidered all over with flowers and birds in very bright colours. I was in a rather unfortunate shade of fluffy blue with red trim – it'd been the best I could find at Big W at short notice. Exotic-dressing-gown woman had a particularly restless and distressed child. Whenever I came into the nursery he was hollering inconsolably. I asked one of the nurses I frequently chatted with why he seemed so miserable.

'He's withdrawing from heroin. His mother was a junkie. She swears she's given it up now.'

That pulled me up a bit. My baby was a few weeks premature and had a bit of jaundice; otherwise she was fine. Other people had much more to deal with.

Mother's Day came around and Polly's bilirubin level had fallen enough for her to be moved from the humidicrib and back into a normal perspex one, but they still wanted to keep her in the special care nursery to keep an eye on things. I went down to see her at one point during the day; I was now allowed to hold her and feed her normally and we were managing surprisingly well.

There were more visitors than usual in the nursery, it being Mother's Day. As well as the mothers – who were also patients – in dressing gowns and slippers, and nurses in their uniforms, there were more people dressed in street clothes. A couple stood beside the crib of one of the babies. The child had obviously had to stay in hospital longer than his mother – perhaps he had been very premature and was now gaining weight, I don't know. Anyway, the couple had an older child, a toddler. Usually toddlers were not allowed into the nursery and anyone who entered had to undertake strict barrier-nursing protocols. We all had to wash our hands before we were allowed in, for example. Because it was Mother's Day, the nurse in charge had allowed the toddler into the nursery.

Mum and Dad were fixated on their baby. The nurse in charge was occupied with the many visitors. The toddler, understandably bored, was running about from crib to crib putting his hands all over everything. What I noticed – and it seems no-one else did – was that the toddler had a runny nose.

eighteen

The doctor was a redheaded man with a scruffy beard and clumsy hands. In them he held my first child, a ten-day-old baby girl who weighed just over two kilos (babies usually lose a little weight after they are born). We'd had her home for only two days.

The doctor listened to me carefully as I told him about her difficulty feeding and the yellow snot I had seen gush out of her nose. He said nothing but took his time examining her. I watched him listen to her chest and peer into her ears, and I realised that he intended to admit her.

We had only brought her to the hospital because it was Sunday and all the medical centres we tried were closed (which wasn't unusual in those days). As we drove across the bridge to the Royal Alexandra Hospital for Children in Camperdown, I'd worried about being thought a panicky new mother and had almost asked Ralph to turn the car around and take us home.

Now there was something about the intense, concerned way this large man looked at my baby that I didn't like. He left the room, saying he wanted to talk to a colleague.

'They're going to admit her,' I said to Ralph.

'No,' he said, 'I don't think so.'

The doctor came back into the small examining room.

'I'm sorry,' he said, 'but I think she ought to be admitted. I think she has a respiratory infection called RSV bronchiolitis. We're in the middle of an epidemic. She's not very sick at the moment, but RSV can be dangerous to premature babies.'

I wept. After losing her to the humidicrib, the special nursery, the lights for jaundice, she had slipped through my hands again. I looked at her sleeping in her baby capsule. She seemed to have been asleep for days – that was one of the things that had brought me to the hospital. She was dwarfed by the capsule; the Velcro band across her middle covering her from her underarms to her knees. I would have cut both my arms off to protect her from danger, but here she was, sick enough to be admitted to hospital, and there was nothing I could do.

We were taken to casualty to await a bed. The nurses stripped Polly of her pretty new Gro-suit and cardigan and put her in a faded, flannelette hospital gown at least three sizes too large. She looked familiar in it. The gown was very like the ones she had worn in the maternity hospital. Perhaps they were government issue.

It took a few hours to get her a bed in Faithful, the baby's ward. When the orderly finally came to get us it was early evening and cold. We trailed miserably along behind the silent man as he pushed our daughter on a trolley, trying to get our bearings and take in our surroundings. The hospital was like a maze, a labyrinth of winding corridors, narrow staircases and more-or-less covered walkways connecting grim, massive buildings that appeared to have been plonked anywhere there was room. No wonder they closed that hospital eventually. It's all been converted to rather fancy townhouses and apartments now.

Faithful Ward was just behind the main entrance and once its heavy double doors swung open to admit us, we were in another world.

It began with a wide corridor bounded on one side by the parents' room (it had a large sign identifying it as such above the doorjamb) and a series of utility rooms on the other. At the end of the corridor stood the charge sister's office and nurses' station, the gateways to the ward. We approached the nurses' station slowly, the wheels of the trolley bearing my daughter squeaking on the lino floor.

I let Ralph take care of all the administrative stuff and turned to look at the ward itself. I saw cot after cot lined up in rows, each bearing a small baby suffering various degrees of illness and injury. Beside most cots sat a mother – some read, some slept, some stared into space. The ward was filled with sound. There was the wet, convulsive coughing of the RSV babies, the electronic beep of monitors, the squeak of nurses' shoes on the polished floor, the rattle of trolleys, the clatter and bang of hard surface meeting hard surface and, of course, the continual crying of miserable, sick and hungry babies. One cry rose above the rest; a strange, plaintive, desolate bleat. I turned to the nurse who was filling out our forms.

'I have never heard a baby cry like that.'

'Oh,' she said, without looking up, 'it's brain damaged. They all cry like that.'

A young female registrar came and suctioned some mucous from Polly's nose. That woke her up; she struggled and cried against the pain. Ralph and I cried too. Then we sat and waited for whatever was going to happen next. Eventually we went to the coffee shop and had a sandwich. When we returned, Polly was no longer in the small cot by the nurses' station but was right up the back in the isolation section with all the other RSV babies. The redheaded doctor's diagnosis had been confirmed.

The only cot available was for an older child and so she was reduced to a small lump beneath the covers who slept and slept and slept. They put electrodes on her chest and hooked her up to heart and respiratory monitors. They showed me how to disconnect the wires so I could change her and feed her without dislodging the electrodes. They told me the rules of barrier nursing; how I must put on and take off a gown every time I entered or left the isolation area. How I must wash my hands before and after touching my child. And how I must never, ever touch another baby. We had entered the kingdom of the lepers.

Ralph went home and I went to the parents' room. Because of the RSV epidemic, it was packed with sleeping women, cheek by jowl on stretcher beds. I found myself a place on the padded bench in the breastfeeding room instead. It wasn't comfortable, but it had a door and I craved privacy.

The next few days were spent sitting beside Polly's cot in a hard orange plastic chair. I read. I slept. I stared into space. I fed and changed my baby. I talked to the other mothers. We swapped magazines, sweets and life stories. Ralph and my mother visited every day and insisted on taking me right out of the hospital grounds for lunch. The hospital was in a part of inner-city Sydney peppered with restaurants. I went wherever they took me because I seemed to have fallen into some kind of trance and just did what anyone told me to do. I didn't have the energy to resist. But when I returned and walked down that wide corridor, I wondered whether Polly was still alive. It was as if I believed it was only my eternal vigilance that was keeping her breathing.

The nurses and the doctors were brisk and reassuring, almost impatient. She only had a mild infection, nothing to worry about, I must stop panicking and imagining the worst – but she was so sleepy. I now knew that the worst complication of RSV was apnoea – a fancy word for stopping breathing – and every time I walked towards her cot I wondered, *Is she still breathing? Or has she died there, silently, while no-one was watching?* I knew that the monitors she was connected to were designed to prevent that happening, but I couldn't rid myself of the dread. I badgered the nurses. 'How sick is she? Is she better? Is she worse?' I was told she was holding her own, that it was just a case of waiting for the virus to run its course. I wanted to believe them. I tried to believe them. I didn't believe them.

I couldn't dismiss the evidence of my own eyes. She was *so* sleepy. Even though she was a premmie baby, she'd been alert in the maternity hospital, bright-eyed and curious. She wasn't anymore. Every evening at about eight o'clock, she seemed to get particularly distressed. They kept asking me how much milk she was getting. A minute this side, I said, two minutes on the other. I had never breastfed a baby before, so what the hell did I know? The monitors went off constantly, frightening Ralph and me.

Our second night in the ward, one of the RSV babies experienced a crisis. Bells were rung and doctors and nurses came from everywhere. The mother and father clung to each other as the professionals worked on their child. He ended up in an oxygen tent. The next morning, at breakfast, I saw the exhausted parents but I avoided their glance. It was as if I had a superstitious dread of them. As if their bad luck was contagious and I must isolate myself from them as much as any germs.

After breakfast, when I returned to the ward, I found that my paediatrician had finally made time to come to the hospital. I was still in my waking trance but my blunt, assertive sister Ann (she is now a school principal) was visiting and she was able to ask him the questions I could not.

'Is she very sick?'

'No, this seems to be a mild case.'

'Is she improving?'

'She seems to be holding her own.'

'How long before she gets better?'

'Probably eight to ten days altogether.'

'When can she leave hospital?'

'Another few days yet.'

Kate and Andy before the 1954 Cambridge May Ball, in Andy's rooms at St John's College. Kate is wearing the dress that cost her twenty-five guineas.

Below: Kate and Andy get married (Manchester, October 1955).

From left: Alfred Booth, Cicely Caro, Andy, Kate, Jean Hartley (Kate's cousin), Terry Caro (Andy's brother) Eva Booth, Jack Caro.

I arrived in June 1957 and my father immediately bought a TV set.

This is the photo shoot where I (politely) corrected the word choice of the photographer.

Me and my new baby sister Ann in 1959.

Kate and me dressed up to the nines in what my mother would have called our best 'rigouts'.

Winning the fancy-dress competition on the boat to Australia. In case you didn't realise, I am the young Queen Victoria.

Aussies now: Andy and Kate with (from left) me, Robert, Ruth and Ann. Must be one of the only times Dad went to the beach.

Fifth class at Chatswood Public School. I am not holding the class sign this time, but I am sitting directly behind the boy who is.

'My Old Black Billy' – a theatrical and musical triumph.

'Virile, virile, virile and virile.' Playing Anne Devastating in the 1975 Macquarie Uni Ancient History Revue.

1978. I look quite sane, even demure. Inside, I am an absolute mess.

Outside the family home in Terrey Hills. Ralph has just arrived to take me out somewhere (the 70s perm helped me avoid helmet hair).

1976. Ralph and I move into the only slum in Killara.

This was taken at USP Needham for a new business pitch. I like to think I once looked like that.

Best looking man I ever went out with – even with a durry hanging out of his mouth. No wonder I married him.

Christmas 1983.

Back row from left: Ralph, Ann's husband Bill, Ruth's then-boyfriend Phil.

Second row from left: me, Ann, Ruth.

Front row: Robert.

Winning that Caxton in 1984. You can't actually see it but my head is exploding.

10 November 1984, Pymble. Ralph and I get married.
From left: Alfred Booth, me, Ralph, Eva Booth.

From left: Andy, Kate, Ruth, me, Robert, Ann.

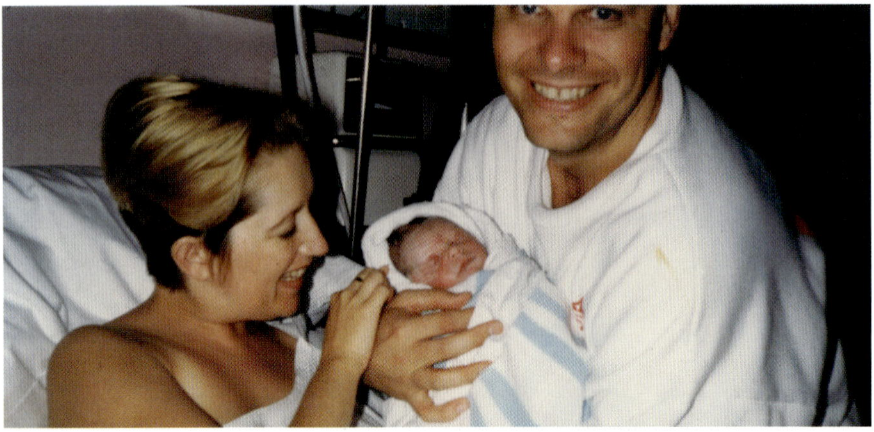

5 May 1988, KGV hospital. Polly Catherine Dunning is born.

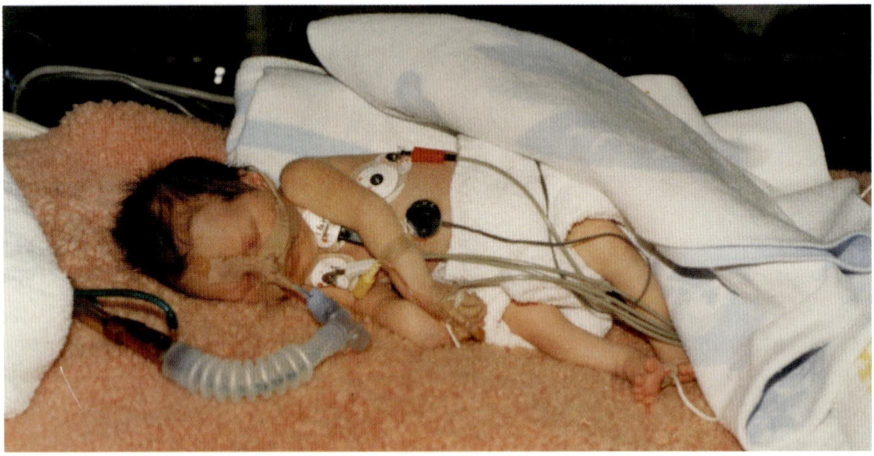

Lower Todman Intensive Care, Royal Alexandra Hospital for Children, Camperdown. Polly gets the last available pediatric intensive care bed in NSW.

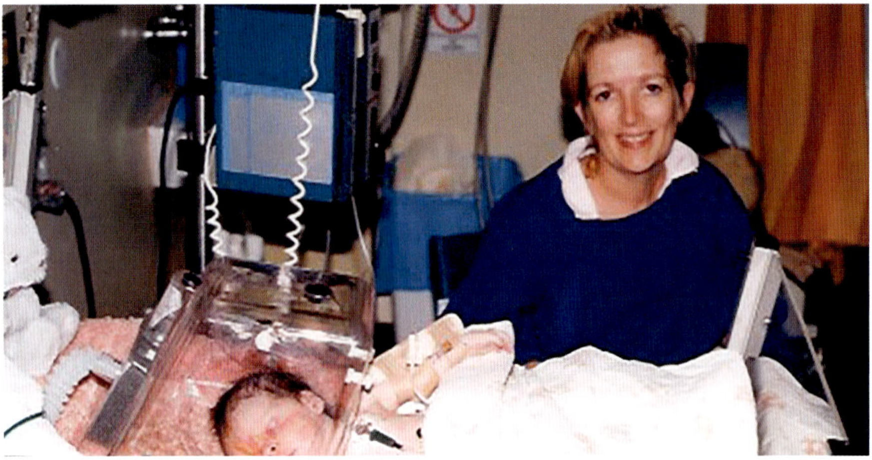

Polly graduates to an oxygen box. I look like I could use one.

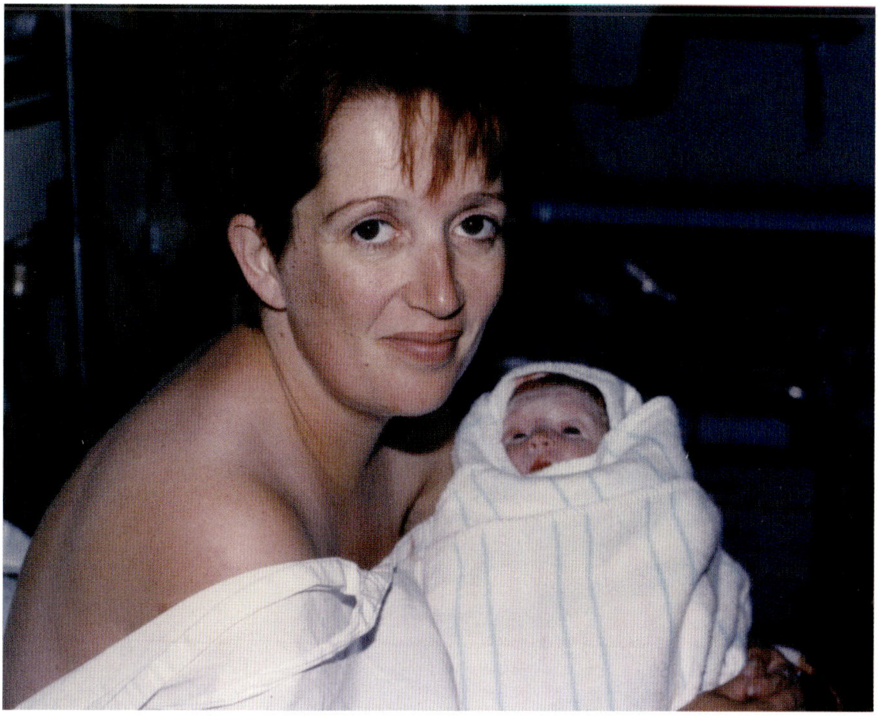

27 March 1991, KGV hospital. Charlotte Frances Dunning is born.

Group on one of our sanity-saving weekends away.
From left: Treen, Ann, Sue, me, Jenny.

Keith Arnold Photography

Taken by photographer and friend Keith Arnold for Ralph's fortieth birthday in November 1994. Polly, me and Charlotte.

At my desk at Saatchi & Saatchi trying to make it up to Charlotte that she's had to come to work with me … again!

The Mercantile Hotel in The Rocks before the 1999 Las Vegas-themed Saatchi Christmas Party. I am the pokie addict, my art director Pic Andrews is pregnant and so – obviously – dressed as Miss Teen Nevada.

'Veuve Clicquot Ponsardin request the pleasure of the company of Mr & Mrs Ralph Dunning (who?) at the Veuve Clicquot Millennium Ball at The Palace of Versailles, Versailles, France, on the 9th of the 9th, 1999.'

Gruen / CJZ Productions / ABC TV

Right and below: A media career at fifty, thanks to the geniuses at *Gruen.*

Gruen / CJZ Productions / ABC TV

Q&A / ABC TV

ABC *Q&A* panel from the 2014 Festival of Dangerous Ideas. It is like flying without a net.

Keith Arnold Photography

Robert, me, Ann and Ruth photographed (again) by Keith Arnold for my parents' fiftieth wedding anniversary.

Andrew Ratter Photography

Me, Polly, Ralph and Charlotte in our garden on 12 April 2014, just before Polly married Adam Howard.

'What is the worst thing that could happen?'

'The worst complication with RSV is apnoea.'

'Is that likely to happen to Polly?'

'No, no – she is holding her own.'

'What about her distress in the evenings?'

'She's tired. Illness always seems worse at night.'

(How could she be tired? She did nothing *but* sleep.)

'So we have nothing to worry about?'

'That's right. We just need to keep an eye on her, that's all.'

Then my paediatrician decided to take Polly off the monitors because he felt they were upsetting Ralph and me too much and, anyway, he was sure she was on the mend. He went away.

As the day wore on, Polly refused to take any food at all. Four hours passed, then six, then eight. I was terrified she would dehydrate. I began to panic and persuaded a nurse to insert a nasal gastric tube so at least she could get a little expressed breast milk.

At 8 pm, when she was due for her next feed, I asked the nurse if I could try breastfeeding her again. I knew that if she started sucking vigorously it was a sure sign she was getting better.

'Sure, why not?' she said.

Over the last few days, when I tried to feed Polly I had only felt a tiny flutter against my nipple, not the urgent, insistent tug I had felt before. Nevertheless, I clung to that flutter as a sign that at least she was getting something.

This time, Polly tried hard to suck. It was almost as if she knew what I so desperately wanted her to do and was trying her hardest to please me. After a moment or two, however, she was spent and pulled off the breast. I looked down at her face, but was distracted by the angry red mark across it where the tape that had held her nasal gastric tube in place had been.

I turned to the young nurse beside me. 'Why has it marked her face like that?'

'I don't know. I'll get Kath.' Kath was the charge sister on duty.

The nurse left and I tried to reposition Polly on my breast. I felt that familiar tiny flutter then she let go. She looked right up at me, into my eyes, and went an odd purple colour. At that moment, Kath arrived beside me. Before I could point out the angry red mark, she held out her arms for Polly.

'Give her to me,' she said.

I handed her over.

Immediately Kath turned her onto her stomach on her palm (Polly was so small, she fitted Kath's hand perfectly) and began banging her quite hard but rhythmically on her back.

'Come on,' she said, in time with each thump. 'Come on.'

I knew what had happened. Ann had quoted those exact words when she told me the story of the crisis of Alice's terrible birth and the agonising moments when the medical staff were trying to get a blue and still newborn to breathe.

'Is she all right?' I said. 'Is she all right?'

No answer. The young nurse, white-faced, was sent to fetch the registrar. The worst had happened: the apnoea they had all mentioned so dismissively; the apnoea they had all told me would never happen. Somewhere, nearby, bells were ringing.

In seconds, Polly's cot was surrounded by doctors and nurses. They stood between me and her so I could not see what was happening. I got off the plastic chair and sat on the floor. It seemed safer to be on the ground. Ralph arrived in the midst of all this and stood and watched and wept. He is a tall man, and he could see over the wall of professionals. He could see something of what was going on.

The registrar emerged from the white-coated cluster. He knelt beside me and put his arm around my shoulders.

'It's the worst thing that can happen,' he began.

Somebody called – low and urgent. 'Doctor!'

He disappeared again.

I don't know if somebody told me she had stopped breathing again or if I just knew. I crawled into a corner behind a pot plant. I wanted my back to be covered. It was instinctive; the world had become too dangerous. Ralph reached down towards me.

'Come out,' he said.

I stayed where I was.

'Come to me, then,' he said. 'Come to me.'

I came out.

They put screens around Polly's cot. Somebody tried to talk me into leaving, but I wanted to stay. If she was going to die, I wanted to be there. But I couldn't see her and there was nothing I could do. Eventually I was persuaded to go. As I stood up to follow the nurse to the parents' room, I saw the mother at the next cot – we had become quite friendly – sitting on her plastic chair, clutching her baby, rocking back and forth, tears streaming down her face. As we walked through the ward, everyone watched us. I knew what they were feeling. They were feeling what I had felt a few nights before; relief that it had not happened to their baby and fear that it might. Some of the women slid their eyes away from mine.

We sat on the lime-green vinyl seats in the parents' room and waited. No-one else came in. The TV blared unwatched in the corner. My parents arrived. Ralph had called them. A nurse poked her head around the door and told us that Polly was breathing again and was to be transferred to another ward – Lower Todman Intensive Care. We learnt later that she had got the last paediatric intensive care bed available in New South Wales that night. We stood in the doorway and watched our daughter being trundled past at high speed. I caught a glimpse of her, between the machines and the medical people, as she flashed past. All I saw of her was a shock of black hair and the healthy-looking but phony tan induced by jaundice. I was now just a bystander.

The young, white-faced nurse who had fetched Kath came in to see us. She sat at our feet on the floor and said, 'I have never seen anything like that before.'

I was angry. Why had such an inexperienced nurse been put in charge of my daughter? And she seemed to want something from me. Forgiveness? Reassurance? Comfort? I had nothing to give her.

'Nor have I,' I said.

She went away.

Much later, near midnight, they took us to see Polly in Lower Todman. I had never been in an intensive care ward before. It was blindingly light and white. I did not take in much more than an impression, but it seemed like the control deck of the *Starship Enterprise*. A greater contrast to the dowdy, old-fashioned darkness of Faithful was hard to imagine. It was like stepping into another dimension. It was just as full of people as the baby's ward but much quieter. People talked in hushed voices and moved briskly but silently. Maybe the nurses wore special shoes in intensive care, because they didn't seem to squeak. The loudest noises were the bleep, bleep, bleep of various monitors and the strange mechanical hiss, burp and whoosh of the ventilators.

Polly lay on a sheepskin, naked except for a bulky cloth nappy. She was no longer in a cot but on a full-sized hospital bed. She had a ventilator up her nose, drips in both arms and electrodes and wires on almost every available surface. I could stroke her right hand, but that was all. Her face was swathed in surgical tape, which was holding the intubator in place. She hardly looked like a baby at all.

nineteen

'There is nothing special about you and there is nothing special about Polly. Terrible things can happen and they can happen to anyone. Safety is an illusion. Danger is reality.'

I obviously looked as shell-shocked as I felt, because Peter Barr had had no trouble identifying me. He walked straight up to me, sat down opposite and, without any niceties, launched straight into the words above. Words that were to change my life.

Maybe it sounds brutal, written down baldly like that, but it was exactly what I needed to hear. Ever since Polly had stopped breathing the night before, I had been obsessively wondering what I had done wrong. Was it that glass or two of wine I had before I knew I was pregnant? Had I exercised too much? Was it stress from losing my job? Was it all the dieting I had done in the past? Then my thoughts turned superstitious. Had this crisis happened because I had been in room 13 when I finally got that private room I'd been so desperate for? What had I done? How had I caused this? What could I have done to change things?

I was desperately trying to hold on to some sense that I was still in control. I wanted to believe that if I could just find the right formula – the right magic spell, if you like – I could keep Polly safe. As Peter Barr spelled out the brutal reality, I gave up that idea. I understood that all I could do was deal with whatever it was I was going to have to deal with. I could do nothing about what was happening to my daughter. It was out of my hands. The only thing I could control was my own reactions and behaviour. The letting-go of control that started at that moment, in that coffee shop, would eventually change everything.

I don't remember anything else about our conversation. I just remember those words. They became the mantra I live by to this day.

When I woke the morning after Polly had been rushed into intensive care, having snatched a few hours' sleep in the breast-feeding room off Faithful Ward (having dreamt I had cancer), I did what I had learnt to do. I reached out for help.

The first person I rang was JuJu Sundin, with whom I had done my prenatal exercise classes. I did this because she had asked all the expectant mothers who attended her classes to keep her posted and I took this as permission to tell her my story. It turned out to be one of the most important phone calls I have ever made.

JuJu listened without interruption before she gave me advice.

'When you get off the phone with me, I want you to call Dr Peter Barr. He works at the children's hospital, so you should be able to find him via the switch. He's a neonatologist, but he's also a grief counsellor. Ask him to meet with you as soon as possible. Tell him I told you to call.'

I did as she said and rang Peter Barr. I told him all that had happened the night before.

'I'll meet you in the coffee shop in five minutes,' he said.

'How will I know you?'

'Don't worry,' he said. 'I'll know you.'

I don't suppose we spent more than thirty minutes together in that dreary cafe in Royal Alexandra, sipping our (not very good) coffees, and, apart from his one quick visit to intensive care, I never saw him again – but in two sentences, he changed my life. I don't even recall what he looked like, but I will never forget him.

* * *

Lower Todman intensive care was at the end of a long corridor with two sets of doors. You could let yourself through the first set to a small area where you washed your hands and put on a gown, but you had to ring a bell and wait to be approved before being buzzed into the actual ward itself.

Polly was dwarfed by the adult-sized bed on which she lay. There was plenty of room for all the tubes, bandages, monitors and drips that so covered her tiny body that only her right hand was left free. Her face had puffed up overnight. It was a reaction, the nurse said, to the oxygen they were pumping into her body. In stark contrast to Faithful Ward, every patient in intensive care had a dedicated nurse. I introduced myself to Debbie, Polly's nurse, and sat by the bed stroking my daughter's free hand. Looking at her poor battered little body, I instinctively started to say something to her that I was to repeat over and over in the days that followed.

'I am your mother and I don't hurt you. I am your mother and I don't hurt you.'

I kept that promise to the letter. I refused to help the staff with any procedures that were painful – and there were many of them. Every two hours, intubated patients had to be suctioned. This meant forcing a tube down into their lungs to suck out the fluid that accumulated as a result of the mechanical breathing. It was horrible. Every time it happened (every two hours, in other words), I got up and left. I did that for two reasons. The first was I couldn't bear to watch Polly fight hopelessly and feebly against the horrible tube. And the second was because I did not want even her subconscious to associate me with pain. At least she was very young and could not anticipate. Watching older intubated babies and toddlers when they realised they were about to be suctioned was really ghastly. They were terrified and struggled and fought as hard as they could.

There were other painful procedures, too; heel pricks and the appropriately but gruesomely named stab gases. Heel pricks were administered by what was called 'the blood nurse'. Ralph rounded on the poor woman one day as she stuck yet another needle into our daughter, making her stir only to cry.

When they weren't hurting her, for those first few days, she was unconscious.

'Do you enjoy your job?' Ralph demanded of the nurse.

It wasn't fair and we knew it, but it was awful to see our defenceless baby constantly under physical attack – even if kindly done and kindly meant, even if only done to save her life. We apologised to the blood nurse later and she was very nice about it. 'Don't worry,' she said. 'You're not the first parent to lash out, nor will you be the last.'

The stab gases were even worse. They had to test for the exchange of gases (oxygen for carbon dioxide) in Polly's blood to make sure she was getting enough oxygen. They had to get a sample of the blood from her arteries as well as from the veins, which were much easier to access. To get to an artery, they literally had to stab her with a large needle. I wept copious tears over that. So did she.

During that first morning, as Nurse Debbie got ready to suction Polly, she warned me I might prefer not to stick around for the process. As I walked down the corridor from Lower Todman, I ran into my paediatrician; the same doctor who – only yesterday – had taken Polly off the monitors because Ralph and I were 'overreacting'. He had the grace to look a little shame-faced.

'Well,' he said, 'I never expected that to happen!'

'No,' I said, 'it seems you didn't.'

And I kept walking towards the public phone.

It's funny. I can still remember what I was wearing on that dismal but eventful day. It was the 1980s and I had an oversize khaki jumpsuit (everything in the 80s was oversize) that – when not pregnant – I cinched in with a wide belt. It buttoned down the front, making it easy for breastfeeding – not that that was an issue anymore. I was back to the breast pump beside a hospital bed. Polly didn't need the milk; all they were giving her was glucose and water.

'She has to concentrate on breathing, not digesting,' Nurse Debbie had explained.

Thanks to the jumpsuit's generous proportions, since having Polly I was still able to wear it with the belt let out a few notches. I'd pulled it on in that grim little breastfeeding room that morning and shoved my hair behind my ears. I moved out of that room that afternoon.

Now that we had a child in intensive care, the hospital provided accommodation for both Ralph and me. It was very basic, just two single beds in a small cell-like room in what used to be the nurses' hostel. There was a window looking out to a grimy brick wall and a phone on the small set of drawers between the beds. (My biggest dread was that phone ringing in the middle of the night; all the parents dreaded it because we knew the medical staff would only disturb us if there was a life-threatening crisis.) There was a shared ablutions block with showers and toilets. Privacy was hard to find. This was difficult, because throughout all this I was, of course, also coping with the permanent period that follows birth and lasts for up to six weeks. Nature doesn't treat new mothers very well. From the state of the accommodation, it was clear hospitals hadn't treated their nurses very well in the old days, either.

Ralph went to work for a few hours each day while I spent all my time next to Polly's bed, with regular interruptions for painful procedures. Ralph joined me there whenever he could. We became familiar with the rhythms and routines of intensive care. Each baby and toddler had a nurse permanently stationed at the end of the bed. Parents – shell-shocked and weary-looking – sat in plastic chairs beside that bed. Children with depressed immune systems were cared for in rooms off the ward. There was a tiny girl from Fiji who'd had a liver transplant in the room nearest Polly. We were on nodding acquaintance with her parents. A young boy was admitted with horrific internal burns that he'd received while playing a silly game with methylated spirits and matches (in shock, he'd breathed the flames in). Ralph became very friendly with his devastated father. Intensive care in a children's hospital is well named. It is an intense place and no-one ever wants to find themselves inside that ward, but there were some good things about it.

The most important was that we never felt fobbed off and our fears and concerns were taken seriously. On that first day, when we were briefed by the intensivist (as the doctors who specialise in intensive care are called), he told us that we no longer had to fear that Polly would stop breathing: 'She has no choice. We are doing her breathing for her.'

He continued, 'We just have to wait out the infection in her lungs. She has a ninety-nine per cent chance of recovering completely and I couldn't say better than that if she had something simple like tonsillitis.'

His words were comforting, even if I couldn't quite bring myself to believe them.

Twice a day, when one shift handed over to the next, the medical staff went from one patient station to another to be briefed. The staff pulled no punches. If your child was improving, they said so. If she was getting worse, they said so. We quickly learnt to trust them. For us, each handover was a relief. Little by little, Polly seemed to get better. We had been told that the first step in the right direction was to wean her off the intubation, put her in an oxygen box – a perspex box that fitted over her head, filled with warm, moist air with an artificially high level of oxygen to help her breathe easily on her own. The next was to get her breastfeeding again. Then she would move from intensive care back into Faithful. After that, unimaginably, the next step was home and real life.

Twice a day, at handover, we could see the intensivist had been right. We just had to wait out the virus. The news for the little girl from Fiji was not so good. Every day the debrief became a little less positive. Her body was rejecting the transplant and the drugs were not having the desired effect. We felt dreadful for her parents, who hung off every word of the briefing, as we all did.

It was a red-letter day when they decided to remove the intubation tubes and put Polly in an oxygen box. She immediately became more wakeful. It also meant no more suctioning. The heel pricks and stab gases continued, unfortunately. They also began to feed her a little of my hand-pumped breast milk via a nasal gastric tube. She had lost a lot of weight, something that became very obvious now she was no longer being artificially inflated by the intubator. The milk I was able to extract was beginning to dwindle, but they told me to persevere. How I grew to hate that breast pump; my wrists and arms ached constantly, but I did it for hours and hours a day. The resulting milk was refrigerated and a small amount was fed to Polly as she gained strength, but most of it was simply poured down the sink.

We had few visitors. My mother came and herded Ralph and I out of the hospital every day to have lunch, just as she had when we were in Faithful. It frightened me to leave – although less so than it had when Polly was in the babies' ward. I knew her every vital sign was being carefully watched now. But it was good to get out of the hospital grounds and see the real world going about its business as if nothing had happened.

One day, much to my surprise, my obstetrician Sue Fleming turned up. She had a meeting with a colleague at the children's hospital and thought she'd drop in to see how I was doing at the same time. I really appreciated that. It was then that I felt my decision to choose a female obstetrician who had children of her own had been a good one.

Very slowly, Ralph and I began to allow ourselves to believe that Polly might really be going to recover and we might finally get to take her home. My life had been nothing but hospitals for more than a month. Then, just when it seemed the end might really be in sight, in the middle of the night, the phone between our beds rang.

'Mrs Dunning?' (It wasn't a name I used but there were much more important things to worry about just then.)

'Yes?'

'Polly's mum?'

'Yes?'

'Can you get down to Lower Todman right away?'

'My husband too?'

'No need. Just you.'

My anxiety subsided a little. If they didn't need Ralph, then it was unlikely she was about to die.

'What's happening? Is she all right?' Ralph was starting to get out of bed.

'I don't know. But I don't think it can be serious; they only want me, not you.'

'I'm coming anyway.'

We hastily pulled on our dressing gowns, and raced through the dark and freezing hospital (it was almost June). Polly had seemed much better only a few hours previously when we'd left her.

Lower Todman was a blaze of light and activity, as always. A male nurse was standing at the end of Polly's bed with her in his arms. I recognised him. He was the nurse who had assessed Polly as the sickest child in New South Wales the week before and given her the last available neonatal bed in the state. She was now squirming in his arms, screaming her head off.

'Mum?' he said, as soon as he saw me.

'Yes.'

'This child is starving. I think you should breastfeed her right now.'

I sat down in a chair and he handed the furious baby over. Once I'd undone my gown and nightie, she practically leapt through the air and latched on. She began sucking vigorously. Everyone nearby burst out laughing. Right from the beginning, we had been told that being able to feed properly on her own was one of the best signs she was on the road to recovery. I had cause to be grateful for my weary persistence with the breast pump. Dwindling though it was, at least I had some milk left to give her.

twenty

'You are all suffering from post-intensive care shock.'

The intensivist who admitted Polly to Lower Todman had come to see us in Faithful Ward. He was talking to two couples, parents of babies who were newly released from intensive care. We were in need of his diagnosis. Our babies had both gone into intensive care due to complications with RSV bronchiolitis and were now back in the general baby's ward. All four of us were rigid with terror now our children were without the security of one-on-one nursing and all that high-tech equipment. We'd hated intensive care, but we'd also relied on it.

'Everyone suffers from it when they make the transition back into Faithful, but don't worry, your children really are well enough to cope. We would not have released them otherwise.'

It helped to know we were normal, but this was the ward where Polly had been – in my eyes – neglected, and where my fears had been belittled and dismissed. I did not like being back there. Faithful had very bad memories for me.

None of the parents from my first stay in the ward were still there. Their children had recovered and they had gone home. Now there was a new set of babies and mothers in the RSV section of the ward. I kept away from them. I did not want Polly to be reinfected (yes, it can happen) and I had nothing to tell them that they would want to hear.

There is no vaccination for RSV or bronchiolitis. Something like 70 per cent of children will have been infected with the virus before the age of three. Most of them will show few symptoms and it is generally not a serious condition for full-term healthy babies and children. As we had discovered, though, it is very dangerous for premature babies. While we were in Royal Alexandra watching our baby fight for her life, we saw lots of other ill and suffering children. To watch little babies and toddlers struggling to breathe or enduring painful and frightening medical interventions is a grim education, but it means you never forget what you have learnt. Whenever anyone has tried to argue the wrongs of vaccination with me, I tell them to spend a week in a paediatric intensive care ward. I was vigilant about making sure my kids were vaccinated and, when they were young and vulnerable, I kept them away from children I knew were not properly protected. I wouldn't wish Faithful or Lower Todman on my worst enemy, let alone a vulnerable child.

We spent a few more days in Faithful, waiting until Polly's chest X-ray showed us that her lungs were clear of infection. In the meantime, she had gone from a baby who was almost permanently asleep to an alert and lively child with a large appetite. She had a lot of weight to regain. I have very clear memories of my first stay in Faithful, as she became sicker and sicker, and also of her days in intensive care, but our last few days back in the babies' ward have faded. I do vividly remember the day we were told that we could take her home.

'Before you go, I have to tell you that it is hospital policy to offer an apnoea mat to every child who has stopped breathing during their stay in hospital.' The registrar who had brought us the good news held out his hand to delay us.

'What does an apnoea mat do?'

'It monitors her breathing or, at least, the rise and fall of her chest, and rings an alarm if she stops.'

'Does she need one? I thought you said her chest X-ray is clear?'

'It is, but I am not permitted to give you an opinion on whether your daughter needs the mat or not – it is up to you to decide.'

Bloody lawyers, I thought. I tried another tack. 'If she was your daughter, would you take one?'

The registrar gave me a long look. 'Well, we know why she stopped breathing: it was due to an infection that she no longer has. So, no, if it was my daughter, I would not take one.'

'Good. Well we won't either.'

It was a shock to come home. The flowers that had greeted our first, but short-lived homecoming weeks before had died in their vases and the house felt stale and dispiriting. But I wasn't as overwhelmed as I had been the first time. I had made a decision about the kind of parent I was going to be. I don't know when I decided; whether it was when Peter Barr stated the bald reality of life to me, when we refused that apnoea mat, or if it was a combination of everything we had experienced since I'd last walked through my own front door. I knew there was only so much I could do for my daughter. I couldn't do Polly's breathing for her, for example. That was just one of the many things she would have to do on her own.

Nonetheless, although my anxiety was under control during the day, it rose at night. The sash window in Polly's room was locked firmly but it was also slightly open to let in fresh air. Night after night, I dreamt that a hand snaked through that gap, picked up Polly and spirited her away.

I also developed a very mild form of post-traumatic stress disorder – or that's what I think it was. Every time I closed my eyes to go to sleep, whether for a nap during the day, or at night, the entire sequence of events up to Polly being resuscitated and rushed to intensive care would play itself out against the screen of my closed eyelids. It felt as if there was a tiny projectionist in my brain and every time the lights went down he or she would start the film. It didn't upset me and, once the film was finished, I went to sleep, but it repeated itself day and night, night and day for about six months. Then it stopped, never to return. I thought at the time, and I still do, that my mind was trying to integrate the experience and make it part of me. I didn't fight it or worry about it. I let it happen.

The second day we were home, I took Polly off to the local baby health centre. Frankly, I didn't really know what else to do and reaching out for help had worked well for me so far. I poured out the story of my traumatic introduction to motherhood to the lovely woman who ran the centre at Crows Nest.

'I think a stay at Tresillian would be a great idea,' she said. 'Let me give them a ring and see if they have room for you next week.'

Tresillian Family Care Centres offer day stays and weekly admissions. Polly and I stayed for the full week and it was fantastic. The first thing the mothercraft nurses noticed was that Polly – who was still so small that triple 0 (that's the smallest size you can get) baby clothes swam on her – was struggling to deal with the sheer quantity of my breast milk. I had what is called 'copious flow'. No doubt it is why my breast milk had not dried up during those wearisome weeks with a breast pump. It may also be why I have such awful memories of engorged breasts. It now meant that milk sprayed out of me like a fire hydrant. Poor Polly gulped and choked as she tried to feed. So I was taught to posture feed. This meant I had to lie down on a bed, a couch, the floor – any available flat surface – and position Polly above me so that she was sucking uphill. Basically, gravity slowed the flow. As I got used to doing this, I became increasingly nonchalant about throwing myself down horizontally wherever I happened to be, baring my breast and feeding my child. Discretion? Ha! Not only couldn't you ignore me, sometimes you had to step over me.

I had one moment of panic during that otherwise very supportive week. A blood nurse came in and wanted to take blood samples from all the babies. From memory, another baby had come down with an infection and I think they wanted to make sure it had not spread. All I knew was that they wanted to do a heel prick. No way. I didn't care what the reason, I wasn't letting anyone stick an unnecessary needle into my baby. (Vaccinations, of course, were not unnecessary and weren't an issue until much later, when my memory was not so raw.) Knowing our recent history, Tresillian accepted my resistance. At least I was able to protect Polly from that.

The best thing about Tresillian was that we both received calm, practical support and guidance. Polly and I also got some proper sleep. The next best thing was that, when our week was up and we were departing, the staff suggested I join their Tresillian new mothers' group.

The group was a weekly meeting of new mothers in the local area. It was ostensibly about mothercraft and advice on caring for your new baby. They provided a crèche and we had a couple of baby-free hours in which to receive instructions and share experiences. I remember very little about what we were taught or what we discussed. The only thing that stuck with me from the formal proceedings was a discussion about the three different styles of parenting: authoritarian, permissive and authoritative. (I've swung between permissive and authoritative, I suspect.) What did come out of it, however, was four (and eventually five) new friends.

Treen was a make-up artist, the same one who had been bubbling over about her pregnancy on that shoot while I was keeping my mouth firmly shut in case I had a second miscarriage. Her son Jackson had been born more or less when Polly was supposed to be. This meant Polly was a couple of weeks older than Jackson, but much smaller. Ann was a New Yorker married to an Australian. She had been a hospital administrator. Her daughter Brooke was more or less the same age as Polly but also much bigger. Sue was a marketing manager and also an American married to an Australian, although she was from Michigan. Her son Luke was the oldest of the babies. Jenny was an architect and Australian-born Chinese. Her son Alex was the same age as Luke. Why we five selected each other from all the other women in the group, I'm not sure. But we made a good decision. The five of us met weekly for a decade. We became six for a few years when Ann's old college friend Polly (always known as Big Polly, for obvious reasons) joined us from Calvary in Canada when her academic husband was posted out here. We gave each other much-needed support.

Mothers' groups get a bad rap and are often painted as competitive and disapproving. We were nothing like that. We were kind to each other and we had fun. We helped each other through our subsequent pregnancies. All of us had a second child and (Big) Polly and Sue went on to have a third. Once our children were old enough (i.e. no longer breastfed) and could be left with their fathers, we went away on weekends together. Maybe our group worked so well because Ann, Polly and Sue were a long way from home and needed support. Maybe it was because we had a lot in common; we were all professional women who had taken time out from our careers (I was the only one who had done so involuntarily) to have kids. We had our differences, too. The Americans were much more concerned about cleanliness than us Aussies, to the extent that they sterilised their toys. All of the other mothers were better cooks and children's activity arrangers than I would ever be, but they were also a lifeline – particularly after our second daughter, Charlotte, was born and Ralph was promoted to a job that meant he spent almost every second week away from home.

That first year of Charlotte's life I had two children under three and Ralph was away twenty-six weeks out of fifty-two. Ralph worked in the wine industry. He'd started out as a sales manager and had then moved steadily up the ranks. Once Charlotte was born, he was promoted to national sales manager, which meant that he travelled around Australia all the time. As a result, 1991 remains one of the worst years of my life, and without the mothers' group I think I really would have gone mad. I remember feeling very glum at the weekly get-together held a few days before my thirty-fifth birthday. As they so often did, someone picked up on my mood.

'What's up, Jane?'

'I'm thirty-five on Friday.'

'Happy birthday. But what's so bad about that?'

'Ralph is away and my parents are busy, so I'll be spending it on my own.'

Needless to say, I instead spent my thirty-fifth birthday having a slap-up dinner at the Bathers' Pavilion with the group. Anyone who tries to tell me women are their own worst enemy clearly has no idea about the warmth and support of female friendship.

But what had happened to my anxiety neurosis throughout all the upheaval and trauma that marked my transition into motherhood? It was still there and still had the power to wake me up at night, but it had faded. I was too caught up with the minutiae and, yes, drudgery of full-time childcare to pay it as much attention as I once had. I had more to think about than the (admittedly weird) permutations of my own mind. I was also exhausted, particularly after I had Charlotte.

Despite our awful experience with Polly – or perhaps because of it – Ralph and I were determined to have another child. We knew in ways that perhaps most other modern parents do not just how fragile children can be. We thought a three-year gap would be reasonable. Polly was thriving by then, still very small and slight for her age but vigorous and cheeky to the point of being fierce. I remember complaining about some recent misdemeanour on her part when Ralph brought me up sharp.

'Yes, she's a fighter. That's why we still have her.'

She was a very early talker. She said her first word, 'duck', while playing with a yellow plastic duck in the bath at ten months. By the time she was eighteen months old, she was speaking in complete sentences. I didn't think she was a genius. I wondered whether it was the positive legacy of having been born prematurely. Her gross motor skills, such as crawling and walking, were slower to develop than many of her peers, but her fine motor skills, such as speech, drawing and building things, were advanced. Is that because she had five extra weeks of being in the stimulating world? She was not a great sleeper, but another stay at Tresillian just before her first birthday had helped. By the time she was two and a bit, we felt brave enough to go through the whole process again. We gave ourselves a bit of extra time, given it had taken us fully nine months to conceive originally. This time, of course, it took no time at all, and three months after we stopped using contraception, I was pregnant again.

twenty-one

I was hanging clothes on the washing line when I felt something that I shouldn't. I was thirty-six weeks pregnant and had been quietly celebrating getting past thirty-five. I should have known better. Something was going wrong again. This time it was blood.

We had moved house when Polly was about eighteen months old to a decrepit two-bedroom Californian bungalow that we'd hastily and cheaply made liveable. Its advantages were a large and sunny north-facing garden and a quiet street. When we'd arrived to inspect the place in the late afternoon, a bunch of local kids were playing cricket on the grassy verge across the road. Their game helped clinch the deal. I was sick of seeing the bruises on Polly's forehead as she learned to walk. Unlike our shabby new house, the Naremburn semi was chicly renovated but every surface was hard. She'd fall on the slate floor and then fall in the brick courtyard. Now she could toddle and tumble about on gentle, forgiving grass.

The Hills Hoist was in the middle of that soft grass. When I felt the ominous gush between my legs, I left the wet laundry in its basket, scooped Polly up and rushed inside to the phone.

Back I went to King George V, back to a hospital bed. This time it was not my waters that had broken early; there was a tear in the placenta. Once again I was spending forty minutes a day monitoring my baby's heartbeat, goggle-eyed with boredom. The nurses who looked at the read-out said they could tell me the baby's sex. I didn't need them to. I was pretty sure I was having another girl – and I was delighted. Polly had taken great interest in my pregnancy and had stubbornly declared to anyone who would listen that the baby was a girl and that her name was Charlotte. When anyone (for example, me) gently suggested she might be having a brother, she simply refused to entertain the idea.

The day after I was admitted, I had to have an amniocentesis to see what was happening inside my womb. I'd rather go to the dentist (and I hate the dentist) than ever have another. I'd rather give birth, have a mammogram (and they make my eyes water) or any number of Pap smears than ever have to have an amniocentesis at thirty-six and a half weeks pregnant again. My fear wasn't helped by the way I was treated.

To have the amnio, I had to lie on my back. By thirty-six weeks it is nauseating to lie in that position because the weight of the baby presses down on your internal organs. I was fighting the urge to throw up. The two women who were to perform the test – one was training the other, I think – were having a lovely chat about their personal lives across my prone body. It was surreal to be treated as just a pregnant stomach. They neither looked at me nor addressed a word to me.

To push an amnio needle into a womb carrying a baby of thirty-six weeks gestation requires some force and also delicate positioning. They had to use an ultrasound to make sure they would not stick the bloody great needle (honestly, it was huge) straight into the foetus. Once they had found the right spot they pushed hard. I felt the muscles in my uterus resist and then a disgusting, utterly nauseating POP! There is something terrifying about your pregnant belly being violated. I wept. Perhaps that's why one of the chatty young women finally noticed that the distended belly in front of them had a person attached.

'Are you all right?' This was said in a tone that indicated it was most inconsiderate of me to interrupt their conversation.

'I'm just a bit worried about the baby.'

'Why? You're not in labour, are you?' This in a tone that implied I was a self-pitying fool.

'Well, I have been in labour off and on for about twenty-four hours.'

'Oh!' (Whoops, probably should have read the notes.) 'Well . . . it all looks okay at the moment . . .'

I say it again: some people really shouldn't work in health care.

I spent three days back in the perinatal ward at KGV. Ralph and Polly visited me daily. Polly was very excited about the imminent arrival of the baby she was still sure would be a girl.

She was also rather enjoying having her dad all to herself. Ralph has always been a very hands-on and nurturing father. When the girls were sick, for example, he was much more sympathetic than I was. As parents we were a bit of a complex mixture. In some ways fulfilling typical gender roles (I was home for five years when they were small, while he was the major bread-winner, for example) and in some ways confounding them (he has always been a more meticulous housekeeper than me, a better cook and a much more protective parent).

The three days I spent in the perinatal ward were frustrating. The first couple of nights, mild labour would begin at about 2 am and last till 6 am before shutting down again. Then, on the third night, the contractions didn't dwindle and shut down, and at thirty-seven weeks I went into labour properly. I was about to have another premature baby. Once again, I was learning just how little control I had.

I am often bemused by the immense effort first-time pregnant couples put into planning the birth – the location, music to be played, food to be prepared, even the perfumed oils and scents to be smelt. Sometimes I gently try to suggest that none of this stuff will matter much and that it's better not to plan too carefully for an event that can be very unpredictable. It is a suggestion that rarely goes down well. But the unpredictability of my experiences taught me a great deal about the illusion of control. I can't help trying to pass it on.

I was very lucky with both my births – which was just as well, given I wasn't nearly so lucky after them. I thoroughly enjoyed giving birth to my daughters, thanks to the inventor of the spinal block. Once I was in proper labour with Charlotte, I gave clear instructions to the midwife: I wanted an epidural and I didn't want to wait too long to get it. When my waters broke, the blissful anaesthetic was administered. Just as I had with Polly, I was able to feel my contractions but the pain was manageable. I worked hard, but when we got to second stage – once the cervix is fully dilated and the baby enters 'the birth canal' (otherwise known as the vagina) – something didn't feel right. I kept apologising to Sue Fleming (my obstetrician for a second time) as I laboured to push the baby into the world.

'I'm sorry . . . I just don't feel like I can get a grip . . .'

And with the next contraction, 'Sorry . . . it just doesn't feel . . .'

And the next. 'It's just not . . . sorry . . .'

'For Christ's sake, Jane, stop apologising. It's not an exam!'

However, when Charlotte emerged – a girl, just as Polly had predicted – I could not help notice Sue flashing a very dark look at the midwife who had been assisting. I didn't pay much attention. I was far too interested in my mysterious new daughter. I had expected another Polly; I thought I knew what kind of babies Ralph and I produced. But Charlotte was completely herself. She was blonde while Polly was dark-haired. She was blue-eyed whereas Polly's eyes were green. Her face was a different shape. She had a different air about her. Don't let anyone tell you babies are blank slates for parents to write on. They enter the world with very definite and individual personalities.

The next day Sue stopped by my room. 'You remember how you kept apologising yesterday and saying you couldn't get a grip?

Well, there was a reason for it. Charlotte was born in the posterior position.'

Posterior means she was born with her face up instead of down, her spine against my spine. Most babies are born anterior – face down. I had a second reason to thank that epidural. Posterior births are much more painful than anterior ones.

Sue was annoyed. 'I'd asked the midwife if the baby had turned and she told me it had.' (Hence the dirty look I'd noticed.) 'It *is* much harder to get a grip with a baby in the posterior position, and much harder to push her out, because you were trying to push her out face first rather than via the top of her head.'

I am so glad I had chosen a female obstetrician who'd had children of her own. It was wonderful to know that my body could be trusted. It was (and I hate this word) empowering to know that the messages it gave me about what was going on were accurate and that my responses had been reasonable. Only another woman who had been at my end of the birthing process would realise how important such a small bit of information could be.

Sue had also more than fulfilled my faith in her when I had gone to see her for my scheduled six-week visit after Polly had been born. She had given me the required physical examination and made sure that I was recovering from giving birth. Then she did something more. She told me how well I had handled the crisis of Polly's near death. Her praise almost brought me to tears. Mothers receive very little praise and much criticism. To be praised by your obstetrician is no small thing and I will never forget how her words gave me courage at just the right time. And here she was again, treating me as an intelligent human being, not as that anonymous cultural icon, 'a mother'.

After a baby is born in New South Wales, a paediatrician is automatically assigned. There were two resident paediatricians attached to KGV. One had his surgery on the north side of the harbour, the other on the south. As I lived on the north it was assumed my baby would be assigned to the north-side paediatrician. Unfortunately, he was familiar to me. He was the same doctor who had dismissed my concerns about Polly and taken her off the monitors just before she had stopped breathing and almost died. When I was told he was to be Charlotte's paediatrician, I remember feeling relieved that I had private health cover and so was entitled to choose my own doctor.

'I do not want Dr X. He almost killed my first child and I am not going to give him a second go at the other one.'

You should have seen the nurse's face.

'But Dr Y is based in Sutherland Shire. That's a long way from you.'

'I don't care. I'll happily drive anywhere rather than see Dr X.'

Dr Y came to see Charlotte a few hours later. He was lovely and did not dismiss or patronise me as Dr X had done. He picked Charlotte up with gentle and practised hands.

'She's lovely, and presents as a perfectly normal full-term baby. I understand she is your second pre-term child?'

Charlotte was born at thirty-seven weeks, which made her one week premature.

'You do know that forty weeks is an average gestation? Some women take longer to cook their babies than others. It looks to me like you just cook them quickly.'

So, it wasn't my fault then? I hadn't done anything wrong? It was just that I had a slightly faster-burning womb. It was also comforting to hear that.

We talked for a while about various things to do with Charlotte and he paid me careful and respectful attention.

Eventually, he asked a rather surprising question. 'Are you a doctor?'

(Sutherland Shire? I'd drive to Melbourne for this bloke.)

'No. But I did spend thirteen days in Lower Todman intensive care with my first daughter and I picked up quite a lot of medical information and terminology while I was there.'

Dr Y and I had got off to a very good start.

Charlotte's technical prematurity was nothing but an advantage this time around. She had no need for a special nursery, no jaundice and so no lights. I had a lovely (quiet) private room at the top of KGV with a great view over Chippendale. The room was full of flowers and I was very content. Ralph and I felt very relaxed with our new baby. One time, Ralph was walking down the corridor holding Charlotte while a matron was giving a how-to-bath-your-baby demonstration to a bunch of first-time parents. She spotted Ralph walking by and grabbed him. 'Come here for a moment.'

He went to stand beside her.

The matron turned to her audience of new parents. 'That's how you carry a new baby!'

Ralph was carrying Charlotte on her stomach. She was lying along his hand and forearm. He held her firmly under her chin and arm while her face was supported by his thumb and forefinger. She was perfectly relaxed.

'Don't treat them like they're made of glass,' said matron. 'The more confidently you handle them, the safer they will feel.'

Charlotte was born just before Easter and as the holiday weekend approached they were sending as many patients home as possible. A male nurse came past my little eyrie and saw me breastfeeding Charlotte, something that was also much easier the second time around.

'You seem to be coping very well,' he observed. 'How about going home tomorrow?'

Going home? Was he kidding? Going home meant coping with a new baby and a not-quite-three-year-old on my own. I knew how hard that was going to be. I intended to squeeze every ounce of benefit out of my allocated five-day hospital stay. I could hand Charlotte over to a nurse if she cried during the night. All my meals were prepared, served and cleaned up by somebody else. Ralph came daily, took my dirty laundry away and replaced it with clean. Yes, I missed Polly, but I didn't miss the drudgery of looking after her.

'I'd love to!' I lied sweetly. 'But Charlotte is premature . . .'

The nurse's face fell. 'Oh well, bad luck.'

Hardly. I still remember fondly that quiet, restful week, high above Chippendale. I knew that as soon as I got home all hell would break loose.

* * *

Three months after we had come home, Ralph was away yet again. In those early days, when he was away I often took the girls to stay with my parents. It was good to have hands-on help, of course, but it was mostly good to have some adult company. Ralph was going to be out of town for a week, so we had moved in with Mum and Dad. Within a day, Charlotte, who was usually a contented baby, seemed restless and unsettled. She was beginning to look strange to me, too – screaming furiously and with red-rimmed, dry-looking eyes. I was worried about her and found myself – alone this time – heading off to casualty at the children's hospital. She was admitted with what they called an NSV, which unhelpfully stands for non-specific virus.

She was admitted into the immunosuppressed ward because good old Faithful Ward was – as it is every winter – full of babies who were RSV positive. The children in the IS ward were generally older than Charlotte. In fact, she was the only baby. In a cot nearby was a boy who was probably a little older than Polly. He had leukaemia and – if memory serves me correctly – the night we arrived he was having blood transfused into his veins. It was horrible. The boy moaned and struggled against the drip continuously. His white-faced and clearly exhausted father sat by his bed all night. All around me were small children suffering from conditions that were painful and frightening.

Charlotte was also ill. She had a high temperature and was restless. They had given her a lumber puncture (true to my policy of not allowing my children to associate me with pain, I made myself scarce while that was happening) to make sure she did not have meningitis. Once we were sure she did not (thank God) she remained in hospital for observation. I was lucky. This time my child was not the sickest child in the hospital. Nevertheless, it was dreary to be back. I retreated into sleep. The chair next to Charlotte's cot was not the most comfortable, but I am a small person and by hooking my feet into the bars of her cot and curling up, I found I could sleep quite easily. I woke to feed her and to see Ralph and Polly in the grounds of the hospital. Polly had a cold (maybe it was RSV, who knows) so she was not allowed into the ward.

At night, I slept with the other mothers in a room that during the day doubled as the schoolroom. The child patients were suffering with AIDS, organ transplants, brain tumours and various cancers. Their mothers were worried and exhausted. We didn't talk much. At 6 am we had to get up, get dressed, pack away our beds, get breakfast in the cafeteria and then spend another day beside our child's bed.

Because Charlotte was only three months old, I was still breastfeeding her at night. I'd get up at 3 am, feed her and settle her down, and then I needed to pee. There was a loo on the ward but it was only for the use of patients. During the day that rule was scrupulously observed. At 3 am it was cold and wet, and the public toilets were a long way away at the end of open walkways winding through the dark and empty hospital grounds. For the first few nights, the night nurses took pity on me and let me use the toilet on the ward. Then, one night, I fed Charlotte as usual and went to the (new) nurse on duty and asked her if I could use the toilet on the ward.

'Certainly not!'

'I only need to pee.'

'That toilet is only for patients.'

'There are no patients using it at the moment.'

'That is not the point. If you need to use the toilet, you must go to the public ones.'

'Do you know how far away they are?'

Quite apart from being cold, wet and windy, it was quite frightening wandering alone through the hospital grounds clad only in my nightie, dressing gown and slippers.

'Not my problem.'

'So you are going to send me out on a night like this for a pee, when there is a perfectly good, unoccupied toilet just over there?'

She nodded and almost smiled. She was quite pregnant.

'Well, if your baby ever has to spend any time in hospital, I hope you meet a nurse just like you.'

The next morning, I was sleepier than usual. It had taken me ages to get back to sleep after my cold, wet walk. I suspect my sense of righteous fury at that smug nurse didn't help. We were woken as usual, but despite the clatter of the other mothers around me, I fell back to sleep. I was eventually woken by that pregnant nurse when she flicked on the bright overhead lights. She stood watching me, her arms folded. Turning on the lights meant that if I stood – the schoolroom being glass-fronted from waist height – I would be fully visible to the entire ward. I had to hunch over and get dressed in a corner to avoid total exposure. That woman was a piece of work.

Later that day, I came back from lunch with Ralph and Polly to see a concerned huddle of medical staff gathered around Charlotte's cot. I was surprised, as she had seemed to be getting chirpier and her temperature had come down.

'You'll have to take this baby home today.'

I still don't know why medical staff (some of them anyway) seem to feel that taking an accusatory tone is helpful.

'Oh . . . okay . . .'

'Otherwise she'll have to go into Faithful – the babies' ward.'

Faithful was full of RSV. No way was she going there.

'No, no, I'll take her home . . . but why?'

It didn't feel like they were saying she could go home because she was better.

'She has diarrhoea!' This was said in tones of horror. And, indeed, I had been told that if she developed diarrhoea she would have to leave the ward.

'Really? I haven't seen any sign of it.'

'While you were out I changed her nappy and it was definitely diarrhoea!'

'Okay.' They were doctors and nurses. I assumed they'd know.

'Anyway,' the doctor took a kinder tone, 'her temperature is normal, she's feeding well and there seems no need to keep her any longer.'

We were discharged, even though it felt a little like we were being tossed out on our ear. I took Charlotte home and watched her carefully for any sign of that diarrhoea. Her poo was completely liquid, but that's entirely normal for fully breastfed babies. They don't eat any solids so they don't shit any solids either. That's when it dawned on me. None of those highly trained medical professionals, who normally dealt with older children, had ever seen a breastfed baby's poo before. That's why they thought she had diarrhoea. I suppose they thought I'd been hiding it from them, hence the accusatory tone.

Sheesh! Not just rude and nasty but bloody incompetent to boot. If you are ever unlucky enough to have a baby admitted to hospital, take my advice: listen to your own instincts.

twenty-two

As I said, 1991 was a lousy year. I had a baby who wouldn't sleep at night, a toddler who wouldn't sleep during the day, and a husband who was away twenty-six weeks out of fifty-two. I was exhausted and the strain showed. I had a cold more or less constantly. Toddlers going to preschool for the first time will do that to a family. They build their immunity by challenging yours. Worse, the navicular bone in my left foot kept coming out of alignment. The agony of this made it very hard to walk or stand, and caring for active kids keeps you on your toes. As I couldn't put my foot down properly this was literal in my case. I was constantly at the chiropractor's having the bone adjusted. Eventually I got orthotics and that helped.

I was a physical mess but not as much of a mental mess as I used to be. Yes, I was still anxious and I still had intrusive thoughts, but – as JuJu Sundin had pointed out to us pregnant ladies in her exercise classes – our brains can only feel one pain at a time, so my foot and the constant fog of exhaustion distracted me.

I had also learnt some important lessons while I struggled with the unpredictability of pregnancy, birth and the fragility of very young children. I was not in control. I can see now that my anxiety was about fear of losing control. I feared suddenly being overwhelmed by homicidal or suicidal impulses. I feared having a panic attack so debilitating I would shut myself up in my house forever. I feared that I would suddenly become out of control. Without knowing it, by giving up the illusion of control I was starting to give up my decades-long anxiety neurosis.

It was never going to be quite as easy as that, of course. First I had to pay attention to a couple of issues I had neglected.

I can't remember exactly when I finally came to grips with my anxiety. I know that my children were still quite small. It may have been after Polly started school. It's one of the gifts that come with having children: you get to vicariously revisit your own past.

I loved sharing the books I'd loved as a child with my daughters and the films, music and games I had once enjoyed, particularly as I felt I was sharing generations of childhood favourites. Just the other day, Polly, now a married woman of twenty-seven, was telling me how she was playing a game with her husband's small niece and nephew that I had also played with her when she was about the same age. It's a well-known rhyming game and many families have their own versions. It involves sitting a child on your crossed lower leg, holding their hands and then bouncing them up and down on your ankle in time to a nursery rhyme.

This is the way the farmer rides:

Bump-bump, bump-bump, bump-bump.

This is the way the lady rides:

Trit-trot, trit-trot, trit-trot.

This is the way the huntsman rides:

Gallop, gallop, gallop.

This is the way the old man rides:

Hobble-dee, hobble-dee, and (while dropping them between your legs) *DOWN into a ditch.*

Her twenty-first-century, iPad/iPhone/iPod savvy niece and nephew shrieked with delight and demanded more, just as she used to.

My grandfather Alfred had played the same game with me. Talking to Polly made me wonder how old that little rhyming game might be. No doubt my grandfather was passing on something from his own childhood that had been passed on to him, and so on back through the centuries. Polly and I wondered how many generations of children have squealed with delight as they've gone down into that ditch.

The passing on of childhood stories, games, rhymes and traditions is one of the pleasures of parenting. But there are other memories that return, some of them not quite so delightful.

I visited another counsellor at about this time. Again, it was a woman I had heard on the radio. I don't know what her qualifications were or what kind of therapy she practised; I called her to make an appointment because she had sounded sensible in the interview and because she'd revealed she lived in the same suburb I did. Patricia and I did not have the same rapport as I'd had with Jytte, but I don't think I needed that intense relationship with a therapist anymore. I just needed someone who could listen with sympathy, without judgment and with intelligence. And she did.

Patricia asked me how I was feeling. This is standard, of course, at the beginning of any therapy session.

'Fine, but, it's funny, I keep thinking about something that happened to me as a child. Something I haven't thought about for ages.'

'Tell me about that.'

'It's not something that I've forgotten, not a repressed memory or anything. It was just a weird thing that happened to me on a school excursion when I was ten or eleven.'

'What was it?'

And I began to tell her about being run over in that motel car park back in 1968. I had related the story very occasionally over the years, but always in a detached, isn't-that-a-bizarre-thing-to-have-happened kind of way. I'd often laughed about it, and told the tale as if it had happened to someone else. In that counselling session, I began to tell the story in that same blasé way, but not for long. I can't remember whether it was something the counsellor said that triggered the flood of feelings or whether it was thinking about how I would feel if something like that happened to either of my own daughters, but I was suddenly in tears.

'Why didn't anyone do anything?' I said to my counsellor. 'How could they just let me be run over like that and do nothing? Why didn't the teachers call the police? Why didn't my parents demand some action? Why was someone allowed to drive into a group of children, run over one of them and then drive away, without any consequences?'

I was sobbing, rocking back and forth, clutching a cushion to my chest while I said these things. Part of me was astonished at my reaction. I'd had no idea I had bottled up this fear and fury for all this time. I had, as the psychiatrists say, disassociated from it. It was only having my own children that made me think differently about what happened to me.

Later, I asked my mother why she had not asked the school about the strange incident. She remembered me telling her about it but she also remembered how I had minimised it and reassured her that I was unhurt. She didn't want to make a drama out of something that I appeared to have dealt with so easily. She also pointed out that it was unusual in those days for parents to make a fuss about their kids to a school – something which had its upside given the readiness of parents these days to march up to their child's school and attack the staff for the tiniest (and sometimes imaginary) dereliction of duty. But it also had its downside and left children much more vulnerable than they should have been. She did say that she half expected to hear something from the school about it and was surprised when no contact was made. I daresay those two teachers who had left us unsupervised had a few nasty days wondering if they were going to be called to account.

Once I had experienced the fear and fury that was attached to being run over – and now it seems quite ridiculous that I ever thought of it as just an amusing dinner party story – I could see some sense in what I had previously thought of as madness. My anxiety neurosis and intrusive violent thoughts had often been at their most intense when I was driving. As I drove past an unsuspecting pedestrian, I would frequently frighten myself by thinking that I could just turn the wheel and . . . The next thought was that there was nothing to stop me. Now, thanks to that sobbing, furious moment in the counsellor's office, I could see that there had indeed been nothing to stop the person who ran over me, except the kerb.

Maybe my neurosis *was* a coincidence, I don't know, but it did feel as if I was beginning to join the dots. Perhaps my anxiety neurosis, far from being a weakness or my enemy, was the healthiest part of me. It had dogged me until I dealt with what I needed to deal with. It had refused to let me go. Whatever the reason, I felt much less anxious after that emotional counselling session. I was still struggling with the drudgery and loneliness of early parenting, but I was not struggling with anxiety in the same way I once had. I was not out of the woods yet, though.

One night, I woke feeling deeply agitated. As I said, I had been feeling much better, but now I felt as if I was once again spinning out of control. In fact, I felt my grip on sanity was much more tenuous than it had ever been. I panicked, wondering if that sense of getting to the bottom of something had been an illusion and, worse, had driven me to the edge of real madness.

Lying in my bed, rigid with panic, I felt as if I was almost hallucinating. Every time I closed my eyes I saw the most terrifying images. One was of a pair of disembodied hands. They were some distance away, floating in the black darkness, illuminated by a strange green light. I was terrified of them. The other was an image from a horror film. I saw a toy monkey looming at me through the dark. It was equally frightening.

I got up and paced about for a bit in a real state of fear. The rest of the house was peacefully sleeping. Why was I collapsing now? I had felt so much better recently. Why now? I searched frantically through my memory of the last few days, looking for something, anything, that could have triggered this mental collapse. They had been ordinary, uneventful days. I could come up with nothing. I struggled against my panic and fear and the nightmarish images that seemed imprinted in my brain. I wanted them to go away . . . why wouldn't they go away? I wanted to shut them out . . . And then I caught myself.

Hang on! Hang on! I thought. If your crazy bits and neuroses are the healthiest part of you, then maybe you shouldn't fight this. Maybe you should stop trying to control and deny it. Maybe you should allow yourself to see those weird images and go with them. Maybe they are trying to tell you something you need to know.

I know this all sounds like psychobabble and maybe it is. I am no psychiatrist or psychologist. I can't tell you what the science of this is or whether I am making any sense at all. All I can tell you is what happened to me. I sat on the couch in our darkened lounge room and allowed myself to really look at the disembodied hands and the looming and nightmarish monkey. There was another vision too, a dead child, behind bars! Oh God! Could it get any worse than this?

Hang on, maybe the child isn't dead, maybe she is sleeping. And the bars are the bars of a cot . . . and the monkey? Maybe it is her toy, hanging half in and half out of the cot. But the hands, what about the hands?

Suddenly I felt I knew what I was seeing. The hands were those of a night nurse in a children's ward in a hospital. She was doing her paperwork at a desk illuminated by one of those green desk lamps. The child was a baby (maybe eighteen months old) in the cot next to me in the ward and the monkey was her toy. I wondered if I had remembered my terror as an eighteen-month-old when I spent that time in hospital in London under observation for gastroenteritis.

In those days, hospitals had rigid visiting times, even for the parents of very small children, and my mother recalled how great was my distress when she left, how I wept in despair. I imagine the sights I saw while alone in that hospital *were* nightmarish to a child who found herself in a very strange place, away from everything and everyone that was familiar. But to the adult I now was, they were unexceptional sights. I could identify them and understand them.

I was suddenly calm. More, I was exhilarated and astonished. It was incredible to suddenly get a window on an experience I'd had as an eighteen-month-old – brought to me by nothing more special or miraculous than my own brain. I felt awed and (sorry to lapse into what some would call the spiritual) almost touched by grace. The return of that memory (if that is what it was) felt like a gift.

Was it a real memory? Is that what I saw when I was an eighteen-month-old in hospital, awake and terrified in the night? I don't know. I suspect some of the images may also have been confused with those I saw as a ten-year-old when I spent a couple of nights in a hospital in Sydney under observation for concussion (I'd fallen into an empty bath head first while larking about). Whatever they were, those intrusive images, visions, hallucinations – I don't know quite what to call them – went from terrifying me as signs of incipient madness to arousing in me a sense of awe and wonder within a few moments. I was also left with a feeling of calm that has never quite left me.

So, did going to hospital as a toddler predispose me to anxiety? Did getting run over as a ten-year-old and having the experience discounted and ignored increase my susceptibility? From my experience of how different I felt once I had reconnected with both those events from my past, I would have to say that they certainly did not help. But I think there was more to my descent into an anxiety neurosis than that.

I think there was a genetic component. Anxiety is a characteristic of many of my relatives and includes different forms of OCD. But I also think that it was my generally very safe and protected existence in a prosperous, loving and intelligent family that made me vulnerable. On some level, I think I knew that I had never been tested or tried and that made me frightened about my ability to withstand and cope with danger and difficulty once it inevitably arrived. I think a lot of young women (and men) struggle with a similar kind of inchoate anxiety. How strong am I? What can I withstand? I've never really been expected to face up to harsh reality, so how will I cope when I have to? The understandable desire of parents to protect children in an already hyper-safe world like middle-class Australia may, therefore, predispose their children to anxiety and neurosis. I suffered from a kind of frantic desperation to catastrophise everything. I was trying to anticipate and imagine the very worst in a pathetic and ultimately hopeless attempt to avoid the collapse and psychic annihilation I really feared. That's why experiencing real danger chased away imaginary danger. I was tested and I survived.

A friend told me a story that illustrated this beautifully. A young woman in a prosperous and comfortable middle-class family had a really serious eating disorder; the kind that can kill, the kind that is every parent's worst nightmare. Her parents despaired and then their daughter's boyfriend, a young man of just twenty, was diagnosed with terminal cancer. The young woman dropped out of uni to nurse her boyfriend until he died, which eventually he tragically did. Along the way her eating disorder completely disappeared, never to return.

I was also what I have discovered is called a 'parentified' child. That is, I identified excessively with my parents. This made it hard for me to separate from them as I grew into adulthood. I admired and loved them (I still do) because they were – and are – admirable people. I did not want to reject them in the way that, for example, Ralph was able to reject his father. They did not deserve to be treated in that way. When Ralph left home (not that he'd ever really had much of one), it was as a result of a huge argument that almost ended in violence. Ralph and

Alan then did not speak to one another for months. (This all happened before Ralph and I knew each other, soon after Ralph had left school.) Ralph was working in a petrol station and one day Alan drove in to have his car filled. That was how they broke the ice and reconnected. But Ralph was very separate from his father and probably always had been. After all, he'd even rejected the name his father had given him.

Alan died on Ralph's forty-fifth birthday and we were away for the weekend at our farm. He was told the news over the phone and, after relating to me what had happened, he fled up to the back of the home paddock. I followed and found him sitting on the steps of the shed. He was crying. I sat down next to him but did not say anything.

After a few moments, he turned towards me. 'I feel sorry for you!'

This was not what I had expected him to say, but I remained silent.

'You like your parents, and if I feel this bad about the death of mine, *you* are going to feel terrible!'

None of us are perfect parents (thank God); we all just do the best we can. My parents were amazing, but I felt protective of them, so maybe, unconsciously, I turned my rebellion inwards against myself rather than outwards against them. To separate myself from them I had to create a barrier they could not help me with. I made myself a bit mad.

twenty-three

I was sitting in my office overlooking Sussex Street in the city. It was mid-morning and I was reading the newspaper. In those days (it was about 1994), *The Sydney Morning Herald* was still a broadsheet, so its pages were spread across my entire desk. My boss, the new CEO of ad agency JWT, was walking past my glass-fronted office. He stopped and came into the room.

'Don't you have anything to do?'

'I have plenty to do,' I said, without raising my eyes from the newspaper.

My boss shifted from foot to foot. I turned another page. He left the room.

It was a small moment but an important one. I did not need to feel guilty or act as if I had been caught doing something wrong when questioned by my boss. This new kind of self-control was very recently acquired.

I had spent the previous five years at home with small children. I didn't like it much. I loved my kids but I did not love the drudgery and loneliness that accompanies parenting. My mothers' group helped enormously. The fact that my sister Ann had left her career in publishing to parent her daughter Alice also helped. But I had felt washed up. My brilliant career (if that is what it was) had gone bung. I did a little freelance work, but over the years it dwindled away to nothing. I was not able to imagine being out of the workforce forever, but was pretty sure a return to copywriting in an ad agency was unlikely. Instead, I retrained as a relationships counsellor.

This was in no small part because I had become – and remain – a convert to the power of good therapy to change lives. I was a living example of it. Unfortunately, once I graduated from the part-time training course, I found I could not fit in actual counselling with the demands of my children and a husband who was away all the time. This meant I never fulfilled the practical hours required to become a fully qualified counsellor. I was disappointed about this at the time, so I looked at going back to university and getting a degree in psychology. My sister Ann had done a master's in education while she was parenting and I thought this might be a way to at least feel like I hadn't completely lost my own identity as a person separ ate from my kids. I enrolled at Macquarie Uni and attended one lecture. It was for a subject called Statistics, a prerequisite for psychology. I did not understand a word of what was said and made a decision never to go back. I was interested in counselling and what makes people tick, but not enough to overcome a lifetime of hating maths. I remained adrift.

I still needed something beyond children and household, however. I joined a book club and a monthly writing group. I also took myself off to a couple of creative writing short courses. One of them, run by Dorothy Porter at the University of Technology, Sydney, helped me to regain a little of my old confidence. She was a demanding but skilled teacher. She expected a high standard from her mixed bag of students. I worked hard for her and she praised some of my work. I needed that praise like I needed oxygen.

But most of the time I felt stymied and useless, and I turned my unused energies in on myself. I was less anxious but probably more depressed. Then, just after Polly had started her first year at school and Charlotte was at preschool, I received a phone call that changed everything.

It has often been my experience in life that just when you think something you've done has had no impact at all, you discover how wrong you have been. I remember the first professional communications workshop I ever ran. It was for health promotion professionals in the Illawarra. It was hard to forget, not just because it was the first I'd done, but also because it was the night of Princess Diana's funeral and the day of unbelievable floods. I watched Diana's funeral on a tiny little telly in the half pre-fab cottage, half motor home that my budget-strapped clients had booked for my accommodation. The rain started that night and continued all the next day. When the workshop ended in the late afternoon, I only just got out of Wollongong before all hell broke loose. As I drove up the steep hill away from the coastal city, I passed huge volumes of water cascading in the opposite direction.

Despite the filthy weather, I left that workshop very pleased with how it had gone. I had hopes of being asked back, but I never heard from Illawarra Health again. My confidence in my first attempt at facilitating a workshop was dented. I must have been wrong to think it went well.

Then, sixteen years after that first workshop, a woman rang and identified herself as a participant. She had risen through the ranks and now headed the program. She had a little money left over in her budget, so she'd had a think about the most useful thing she'd done in her career and – you guessed it – it was my little comms workshop. She booked me again to deliver it to her staff, after more than a decade and a half. Never say never.

The same thing now happened, although without the extreme of sixteen years between event and follow-up. Before Charlotte was born (indeed, I think I was pregnant with her at the time), I had done a few weeks freelance at Saatchi & Saatchi, working on a pitch for feminine hygiene products with an art director called Jenny Eborall. It was a hard brief to crack, particularly as we were tasked with selling sanitary napkins rather than tampons. The 'consumer insight' (wanky language which just means how the people who use it feel about the product) in the brief said that it was older and more conservative women who chose pads over tampons and that the key thing about these women was that they objected to any public mention of menstruation at all. Hmmm, that created a pretty high degree of advertising difficulty.

Jenny and I struggled with this for some time, but eventually we found an answer. As usual, the breakthrough came when we finally got down to the nub of what users were looking for. In a word, with sanitary pads, it is protection. What we developed was scripts for a series of TV commercials that gave women advice on how to protect themselves in all sorts of situations. We wrote one featuring Wendy Harmer giving women tips on how to protect themselves from sexist remarks, another with a self-defence expert advising women on how to protect themselves if attacked, and a skin cancer specialist giving advice on how to protect your skin from the sun. The line at the end of the campaign was: 'This message is brought to you by Stayfree. Because we have always believed women should be well-protected.' Way to promote sanitary pads without mentioning menstruation! We high-fived one another around the office.

We'd done a terrific pitch, if I do say so myself, and Saatchi used it to win the business. They never produced any of the work, however (this is quite normal – sigh), and apart from receiving a much-needed cheque, I had not heard from Saatchi or Jenny Eborall again. Until early 1994, that is, when I received a call from a new art director at ad agency J. Walter Thompson. Her name was Jane Evans and she needed a freelance writer to come and work with her while she looked for a full-time creative partner. Jenny Eborall now worked at JWT and, bless her, she had recommended me. I told them I could work Charlotte's preschool hours – in other words, three five-hour days a week.

They agreed. It was only temporary and such limited hours meant that I would be very cheap.

Jane and I hit it off and I loved being back in the workforce. Colleagues are generally polite to you (toddlers are sweet but neither polite nor predictable) and work has a pay cheque attached. But that wasn't the only attraction. I felt wanted again – as if I had a contribution to make that might be of value. My appetite for the work was enormous and we churned through briefs with enthusiasm. When you get the right creative partner in advertising, it can be a very exciting and stimulating job. I knew it was only going to continue until Jane found a full-time writer but I didn't care; I was going to make the most of getting out of the house and back into my profession while it lasted. The quality of the work we were doing together was high (enthusiasm and excitement will do that for you) and my confidence soared.

Then, after three months, Jane and the management at JWT told me that they'd looked at lots of other copywriters but they didn't like anyone as much as they liked me. Would I consider making the part-time arrangement a permanent one?

'You're getting through more work in fifteen hours than the other writers are in forty.'

The other writers were all male, of course; if you need something done fast and enthusiastically, ask a working mother – particularly one who has just escaped from non-stop drudgery at home.

Would I accept a permanent part-time job back in the industry I thought had done with me forever? You bet I would.

I leapt at the chance. In fact, I think I pioneered permanent part-time work in advertising creative departments, at least in Sydney. I have no proof of this, but I have never come across anyone else who was doing it then. It is, I hope, much more common now.

My daughters were six and three when I went back to work. Polly was at school and Charlotte was at preschool. It would be a juggle, particularly as Ralph was still travelling all the time with his job, but I didn't care. Ralph was as pleased as I was about the offer – not that I would have asked his permission or taken any notice if he had reservations. Frankly, I would never have married a man who felt he had a right to exercise that kind of control over his wife. I was an adult. I got to decide. If he'd had a problem, I would have suggested he cut back his own hours and pick up the slack. Thanks to all the work I had done on myself, I knew what my rights and responsibilities were and I did not feel at all guilty about asserting them. Ralph and I were co-parents – we had equal responsibility for our children. I was also lucky that I came from a feminist family. There was simply no judgment and no discussion about my decision to return to work. It was my choice and they'd support whatever decision I made.

My mother had not been so fortunate. When she decided to return to studying and do her HSC and then go to university, thanks to Whitlam making higher education free, her father – but not her husband – was very disapproving. I was sixteen when she went to tech, my youngest sister Ruth was nine, but the more her father tut-tutted, the more determined my mother became.

Oh, and just an aside here, but it drives me nuts when I hear the current federal education minister, Christopher Pyne, say that the people who benefited from free university education in the 1970s were almost all from the ranks of the better off. What he doesn't say is that they were also mostly women who had been denied the chance of a university education by their fathers, who had preferred to pay the fees for their sons rather than their daughters. Whitlam's higher education reforms were hugely important for women from the generations before mine and that has had equally important positive results for them, their daughters and our whole society. We should not forget that. Rant over.

As a beneficiary of that feminism, in 1994, I went back to work (almost) without a backward glance. It was only for fifteen hours a week, after all.

Art director Jane Evans and I then embarked on a very productive period. Our creative director, a nice man called Pete Townsend, left, and we had no-one in the position for nine months. The agency was scouring the world for a replacement. Good creative directors (who are as rare as hen's teeth) can help creative people do their best work. Bad ones (common as muck) are just another hurdle you have to climb over. Nine months without a creative director saw JWT Sydney produce some of the best creative work in Australia at that time. Brian Jones created the long-running 'Iron Man Food' campaign for Kellogg's Nutri-Grain during that period, for example.

With no CD, the creative teams worked directly with their allocated clients. Jane and I got the Unilever account and I found myself working with the fabrics group at Lever & Kitchen. Funny how sometimes the world goes full circle. No-one remained of the people I had worked with a decade previously, but I understood the client and their world better than any other copywriter in town. It was the beginning of a beautiful friendship.

Things had come a long way since the late 70s at Unilever. For a start, the marketing manager of the fabrics group was a woman. This was still relatively unusual, but she was American. I have noticed that the positive assumptions Australians make about American executives can wipe out the negative assumptions we make about female ones. I wonder if that works in reverse in the US? I liked her very much, particularly when she gave us the following brief for L&K's premium laundry detergent brand, Drive. Its major claim was that it got difficult stains out in the wash.

'For God's sake,' she said, 'don't give me happy little housewives thrilled to get the stain out of hubby's shirt.'

And she had a point. Some time later I put together a reel where I cut together all the laundry detergent commercials from all over the world from that year. No matter the part of the world they were made – from Africa, Asia, Europe, the Caribbean or the Americas – they all followed an unwavering formula. The stain got on the clothes thanks to a kid or a husband. Mum pulled a wry 'oh no' face. We saw her using the advertised product on the stained clothing, followed by some sort of animated sequence illustrating how the 'exclusive scientific ingredient' lifted the dirt from the clothes. Then we saw the clothing completely stain-free, Mum exclaiming in delight (this looked hilarious in the cut-together reel, I wish I still had it), then kid and/or Dad staining the clothing all over again. It was a sexist view of Mum as servant, all right, but it was also boring, predictable and lazy advertising. To be honest, if you wanted to subvert a category and so make a name for yourself, laundry detergents were the way to go.

We grabbed the opportunity with both hands and wrote a campaign of three forty-five-second TV commercials. One was about a young guy who meets a gorgeous girl in a bar. She writes her phone number on his white T-shirt in lipstick. Next morning, he wakes to find his flatmate (another bloke) has washed the lipstick out in the wash with Drive. The stain came out in the wash – get it?

The second ad was about a young couple on the first night of living together. They are tiptoeing around each other due to the newness of it all. He is a mechanic working with big motorbikes. He puts a load of washing on using Drive. A little later, she notices he hasn't put his overalls in with the rest of the wash. Thinking she is doing him a favour, she interrupts the washing cycle and pops them in. The ad ends with him, back at the bike workshop, surreptitiously reapplying grease and oil to his now far-too-clean work clothes.

The last commercial featured a divorced dad bringing the kids back after an access visit. He makes slightly awkward conversation with his ex-wife as she does the washing. He compliments her – rather dorkily – on how clean she gets her washing. He pulls out an item to demonstrate his point, only to notice it is a man's shirt. Clearly his ex-wife has moved on . . .

Our forthright client loved the scripts, but there were the usual hurdles to overcome. It took a while before we had approved scripts (they had to go through the focus group research nonsense) and an approved budget. A number of directors pitched their ideas on how to shoot them. We chose a director from New Zealand and then Jane and I were off to Wellington to make all three. I was also travelling occasionally now – nowhere near as much as Ralph, but we did start to confront some of the very real problems that face a dual-career family. Ralph was rarely able to step into the childcare breach thanks to the view that men must always put their work first and their families second. I mostly put my family first (I was working fifteen hours a week, remember), but when I had to travel I felt entitled to put myself first occasionally. My parents minded the girls when they could.

My mother did most of the childminding, but my father adored his grandchildren. They have six now, all girls. One evening, my mother was taking Polly to something after school and Dad stayed home with three-year-old Charlotte. Charlotte was rocking back and forth a little too vigorously on a small, child-sized wicker rocking chair in front of the telly. She toppled over backwards and hit her head against the metal runner of the sliding door behind her and began to wail. My father dashed over and picked her up.

'Oh dear, never mind, at least you aren't bleeding – oh! OH!'

It was then he noticed the blood running through her blonde hair and dripping through his fingers as he held her. She had cut her head open. My father is not very good with blood (that's putting it mildly) but he did exactly the right thing, rushing her to a nearby medical centre, where she had a few stitches.

I took her back a few days later as instructed to have those stitches removed. I saw the same doctor.

'Oh, good, yes, this has all healed perfectly. No harm done.' He smiled at Charlotte and gave her a sweet for being so brave. But then he turned to me with a much more concerned expression.

'But, tell me, *how* is her grandfather? He was very distressed when he brought her in.'

I could imagine.

My parents were great but I did have to hire live-in child-minders on a number of occasions. I always went through reputable agencies and tried to use the same people when I could. When my working hours increased, I eventually hired a nanny for after-school care. Jan stayed with us for six years and the girls adored her. I'll say it again – when I needed help, I asked for it and it was always available. I have never seen any virtue in pretending you can – or should – do it all on your own. Of course, I was also very fortunate in that I could afford good help, although I do remember in the early days sometimes going to the ATM to withdraw the nanny's salary and realising I only had a couple of dollars left to last the week. But we managed, we didn't go hungry and, while I might have been working just to pay the childminding fees at first, I was happier, healthier, more energetic and – as a result – a much better parent.

There was a downside, of course – there always is, to everything. And it was probably Charlotte who bore the brunt of it. Once the agency sent us a minder who seemed lovely in the interview but who – according to Polly – made Charlotte cry and who was late to pick up Polly after school. Nothing terrible happened, but I reported the woman to the agency and we never used her again. Charlotte also had too many carers at one point when my childcare arrangement suddenly fell over. I solved the problem thanks to a neighbour. Charlotte's best friend was Laura, who lived (still lives) across the road. Her mother also worked. Her kids were all minded after school and preschool by a lovely local woman who now had a vacancy. Charlotte was thrilled to be spending her afternoons at 'Diney's' (the woman's name was Diane) with Laura. All went well until an incident that I didn't hear about until many years after the event.

Diney's kids were almost grown and her two daughters were delightful and often pitched in with the childminding. Her son was in his teens and, as I found out later, resented the little children his mother minded in the afternoons. One day, angry with Charlotte over some misdemeanour, he locked her in his bedroom and hid the key. His mother was frantic and Charlotte was distressed but sharp-eyed Laura, all of four, had seen where he'd hidden the key and Charlotte was only imprisoned for a short time. I was not told about this and I should have been. Years later, I was driving Laura and Charlotte somewhere and they were chatting and their days at Diney's came up. Most of their memories were very good ones, until they turned their attention to Diney's son and how much they had both disliked him. That's when the story emerged. I was horrified.

Was any permanent damage done as a result? I don't know. But then, as I knew only too well, damage is always done, no matter how you parent. My mother was a stay-at-home mum until I was sixteen and I developed a serious anxiety neurosis in my twenties (not that I blame my parents for that). I went to work when Charlotte was three. She is twenty-four now and shows no signs of an anxiety neurosis (to be honest, she's so laidback I sometimes wish she had a little more anxiety). Polly is much more driven and anxious, but not in the bizarre way I was.

Danger is reality and safety is an illusion. To develop resilience, kids need to experience some difficulty – even, perhaps, a little bit of danger. Ten minutes alone locked in a bedroom? I'm not thrilled that it happened, but nor am I going to beat myself up about it. And my sense of justice can't help asking has beating himself up about such a thing even crossed Ralph's mind? If this was his memoir, would anyone expect him to justify why he left his kids to concentrate on work? It remains mothers who get judged for things like this and that's neither fair nor reasonable.

Guilt was a constant, even though I was by this time pretty good at not allowing the judgment of others to affect me as much as it once had. As my work ramped up, childcare generally worked pretty well, but whenever the kids got sick, that's when the wheels fell off. I remember poor Charlotte waking up with a tummy bug on the worst possible day. I was in post-production for a commercial and hundreds of thousands of dollars relied on me turning up. My mother and Jan were unavailable and Ralph was away. There was nothing for it; Charlotte would have to come with me. I dragged her from sound studio to edit suite to post-production facility. I carried a bowl and every time we got in the car, she would throw up into it. At each venue, I dashed to the loo, gave her a glass of water and washed out the bowl. She was remarkably uncomplaining, poor little thing. Finally, we arrived at the edit suite and there was no-one at reception. I had been there many times before, so I dashed to the ladies and whooshed the vomit into the sink and turned on the tap. No water! I tried another tap. Still no water! I rushed out to reception. The desk was now occupied.

'There's no water in your ladies!'

'No, we're having some plumbing done and they've turned the water off for a couple of hours.'

I didn't like to tell her about the congealing vomit.

***

My life had changed utterly. Instead of me being the sad stay-at-home while my husband gadded about the world, I was travelling too. Okay, my trips weren't quite as glamorous as his. I still remember him calling me from Italy and waxing lyrical about having spent the day at the fifteenth century Antinori winery in Tuscany. At the end of his (justifiably) fulsome description of his day, he remembered to ask me about mine.

'What did you do today?'

'Canteen duty. And you will owe me for life.'

All of this meant that I was rather looking forward to going to Wellington to shoot the Drive commercials. I had already been to New Zealand once that year, to Auckland. Sitting at my desk in Sussex Street one morning, I received a phone call asking me if I would judge the New Zealand national advertising awards (AXIS). I was astonished.

'Are you sure you have the right Jane Caro?'

I'd only been back in the business a few months, I didn't have any work to show for it as yet, and anything I did have was over five years old. I seriously wondered if it was a case of mistaken identity. The guy on the end of the phone had the grace to chuckle.

'I have the right Jane Caro. We want you.'

It was an all-expenses-paid week in Auckland, and all I had to do was swan about passing judgment on other people's work. It would also look good on my CV. I didn't hesitate. Ralph being away yet again, I left the girls with my mother, got a neighbour to feed the cat and packed my bag.

I felt even more like an impostor when I got to the airport. Air New Zealand was a sponsor of the AXIS awards (those were the days when advertising still mattered) and the Australian judges were all upgraded to first class. As I boarded the plane, a steward took my coat to hang it among the leather and furs of the other passengers. My coat was, shall we say, very different. I'd bought it in Leura on a weekend away with my mothers' group. It was brightly coloured, made from knitted cotton with a fake sheepskin collar and was designed for a twelve- to fourteen-year-old. It fitted me perfectly. I am also very short of leg (I often say I have backseat legs), and when I took my seat it was so deep I could not bend my legs; they stuck straight out in front of me.

It was only once the plane had taken off that I could change the angle of the seat and engage the footrest. The fact that the first-class seats were literally too big for me did not help my feelings of being a fraud. I was in 1A and in 1B was a fellow AXIS judge. Paul Jones had written the iconic 'It's Time' campaign that helped Gough Whitlam win government in 1972. It is still considered one of the best political advertising campaigns ever written. I was out of my depth in every way possible. But I was having fun, lots of fun. Paul Jones was very good company and judging other people's work is much easier than actually creating any yourself, so I made the most of being an international advertising judge. You can perhaps see why my confidence began to return.

A few months later, while we were in Wellington shooting the Drive commercials with director Roger Tompkins, Jane Evans and I were able to have a little time for ourselves. Jane remembers me suddenly looking at her, while we were trying on interesting (but expensive) clothes in Zambesi, and announcing, 'Jane Caro is back.'

And it did feel like that. The person who had become lost beneath mounds of laundry, grocery shopping and scattered toys had re-emerged. I felt like me again. I lost weight. I regained my energy and purpose. My low-grade depression dropped away. I was earning my own money – not a lot, because I was working part-time, but I once again felt entitled to buy things for myself.

I bought an expensive shirt at Zambesi and wore it till it fell apart. It wasn't that Ralph had ever questioned my spending, it was just that I didn't feel free to spend money on myself when I wasn't actually contributing financially.

When I travelled – which I didn't do all that often but enough to make life interesting – I missed my daughters very much. While they were small, I always left them both a letter so that if anything happened – like a plane crash – they'd have a memento of how much they both meant to me. But I also loved being just myself for a few days, rather than Ralph's wife or Polly and Charlotte's mum. And coming home was wonderful. Is there anything more fabulous than arriving at your front door and having two little girls – one dark, one fair – scream your name (well, 'Mum', anyway) and run helter-skelter down the hall and jump into your arms? Despite the cobbled-together childcare and the (occasional) guilt, it was worth going away just for that.

There was judgment, of course. Once the girls were both at school it was impossible not to notice how many of the mothers divided themselves into two groups. Some of the stay-at-home mothers emanated a combination of judgment with a sense of competitiveness. Some of them seemed very defensive. Not all of them, of course; there were many women who couldn't care less what other mothers were doing. We didn't see the full-time working mothers, not that there were many of them in those days, especially when their children were very young. It was us part-time mothers who were always rushing from pillar to post trying not to let anyone down. Worse, we were also trying not to let anyone see how hard it all was, because that would just lead to more judgment.

I remember a single, childless woman I worked with saying to me over lunch one day, 'Well, you've really got it worked out, haven't you? You've got interesting work, kids and a husband – a balanced life.'

'You know what a balanced life really means, don't you?'

'No, except it's what everyone wants.'

'It means you don't get *all* of anything.'

But to return to 1994, when I was at the wobbly edge of all that balancing, the Drive commercials we made in Wellington hit the airwaves and suddenly, at least in the advertising world, Jane Evans and I were famous. We were called the two Janes – she was big Jane and, inevitably, I was little Jane. The commercials, particularly 'Lipstick', won awards all over the world. They were written up in editorials – and that's exposure you can't buy (you couldn't then, anyway). Jane Cadzow wrote a small piece in the *Good Weekend* about what she called the 'intriguing' 'Ex-wife' commercial. A woman took the trouble to call Lever & Kitchen and thank them for making her – a divorced woman – feel like a normal part of the community by running an ad that treated a divorced couple as just another kind of family. Who knew laundry detergent ads could have such an effect on people? The people they had the most effect on, of course, were Jane and me.

It was exciting to turn up at the office and find our Drive campaign had won prestigious international awards overnight. It was even more exciting to win them in person.

Like the Oscars, finalists in advertising awards are always announced before the ceremony. In 1994, the Drive ads were finalists in all sorts of awards. We had the greatest number of finalists in the Australian TV awards, called FACTS (Federation of Australian Commercial Television Stations) at that time (it's now FreeTV). On arriving at the venue, Jane and I couldn't help getting excited when we were shown to a table right down the front.

The first category was announced (by Kerri-Anne Kennerley, if memory serves me correctly) and Drive 'Lipstick' won. Jane and I rushed to the stage to accept our trophy. As we turned to leave, Kerri-Anne told us not to go far. We proceeded to win the next few categories (including best use of humour). After accepting each trophy, we'd walk into the wings and then straight back out again to win another. We – as they say in the laundry detergent business – cleaned up. It was incredibly exciting.

It was also thanks to the Drive campaign that I got my first public speaking opportunity. It was an event about women in advertising; a topic that has ebbed and flowed in the industry for decades. As far as I can see, however, despite all sorts of initiatives and good intentions, nothing much ever changes. There have never been many of us – in creative departments especially – and the few there are very rarely get ahead.

I think the reason so few women get promoted in advertising – particularly as creative directors – is the same reason they find it so hard to get promoted everywhere. It is my observation that all of us absorb some elements of misogyny as we grow up. It is hardly surprising, as we are brought up in a society that preferences men in almost every area you care to name, particularly when it comes to wealth, power and prestige. The Sex Discrimination Commissioner, Liz Broderick, describes misogyny as being like asbestos in the walls; we absorb it without realising it. That is why sexism is not just something men do to women; it is also something women do to one another and, most damagingly of all, to themselves. The result is that we unconsciously assume that men – particularly white, middle-class men – have merit until they prove otherwise. I have seen this over and over when very ordinary men get promoted far beyond their level of competence, not just once or twice but continuously. Most of the bosses I have had who failed at their job were kicked upstairs. That rarely happens to incompetent women. This is because that same unconscious misogyny leads us to assume that women *don't* have merit until they prove otherwise. Worse, just as men assumed to have merit will be given the benefit of the doubt long past deserving it, so women will have to prove their merit over and over and over again. Exceptional women can and do get promoted, but any mistake or lacklustre performance will be taken as evidence that not only are they hopeless but, just as we thought, so are all other women.

Before my first-ever speaking engagement, I was nervous. A friend suggested I take a prop to give me something to do with my hands. The event was scheduled for one of my non-(paid) working days, and as I had been asked to speak about the Drive campaign, I decided to take a basket of clean washing that

I would fold and sort as I talked. The thesis of my talk was that while doing the washing is boring, the people who do it are not and therefore ads about it shouldn't be either. Another friend suggested I visit the venue (the theatre in the Maritime Museum) prior to the gig so I would feel familiar with the physical environment. That was a good suggestion too. I gave the speech and not only did it appear to go down well, but I enjoyed myself. I had no inkling, however, that one day I would earn the majority of my income from public speaking. That, as yet, lay a long way into the future.

* * *

When I look back over my working life, particularly when I was not (as I now am) self-employed, there are a few periods that really stand out as special. The first year at FMH when I was teamed up with Rocky is one, and those first couple of years working with Jane Evans at JWT is another. But, good or bad, nothing ever lasts.

Despite winning more awards – we wrote a long copy magazine campaign for Nature's Way that also did well – our success started to weigh against us. Far from rating Jane and me for doing so well, it soon became clear that some in senior management felt threatened.

It is the classic double-bind of the working woman. I'd been there before at the Palace. If you are not considered brilliant, you are discounted and undervalued and often the first to be let go. If you *are* considered brilliant, you are seen as scary and difficult. I was undervalued at the Palace because I wasn't winning enough awards. Now I was seen as threatening because I was winning too many.

This double-bind has since been backed up by research. The famous Howard and Heidi experiment (referred to by Sheryl Sandberg in her 2013 book *Lean In*) shows that the higher men are rated on skills, the higher they are rated on likeability. The higher women are rated on skills, the lower they are rated on likeability. Neat, isn't it? And Jane and I began to suffer from exactly that.

The first indication that we were no longer wanted occurred when JWT Sydney moved from one office building in Sussex Street to another and, as described in the prologue, I arrived at the new premises to find I had not been allocated a permanent office or even a desk. I staged a polite but pointed protest and Jane and I were grudgingly allocated a large and airy office they had been keeping vacant for the prestigious international team (or so they said) they were intending to hire. We were told we could only stay there until the new team were hired. We occupied that office for a couple of years and no such team ever materialised.

It was just as well they miraculously found available space, because the Drive campaign promptly won the Unilever Grand Prix for the best advertising campaign produced for one of their brands anywhere in the world. It would have been very embarrassing if I had still been working in reception. Our bosses may not have liked us, but the client certainly did.

But bosses have power and if they want to make your life difficult, they can. Suddenly, all creative teams were being asked to pitch for every brief. Jane and I complied, but time and time again, we lost to work that both of us felt was inferior. After the eighth consecutive rejection, it started to feel personal. It got worse when a Drive script was written about a Chinese laundry. I warned the agency that it was racist. They ignored me and rejected our (much better, in my opinion) script. The Chinese laundry TV commercial was made and, the minute it went to air, the client was inundated with complaints that it was – you guessed it – racist.

I did get a moment of satisfaction when I was asked by the chastened client to revise the TVC so that it was no longer racist. This I did, but there was no turning it into a good ad. I began to look around for another job.

twenty-four

It was the school holidays and I'd taken a week off to spend some time with the girls. It was lovely to be out of the pressure-cooker that JWT had become. Jane was not reacting well to the stress and that was making everything worse. With two small kids and a husband who was almost always on a plane, I knew I needed to leave.

On the first day of that holiday, my old boss from the Campaign Palace, Bob Isherwood, called me out of the blue. He was now the CD of Saatchi & Saatchi worldwide (talk about falling on your feet) but based in Sydney. He had a problem with a series of ads that had been made for a major client and had failed to cut through. They were aimed at women with children and Bob couldn't think of any other woman with children who also wrote ads (nor could I), so he rang in a panic and asked me if I could come in and try to rescue the (very expensive) campaign. In my first ten years in advertising, being a woman had been nothing but a disadvantage. In my second, it was proving to be nothing but an advantage. People – even male people – could see some logic in getting your target audience (most ads are aimed at mums) to write your ads.

So, instead of spending the week with my daughters (yes, I know, I am a very bad mother), I spent it at Saatchi making the ads more relevant. Rejigging those ads was another example of how my feminism helped me to think differently. The TV commercials were for Red Rooster and were lovely evocative films of mothers and kids with the Stones song of the same name for a soundtrack. They were too subtle, however, and had gone to air without anyone really noticing them. All I did was include a rolling super (words superimposed over the picture that slowly roll up the screen – rather like credits at the end of a movie) that listed some of the stats from the annual household work survey on the number of hours women spent doing the laundry, vacuuming, cleaning, cooking and childcare. The idea was to give women permission to get Red Rooster for dinner occasionally – because they had earned it. Bob and the client service team loved the solution.

At that time, women did the lion's share of housework, whether they were also in the paid workforce or not. Sad to say, twenty years after writing that campaign, I could find little evidence that this division of labour has changed very much. There may be fewer household tasks done overall, but women continue to do 70–80 per cent of them, particularly after they have kids. I remember joking to a friend that when Ralph and I first lived together we divided the household chores fifty-fifty.

After Polly was born it became thirty-seventy, and after Charlotte ten-ninety.

'I'm not having any more children,' I said.

To be fair to Ralph, now the kids are grown and have moved out and we both work from home, he does the vast majority of the household chores. I don't feel guilty about that. I did most of them for two decades.

This was a rare moment when the depressing reality of the domestic workload imbalance and my feminist awareness of it worked in one woman's favour (mine) at least. I remember taking the revised Red Rooster TV commercials into the final presentation and suddenly realising, as I walked through the door, that if I made a good stab at the meeting, Saatchi would offer me a job. And that is what happened. The minute the presentation ended, Brian, the CEO, asked me to step into his office for a moment. I came out with a four-day-a-week job at one of the hottest creative agencies in town (and the world) plus a higher salary.

Actually, it's worth digressing for a moment regarding that salary because, even though it was more money, I still managed to do myself down. Like a lot of women, I find it very hard to put a value on myself – a monetary value in particular. When Brian discussed the job with me, he asked what kind of salary I was looking for. I froze. In rapid-fire succession my brain debated the following questions: What does he want to pay me? How much is too much? How much is too little? In the end I told him (I know, I'm an idiot) what I was earning and said I'd like to be paid between $5000 and $10,000 more. He immediately offered the upper end. Bugger. As we all know, if they agree to your price too quickly, you've pitched too low.

There was another reason why they were keen to hire me. Bob and the senior management team were doing some badly needed repairs to the agency culture. Only a few months before, Saatchi Sydney – and the industry in general – had been rocked when a senior member of staff was accused of sexual assault. The executive was arrested on the premises, although all the charges were later dropped. The agency went into crisis mode and the first thing they decided to tackle was any suggestion of a sexist or sexualised culture. They hired well-known feminist businesswoman Sandra Yates as non-executive chair and I was another well-known feminist (in advertising circles, at least). They wanted me because I was good at my job, certainly, but they also wanted me to help signal a change of culture. And I must say I never saw any sign that Saatchi was either sexist or sexualised while I was there.

Whatever their reasons, I was delighted to escape JWT and return to working for Bob Isherwood. I was sad to leave Jane – I had loved working with her and we'd done great work together – but, as Rocky had done when he'd left me at FMH, I had to grasp the brass ring I had been offered. They already had an art director they wanted me to work with, so I couldn't bring Jane with me.

The five years I worked at Saatchi remain the best time I ever had working for other people. Well, the first four were, anyway. But five years is the longest I ever worked anywhere and even when it all went pear-shaped, I still felt respected and valued in my workplace. That has been such a rare experience for me throughout my working life, yet it is so important if you want to do your best work.

It isn't hard to show respect for your employees. At Saatchi my ideas were listened to carefully. I was taken seriously and I was trusted to do and say the right thing. By and large, I lived up to that trust. My mistakes were forgiven, my successes praised and publicly acknowledged. I didn't always get my ideas approved and they weren't always the best in the department, but my colleagues and I were generous with one another. If we liked someone else's idea we said so. I have found this to be universally true of people who are good at their job; they are not threatened by other talented people. If you find yourself working in an atmosphere brittle with fear, where everyone treads on eggshells and intimidation and humiliation are rampant, my guess is you are working for people who are not very good at their jobs. There is only one solution to this: get out.

It shouldn't be rocket science that respecting your workers helps them to be more productive but it happens so rarely. Or does it only happen rarely for women? I am not sure. I think my husband mostly felt he was respected in his workplace, although he did have one psychotic boss early in his career who undermined him relentlessly until Ralph left. For me the opposite was true. That sense that I was valued was rare and very special. I responded by working my guts out for the agency and my clients. I had a new art director, Pic Andrews, and she was young and smart and we got along famously. We wrote some terrific ads, some good ones and some bad ones.

We never set out to write a shit ad but it happens. The more fingers that are allowed to get into the creative pie, the more it happens.

I had a favourite client – the NRMA – for whom I did some of my best work, but even they had layers and layers of approvals that had to be worked through. Pic and I would write the ad in response to the brief, it'd go to the junior clients and it would come back with 'feedback' (I HATE feedback), you'd respond, it'd go to the next layer, more feedback, more changes, another layer, more feedback, until eventually the ad looked nothing like the one you'd originally created. To fix this, I came up with a solution. Ads went to the clients with an overlay. They wrote their comments on the overlay but no feedback was responded to until every layer of approval had had their say. At the very least, people got to respond to the original ad rather than the dog's breakfast it had become.

I did something similar when I was at JWT. Our most difficult client was Kellogg's. For some of their brands we wrote upwards of seventy scripts, all of which were rejected. The requirement was that we had to write three different scripts, all approved by unbelievably anal clients (what is it about people who market breakfast cereals? I always thought they should eat more of their own products to help them . . . um . . . loosen up) and put them into research via a storyboard. The trouble was, whatever won in research had to be shot exactly as it had been storyboarded, no deviation was allowed, which was why most of the Kellogg's ads of the period made no sense at all. A research storyboard is not the same as a shooting storyboard.

I tried to fix that by getting the potential directors of the three approved scripts to work with the storyboard artist to create a shooting board to go into research. That way, whatever got through research would at least make a modicum of sense as a TV commercial.

Honestly, I should have been a creative director. I would have been a good one.

I wouldn't do it now, even if you paid me the sort of ridiculous salary blokes in that position get paid. My experiences of the foolishness that happens in private enterprise – particularly from so-called managers, particularly in large multinationals – may be one of the reasons why I am not as much of a worshipper of the efficiency of the (ahem) free market as many of my contemporaries. Most of the biggest evangelists for market forces as a solution for every problem have rarely spent much time actually working with them. I was at the coalface of market forces for thirty-five years. I have often referred to myself as the high priestess of choice. Most of the time I was not very impressed with the brains, efficiency or even basic common sense of those operating the levers of the free market. Sometimes, at my most cynical and frustrated, I would mutter darkly about scum rising to the top.

Back in the late 1990s, however, while I was at Saatchi, I still had ambitions in advertising. When Pic left to have a baby, I started working with a pair of young art directors from the UK. Jason Mendez (the cousin of *American Beauty* director Sam Mendez) wanted to move into copywriting, so I was assigned to mentor Jason until he and his partner, Jill Bull, could operate as a team on their own. It was a great arrangement and vindicated my belief that putting a senior creative with juniors was much better than forcing two juniors to work together and compete. Our collaboration led to probably the best moment of my advertising career.

It was for my favourite client, the NRMA, and the job was briefed in during the period the organisation was demutualising. This basically meant it was being divided into two organisations. The roadside service arm and motoring lobby group remained the NRMA (National Road and Motorists' Association), but the highly profitable and lucrative insurance side of the business became the IAG. Members of the association (at that time almost every driver in New South Wales) were offered shares in the insurance company, but there remained considerable anxiety about the demutualisation because the members had to vote in favour before it could happen. The push was on to persuade them to vote yes.

Our brief was to reassure the members that the NRMA would remain true to its core values rather than morph into just another corporate insurance company. At that time, the NRMA, thanks to its roadside service, was the only insurance company with a positive image. Its slogan – N.R.M.A for H.E.L.P – was believed by the public because most of them had actually been helped by the NRMA when their car had broken down. The slogan was written by my then creative director, Mike Newman – who was, coincidentally, the partner of Jenny Eborall, the art director who'd rescued me from the depths of motherhood. Mike was the best CD I ever worked for. He was a terrific wordsmith himself, particularly in print. As a creative director he hired well (I would say that, wouldn't I?) and then got out of the way and let people do their job. When I worked at Saatchi Sydney, it was one of the only creative departments in Australia that was not wall-to-wall white men of a certain age (between twenty-eight and forty-eight), many of whom were Poms. During my time, Saatchi had four female creatives, a Chinese art director, a gay writer and only two Englishmen. Unlike almost every other boss I have ever had (all of whom were blokes), Mike did not hire clones of himself.

To return to the NRMA and its demutualisation, I'm not going to make a case that the company remained true to its core values. I suspect no-one even remembers today that the IAG was once part of NRMA and it has become the very thing it swore blind it never would. However, a copywriter's job is not to reason why. We are like barristers, hired to put our client's case in the best possible light, and that is what Jason, Jill and I did. Also, just like barristers, we don't have a crystal ball. I admit I feared that NRMA insurance would leave its soul behind, but in the face of constant protestations that this would not happen I shrugged my shoulders and got on with my job.

Jason, Jill and I wrote a commercial we called 'Job Seeker' about a young guy nervously heading off for a job interview. We know he's been looking for a while because his mum waves him off saying, 'I've got a good feeling about this one, darling.' It's pouring with rain and a woman with two kids in the car breaks down in the middle of an intersection. Our hero is running late, but he can't leave her stranded, so he gets out, pushes her to the side of the road, fiddles about under the car's bonnet and gets her going again. Then, soaked and oily, he arrives late for his interview. The final shot is of an NRMA van driving up to his house. He jumps out in his uniform, looking delighted as he hugs his mum. We hear a voiceover: 'NRMA. Because we always have been and always will be dedicated to helping people on the road.' It remains the best-loved commercial the NRMA has ever done, both internally and externally. If you want to see it, it is number 48 in the 100 best automotive commercials of all time, and you can find it easily with Google.

The script sailed through the client and through research. Director Ray Lawrence was assigned the job and we were asked to create a sixty-second TV commercial with a forty-five-second version. The number of sixty-second ads you get to make in your career you could count on one hand (they're like double-page spreads; I've never done one of those) and even forty-fives are pretty rare. The thirty-second length works best for the TV station's scheduling purposes, so they make it the most economical length to buy, but it's a shithouse length creatively. It's too long for a gag and too short for a story.

Anyway, we cast a very young Leon Ford as the job seeker and everything was easy after that. The shoot went well, even to the extent that it rained on cue. Well, it was great for the commercial, but the days spent in cold, wet tents watching a split (the screen that shows the creative team what the camera is seeing) gave me a nasty dose of bronchitis which turned into pleurisy. No matter, I wasn't going to miss out on seeing this script come to fruition. I coughed away happily, dosed up on cold-and-flu medicine.

One of our locations was then New South Wales premier Bob Carr's office. We filmed there on a Saturday. Carr was allowing his office to be used as a location in an effort to encourage the local film industry, and it had just the right level of slightly intimidating grandeur and importance that we required. Shooting indoors was warm and dry but it had one downside – space was limited, and there was a lot of cast and crew. Ray asked everyone who wasn't necessary to the shot to make themselves scarce. Keen to oblige, Jason took himself off down a corridor. He noticed a door to a conference room was open and went in to admire the spectacular view of Sydney. He and Jill had only been in town for a few months. Unfortunately, the conference room he had chosen was the state cabinet room. There was meant to be a guard on the door, but she'd been tempted away to peek at the filming and that's why Jason had been able to just wander in. When it was discovered that Jason was a citizen of Jamaica, not Australia, panic ensued. Apparently, the state cabinet room is off limits to everyone but those with special security clearance. Saatchi and the film production company had to work quite hard to convince the powers that be that Jason was not a spy, just a copywriter trying to do the right thing and get out of the way. This incident happened in 1997. If it happened today, I can't imagine what the consequences for Jason – and indeed all of us – might have been. I suppose Jason and Jill would probably have found themselves deported. Twenty years ago, fortunately, we were less paranoid and common sense prevailed.

When we went to see the edit of the commercial once shooting was finished, Ray showed me the sixty and the forty-five. They were both terrific. He wasn't finished, however.

Ray and the editor played me another version. It was ninety seconds long, an unheard-of length for a TV commercial – but where the others were terrific, this was brilliant. It gave the tale all the time it needed to unfold.

'Do you think they would run it in cinema?'

'I don't know, but I can ask.'

That evening, I presented the commercials to the client just as Ray had presented them to me. I showed them the sixty and the forty-five, and then I told them there was more.

'Ray has done a ninety-second version and, frankly, it is brilliant. We were wondering if there is any chance we could run it in cinemas. Anyway, have a look and see what you think.'

I played the commercial and there was a long silence. Then one of the clients, Gary, leant across the table towards me.

'We paid a university professor a lot of money to analyse our media spend and he told us that we should never advertise in the cinema.'

Oh well, I thought to myself, I gave it my best shot.

'But,' Gary continued, 'I'll tell you what we will do – we'll run it on TV.'

I loved the old-fashioned marketers at the NRMA. They had hearts, souls and, most importantly, guts. They took risks. The sanitised, pseudo-science that is marketing today is a pale imitation of the old-style instinctive marketers I was lucky enough to work with.

It remains one of the only times in my career when all the planets were in alignment, and to create a really great ad – or a really great anything – it seems you need all those planets on your side. When the ninety-second version of 'Job Seeker' went to air I was quick to caution Jason and Jill that this was a rare experience in advertising. They must be the only creative team ever whose first TV commercial was a ninety-second award winner.

For obvious reasons, I was very happy at Saatchi. I was doing work I was proud of and I felt well managed. At JWT, when I went to meetings I sometimes felt embarrassed by things some of my colleagues would say. I never felt like that at Saatchi. The agency was run by smart people who hired smart people and its culture, after the quick and effective action taken by Bob Isherwood and the rest of the management in the wake of the scandal, was becoming famous and admired. I remember being asked once by a new employee who the arseholes were. I thought for a while and then admitted I couldn't think of any. How rare is that?

We were good at having fun, too. The Saatchi Christmas party was justly famous. Every year the garage beneath our premises in George Street in The Rocks was transformed. While I was there it became a Chinese market, complete with live ducks in cages, a Las Vegas casino, a tribute to love, and a school. Everyone dressed up according to the designated theme and my colleagues and I competed as to who could come up with the most creative costume. For the 'love'-themed party I went as the consequences of love, equipped with a bucket, mop, cleaning products and naked baby dolls strapped to my arms and legs. For the Chinese-themed party I borrowed a cheongsam and bought a cheap black wig. Sadly, with my particularly round eyes, I just looked like a cheap and nasty Cleopatra, and the eyeliner I used to try to give them an Oriental slant just made it worse. My best two costumes, however, were for the Las Vegas party and my final hurrah – the back-to-school extravaganza.

My art director, Pic, was heavily pregnant with her first child the year of the Las Vegas party, so of course she went as Miss Teen Nevada, complete with sash, tiara, sceptre and tight blue dress emphasising her belly. We had a James Bond in a (very short) towelling robe, and showgirls and Liberaces galore. As I was in my forties by this stage, I knew I couldn't compete with the showgirls and I'd had some success with my cynical take on love the year before, so I decided to go as the real Las Vegas. I wore leggings, cheap high-heeled mules that went clack, clack, clack when I walked, a loud nylon shirt, cat's-eye glasses on a chain and a curly grey wig. I carried a polystyrene cup full of change and a lipstick-stained cigarette.

Before the party, a bunch of us went to the pub across the road for a drink. A couple of American tourists came in. In The Rocks, tourists were an occupational hazard. The Americans were very taken with everyone's costumes. I had seated myself in front of the poker machines for extra authenticity. Anyway, the Yanks wanted a photo of everyone. As my colleagues gathered into a group I got up and attempted to join them.

The Americans tried to block my approach until my friends cried out that I needed to be in the shot too.

'Oh! You're in costume!' said the American woman.

Uh-oh, perhaps my transformation was too convincing.

After our drink, we all trooped back across the road to join the party. Sharon Skeggs, who headed up the retail arm of Saatchi, spotted me immediately.

'Jane, there's someone I want you to meet.'

At that time, pre Megan Gale, international supermodel Lauren Hutton was the face of David Jones, and that's who I found myself facing while dressed as a poker-machine-addicted old lady.

'Lauren, this is Jane Caro. She's one of our best creatives.'

Lauren Hutton looked me up and down slowly. 'Well, you're certainly a good, brave girl.'

Thanks. I think.

My back-to-school costume was equally successful. I was leaving Saatchi to go to a new agency called Principals (that was a mistake, but more about that later), so my costume was obvious. I merely hired a mortarboard and academic gown and found a long, wicked-looking piece of bamboo. With my glasses on the end of my nose I was the living embodiment of a stern female principal. Which was fine, except for the weird way so many men reacted. I was surrounded by half-pissed blokes wanting me to cane them! At first it was funny, but after a while it started to feel rather creepy. To escape the blokes with the strange glint in their eyes, I fled to the quieter bar that had been temporarily established upstairs in reception. There I found my current art director, Stuart, morosely nursing a beer. He and I got on all right, but we had very different approaches to work, to life, to just about everything. Nevertheless, at least he wasn't asking me to beat him.

'Shit,' I said sitting down beside him. 'This costume has a weird effect on men. I haven't pulled like I have tonight for fifteen years!'

'What, you?' Stuart clearly thought I was delusional.

Just then the lift door opened and the newest creative team stepped out and came over to the bar. Justin Drape and Scott Nowell (now the creative brains behind The Monkeys, Australia's hottest ad agency) were not just talented but young and very good-looking.

'You know, Jane,' said Justin, as he sat down beside us, 'you are quasi-erotic in that outfit.'

That shut Stuart up, but I couldn't help wondering about the 'quasi'.

I daresay there were lots of drugs at those parties, mostly lines of coke, but I have always preferred wine, so I kept away from all that. I was never interested in drugs, perhaps because of my experience with anxiety. My mental stability had been hard won. I didn't want to risk it with chemicals. But my wariness around illegal substances is not necessarily the norm. Very conservative clients would often arrive at the Saatchi parties hoping to be supplied with not just drugs but girls. I was often called on by other more sensible colleagues to rescue some pretty young thing from the drunken and/or drugged lascivious advances of a client – a job I was expected to do without risking the account. There is no doubt that a confident older woman can dampen the lust of a man who knows he is doing the wrong thing. I suppose that's why they turned to me. It was also, in an odd way, an expression of respect. I was trusted to do even this difficult and delicate task adeptly, and I did. My intervention – I never said anything directly – was to start up a conversation about work, allowing the girl time to make herself scarce without anyone losing face, or anything else.

It was while I was at Saatchi that I was made the first female chair of judges for AWARD (the Australasian Writers and Art Directors Association). I was elected to the committee and our first meeting was spent dividing up the various positions for that year. Female committee members usually were appointed to run AWARD School (you know, because 'nurturing'). A number of women in the business had given me strict instructions that I had to try to get the job of chair of judges; they were sick of it always going to a bloke. I was nervous about it. It was the most prestigious job on the committee and I was sure that not only would I face lots of competition but that the other committee members would laugh at me. (It seems I had absorbed that lesson about women being assumed not to have merit just as much as everyone else had.)

The way the jobs were divvied up was simple. They called out the job title and those who wanted it put up their hand. When they called out, 'Head of AWARD School,' everyone looked at me, but I kept my hand firmly by my side. Someone else got that role. Then they called out, 'Chair of judges.'

I screwed my courage to the sticking-place, closed my eyes, put my head down and put up my hand.

'Okay, that's Jane, then,' said Les Gock, the then president of AWARD, and he moved on to allocating the next job.

I couldn't believe it had been that easy.

twenty-five

It might have been easy to become chair of judges, but that was the only thing easy about it. I decided that as the first female in the position, I had to do it a bit differently. What I tried to do was broaden the profile of people asked to judge the different categories. You had to be a full AWARD member to be a judge and you had to have had something accepted in the annual AWARD book to be eligible to be a member. To be chosen as a judge, you also had to have won a few national and international awards yourself. Of course, most people had won a lot of awards for the same couple of ads, but nobody seemed to worry too much about that.

I wanted to choose more women, more young people and fewer of the usual suspects. I think this is what's now called 'diversity' and is believed to deliver richer and more creative results. It wasn't seen that way by the advertising 'creative' community back then. Far from it. Choosing judges from a larger pool of eligible candidates got me into all sorts of trouble. Even though the highest percentage of women I could get (on the print jury) was 40 per cent, the guys in the industry went into orbit. The list of judges was printed in the industry trade magazine, *Campaign Brief*, with all the women's names in pink and all the men's names in blue! There were editorials written excoriating me for not choosing judges on – ahem – merit! The irony of that was entirely lost on these supposedly clever men. None of them had ever wondered how it was that women had so little merit and men, particularly men just like them, had so much. Maybe they thought they were just naturally superior.

I was even rung at home by one particularly pompous arse. He proceeded to lecture me about the error of my ways and my prejudice and biases! He wasn't just criticising my choice of women, but also some of the younger creatives. I was relieved that the young man he chose as an example of someone who had not paid enough 'dues' to be a judge turned out to be a past D&AD winner (D&AD was the Holy Grail of advertising shows, being the British equivalent of AWARD). I refused to be bullied or intimidated. I stuck to my guns. The show went well. In my opinion, the right work won. It did not do me much good.

Tenure on the AWARD committee was for two years. In your second year, you handed over your position to a new member of the committee (half of the committee retired every year) and you worked as a mentor or helper, passing on your experience from the year before so that the wheel did not have to be reinvented constantly. The guy who followed me as the new chair of judges made it clear from the beginning that he regarded what I had done with disdain. Nevertheless, due to protocol, I was asked to attend the first meeting, where the shape of the next annual judging was to be discussed. This chap laid down the law to the rest of us (the executive of AWARD were all women) in no uncertain terms.

'This year I want to do it completely differently,' he announced. 'I intend to get the members to nominate and vote for the judges so there won't be the kind of problems we had last year.' This was said with a very pointed look in my direction.

'Good for you,' I replied. 'That's exactly the attitude I took as chair of judges.'

My successor was both appalled and astonished. 'But I totally disagreed with everything you did last year!'

'I guess that's what happens when you do things differently. Some people don't like it.'

Being Chair of Judges was often controversial because those whose work did not get a guernsey often took out their disappointment on whoever was in the hot seat that year. A few years after my tenure as Chair, I was accosted by a woman who informed me loudly that I was the worst AWARD chair of judges ever.

'Why do you say that?' I asked her.

'It was outrageous that the bronze award winners did not get to go on stage.'

'That was not my year.'

'Yes it was.'

'No, it wasn't, and I can prove it.'

I leant towards my art director, Pic Andrews, who was sitting nearby.

'Pic, the year I was chair of judges, did you and I win a bronze award?'

'Yes, for that New South Wales Police radio commercial.'

'And did you get up on stage to collect it?'

'Yes, I did.'

'Did all the bronze award winners get to go on stage and collect their pencil that year?' (The award is in the shape of a large bronze, silver or gold pencil.)

'Yes, of course.'

I turned back to the woman who had been having a go at me. Her mouth was hanging open.

'I always thought it was you,' she said, sort of apologetically.

'I don't mind being blamed for my own mistakes,' I said, 'but I'll be damned if I'll take the blame for those made by other people.'

But worse things were happening than a bit of conflict over how to run advertising award shows. Mike Newman had left Saatchi and the agency was looking for a new creative director. I decided to put my hand up for the job.

Bob Isherwood was in charge of the search. When I told him I was interested, I could see he was surprised.

'Really?'

'Yes. I think I'd be good at it.'

'Well, you see, I asked all the creative directors around the network to recommend people and your name wasn't mentioned by any of them.'

'Were any women suggested?'

'Um . . . no.'

I shrugged.

'Okay, I'll put your name into the mix, then.'

I knew when I left his office that I was never going to be seriously considered. In fact, I knew before going into his office I wasn't going to be seriously considered, but I felt that the powers that be needed to face up to the fact that they never even thought about promoting women, and putting my own hand up was the best way I could think of to do that. To be fair, some years after I had left the agency, some ex-colleagues did approach me about the job of Creative Director of Team Saatchi (the retail agency). I did not get the job but the successful candidate was a woman. But that was still in the future.

I felt particularly motivated to go for the job of Saatchi Creative Director because of a rather strange little internal survey I had been asked to participate in. It began with a phone call from our office in New York. A very nice American woman was on the other end of the line. She was not someone I knew, but she introduced herself to me as being part of the planning department.

'Kevin' (the chief kahuna of Saatchi worldwide at that time) 'has asked me to conduct a survey among the senior women in the company about our lack of women at the top. As a senior creative, I wondered if you would be happy to participate?'

'Sure . . . but . . . um . . . pardon me, given that Kevin is the head of the company and has the final say-so on who we hire, shouldn't he really be asking himself that question?'

There was a hush on the end of the line and then a rather knowing chuckle.

'Yes, well, you're not the first person I've called who has made that same point.'

I have always found it almost amusing that senior men often look with bewilderment at the lack of senior women in the ranks, as if somehow such an imbalance has absolutely nothing to do with them. It's as if they think we just keep selfishly knocking back all those offers of glamorous, high-paying positions they keep thrusting upon us. Remember, I am the creative who has never been rung by a headhunter about a job.

Nevertheless, the nice American lady and I had a good chat, and she even asked me about quotas. Then, I thought quotas were a step too far and instead recommended that no shortlist or longlist of possible candidates for senior positions be accepted unless they included at least some women. Now, I would suggest quotas. Frankly, I don't think anything else will actually work. And obviously my mild suggestion of women always being included in lists of candidates was not accepted, as there were clearly no women being considered as a possible CD of Sydney until, I guess, I pushily inserted myself.

A few weeks later I received a beautiful bunch of flowers from Kevin to thank me for participating in the survey. Which was nice, but I'd much rather have been made creative director.

Of course I didn't get the job. Which would have been okay if the creative director they did choose (with the correct anatomical arrangements) had not been so badly briefed.

The very first email our new master sent held the clue. 'I want every creative to gather in the bar at 12 pm sharp.' It was the 'sharp' that sent a shiver down my spine. This guy wasn't interested in making friends.

We gathered as requested on the dot of twelve and we waited . . . and waited . . . and waited. A good ten minutes after the appointed time, our new boss arrived. He marched into the centre of the room and grimly surveyed us all.

'Welcome to your new jobs. As of now, you are all on three months' notice. You have that time to prove to me why you deserve to work here. As far as I am concerned, you have no past, you have no history. I don't care what you have done before, I only care about what you are going to do in the future.'

If I hadn't been waiting for my stock options to mature, I would have resigned on the spot. I had a past. I had a history. I had worked damn hard for both. Most sane people called them a track record, and I wasn't going to pretend for a moment it didn't exist.

It was not an auspicious beginning.

The Saatchi stock options, if you are wondering, were a result of the agency buying itself back from its owners a year or so previously. The staff had all been encouraged to buy options via a tax-efficient salary sacrifice. Urged on by an always financially savvy Ralph, I had taken the maximum allowed. They matured in December and, if I wanted to realise their full value, I couldn't leave before that time. It was May when the new CD arrived. It was going to be a long seven months.

The atmosphere in the creative department changed utterly. People were working almost constantly, desperate to hold on to their 'new' jobs. One copywriter came to work even though his toddler had been rushed to hospital with a serious illness, he was so terrified that his absence would result in him being fired. I was still supposed to be working four days a week but began to joke darkly that working part-time at Saatchi now meant that you got to go home occasionally. Working full-time now meant you never got to go home at all.

Even though the department was working all hours, it was almost impossible to see the boss and get him to approve our work. There was always a queue of people outside his office waiting for meetings they'd booked in his diary but which he never actually attended. I guess that 'sharp' only applied to underlings. I was luckier than many of the men I worked with who were the main breadwinners. Ralph was in a secure job and earning a good salary, and I had a past (aka track record) and I was pretty sure I could find another job. And our boss's dictatorial, yet strangely chaotic, management style brought out the defiance in me. I refused to join the queue. If Stuart and I were supposed to show him our scripts at 6 pm, we would turn up at the appointed time, scripts (or layouts) in hand. If he didn't appear by 6.15 (he never did), I'd leave the scripts in a pile on his chair and a note with my phone number on it and – yes – go home. To be fair, he didn't seem to mind.

In fact, I think that after a while it began to dawn on him that this management style was not in his own best interests. The culture that had been so famous was shattered and some of the big clients started to get restless. The CD brushed aside the scripts Stuart and I had written to follow up on the 'Job Seeker' spot for NRMA. I won't say anything directly about the commercials that were made instead except that, the morning after they first appeared, I was phoned by creatives from other agencies asking me if I'd had anything to do with them. I was pleased to be able to deny it. Eventually, Saatchi lost the account.

Understandably, our boss began to soften. Beneath the dictator who put the fear of God into people, I glimpsed an inexperienced creative director who, out of insecurity, had taken the wrong advice. He was also exhausting himself. I remember the last TV campaign I made for Saatchi. It was for Lexus. One of the ads required shots of a car driving at night. To facilitate this, the Sydney Harbour tunnel was hired as a location and was closed to traffic between midnight and 5 am. (When you see the tunnel is closed at times like that, it may be for maintenance or it may also be because it is earning New South Wales money as a film location.) This meant an all-night shoot, never my favourite activity. Dutifully, I sat in the Domain carpark from midnight on, swaddled in blankets (it was winter), staring at a blank split. It was blank because the camera on the truck towing the hero car had broken down and time was being spent fixing it. At 2 am, my boss arrived. He said he was on his way home from the office. I believed him. He sat there with me, staring at that split for two hours. Why? I have no idea.

Despite the dreary night shoots, the ads themselves turned out well. I went on a week's holiday just before they were finished. When I left, they had looked like beautiful, glowing jewels – the film art director had done a terrific job. When I returned, they looked flat and de-saturated.

'What happened to all the beautiful colours?' I asked Stuart.

'Colour is so 1980s, don't you think?' Honestly, only an advertising art director would ever say anything like that.

The day my stock options matured, I resigned. A year or so later, so did the CD. Saatchi Sydney have still never had a female creative director (except in the retail arm, and they eventually fired her, too). Hardly any advertising agencies ever have. Funny that.

twenty-six

I did not regret leaving Saatchi, even though I had been there for five years and had – mostly – enjoyed them. Even my last boss had improved on acquaintance. When I left, he organised a wonderful farewell present for me. It was a variety of different fruit trees – apples, mandarins and five different kinds of olives. The present was particularly appropriate because Ralph and I had come into a small legacy and, instead of using it to buy a bigger house in a flasher suburb, we decided to buy a (very) rundown farm in the most beautiful part of New South Wales – the Upper Allyn, about three hours north-west of Sydney. The girls loved it there, riding through the forest on one of our motley crew of horses or mucking about for hours in the river. We'd spent every spare weekend for the last few years renovating the old weatherboard farmhouse and establishing a garden. Ralph had wanted to breed cattle for decades and he'd bought a small herd.

The trees were a lovely, generous and imaginative present. My boss also made a short video about how good it would be when Jane finally decided what it was she wanted to do when she grew up. It was funny but also perceptive, because I did feel restless. Partly, it must be said, due to my latest boss but mostly because of what I now saw as my inability to get ahead. I was feeling bruised from banging my head up against that famous glass ceiling or, as American feminist Laura Lissey prefers to call it, that thick layer of men.

I had also started writing occasional articles and submitting them to newspapers. Fatally, I was quite successful. The first eight I submitted to *The Sydney Morning Herald* were published. I mostly wrote about the importance of public education. My first published article (still available on the internet, despite having been written fifteen years ago) was called 'Ten reasons why you should always send your child to a public school'. But I also had articles accepted on feminism and one on the 9/11 catastrophe that was published only a few days after the event. Even I couldn't quite believe that.

I have never had a hit rate quite like it since. The girls were growing and both were now at school, so, tentatively, I began stretching some muscles I hadn't been using. My most successful subject was my passionate support for public education. Ralph and I had followed through on our beliefs and sent our girls to a nearby comprehensive, co-ed public high school. Even though it was a school in a very well-heeled area, we had been warned subtly and not-so-subtly that by choosing a public secondary school for our daughters we were sending them to hell in a handbasket.

'Polly goes to high school next year, doesn't she?'

'Yes, that's right.'

We were at a suburban dinner party and my interlocutor could not see our hostess making desperate hand signals warning her off this particular topic.

'And where are you sending her?'

'Mosman High.'

The reaction to this announcement was always the same: an inadvertent recoil, followed by a rictus smile while the gobsmacked middle-class mother tried to think of something appropriate to say to this utterly unexpected and unacceptable yet somehow vaguely threatening answer.

'Ohhhhhh . . . I hear it's a very good school . . .'

'Yes, that's why we chose it.'

'Only if you don't mind the drugs . . .' This was muttered sotto voce by a fellow guest whom I assume didn't realise I could hear every word.

Interestingly, some years afterwards we ran into this woman and her husband again, and slap me upside of the head if they hadn't moved their child to Mosman High! They now loved the school and had completely forgotten their original attitude.

It wasn't the only time I was warned off Mosman High because of a supposed (but completely imaginary) drug problem. An ethicist, whom I will kindly not name, was meeting with me about another issue entirely. We were both mothers of similarly aged children living on the Lower North Shore. After a while, for reasons I no longer recall, we got around to talking about schools.

'Of course,' this supposedly super-ethical person (well, she had a piece of paper to prove it) said in hushed, conspiratorial tones, 'Mosman High has a terrible heroin problem.'

'How do you know that?'

'Everyone in the area knows that.'

'Really? My daughters attend Mosman High.'

I had the satisfaction of seeing all the blood drain from her face.

'And I can promise you there is no heroin problem at the school. Many school-aged kids – from all kinds of schools – experiment with drugs' (I knew that from my own school days) 'but few do so at school. Schools have rigid timetables and they are well policed. Generally, it is much easier for kids to experiment outside of school hours, often at home or at the homes of their friends.'

She was still too mortified to say anything so I happily rubbed her face in her stupidity a little more. (I know, I'm sorry, but really, I'd had enough of this baseless rumour-mongering.)

'Anyway, I don't know about you, but if I was a drug dealer and I could stand outside the school that charges no fees or the school that charges twenty thousand a year plus, I know where I'd be concentrating my efforts.'

I now believe that people who spend thousands of post-tax dollars on something they could get for free have to tell you that all the nearby public schools are ghastly because otherwise what kind of fool are they? Moral of the story: never believe the scuttlebutt about public schools. Mostly it is people justifying their own decisions. Go and see the school for yourself – it could save you hundreds of thousands of dollars.

This damaging and self-justifying desire to talk down public schools infuriated me and I began to write about it. It turned out that there was a need for a new voice in the schools debate, particularly one without a particular vested interest (I was neither a teacher nor a member of the union) and so my timing was right.

Unfortunately, despite my fledgling forays into other kinds of writing, I had to make a few more missteps before I escaped advertising all together.

* * *

I left Saatchi to take up a position at a relatively new agency called Principals. Its philosophy was that everyone employed was senior and I was (at last) given the title of creative director, though it was a pyrrhic victory because so were all the other creatives. Mind you, they really were very senior. One of them had once been Australia's most awarded art director – David Barnes – and another was my old boss from Campaign Palace days, Jack Vaughan. I enjoyed working with Jack and David very much, but the agency itself was going through a transition and, after only a year, the strategy planners who ran the place let all the creatives go – even Jack and David, who had been co-owners! They wanted to concentrate on strategy and creatives just got in the way. What all that advertising strategy was for, if not to help craft actual ads, I'm not sure.

David and I decided to start our own small agency – Caro & Barnes – working out of a spare office in his brother's law firm. We did all right – for a while. Meanwhile, I had been invited to join the Advertising Federation of Australia's Ethics Advisory Committee and, in that capacity, I was asked to appear on the Channel Seven program *Sunrise* to defend some beer ads (surprise, surprise) that were being criticised for sexism. I did, and I must have come across quite well because the new producer of the revamped breakfast show – Adam Boland – rang and asked me to become their regular marketing commentator. They'd just changed hosts, taking a risk on the financial reporter David Koch (whom, coincidentally, I'd gone to school with at Forest High) and news journalist Melissa Doyle. They couldn't afford to pay me, but Barnsey and I decided it was great publicity for our nascent agency. Turns out it wasn't. What it was, however, was great publicity and training for me.

After running Caro & Barnes for about eighteen months, I did something I had never done before and will never do again: I took a job purely for the money. It was a huge mistake.

I went to work at another large multinational agency but, unlike JWT and Saatchi, this one was pretty much on its last legs. The few remaining staff sat huddled together in what were now mostly empty offices. The once-great agency was down to a handful of clients, most of them internationally aligned. In other words, they weren't with the Sydney agency by choice. After a few months working there I began to see why. Some of the senior managers were difficult people. Nice enough socially, they didn't set out to undermine your confidence but, nevertheless, they did. I had joined the agency a bit full of my own importance, certain that I was now old enough and tough enough that I could no longer be undermined. It was a painful but salutary lesson to discover that I was just as vulnerable to feeling like shit as I had ever been. My daughters remember me referring to the agency as 'the sad place' and that is exactly what it felt like. I began to wonder if I had any creative ability left at all. My new bosses were kind enough, but somehow I left any interaction with them feeling as if all the oxygen had been sucked out of the room and out of me. I felt constantly deflated. As you can imagine, the agency churned through creative people. I managed to stick it out for eighteen months.

One of the reasons I stayed was because I got some opportunities to work internationally, something that had not happened before. The US head office of the agency would gather groups of creatives from around the world to work on a particularly sticky problem and I soon found myself in demand for what were called 'rumbles'. Not only was it exciting to travel overseas for work, but the fact that I was often invited to be part of the program helped to soothe my bruised ego. I went to Singapore on rumbles a couple of times and then, most excitingly of all, I got to spend eight days in Chicago. It was quite an experience.

Eight creative teams were flown in to the city early on a Sunday morning. There were teams from Australia (obviously), China, Latin America and the US. We all assembled on the Sunday, in various stages of jetlag, to be comprehensively briefed. Bigwig strategy planners, researchers and account service people from Asia and Latin America had also been flown in to give us every detail of the communication problem we were to spend the next week trying to solve. The briefing session was so detailed and comprehensive it took up almost the whole day. The next morning, we reassembled and got to work. By the end of the week, we'd had a lot of fun and had eight different campaigns to present. Surely one of them would be the answer to the client's communication problem. On the Friday, we were to present our work at the client's offices in neighbouring Wisconsin.

We hadn't just worked all week, of course. That was one of the things I liked about rumbles – the chance to meet and socialise with smart, interesting and creative people from all over the world. During the week, I had eaten in all sorts of places and attended a Cubs versus Red Sox baseball game at historic Wrigley Park. We'd sat in the bleachers and I'd even had beer spilt all over me, which just made the whole thing feel really authentic. I am usually completely indifferent to sport, but this wasn't sport – it was history, it was American culture, it was theatre. Before the game they played 'Take Me Out to the Ball Game', everyone stood with their hand on their heart when they played 'The Star-Spangled Banner', there was a minute's silence in tribute to 'the fallen' in Iraq and, on the streets outside, kids played in the fire hydrants. I loved it. Even better, it was an historic game because the Cubs (from Chicago) and the Red Sox (from Boston) usually play in different leagues and so had not played each other since 1919. This was special in every way.

The hotel we were staying in was also playing host to the annual draft of the American National Basketball Association (NBA) and so was packed to the rafters (literally) with the most enormous young men I had ever seen. Since I was a very short, middle-aged white woman, they just looked straight over the top of me if we shared a lift or waited together in line at the reception desk. When we did interact, however, I was very impressed with their rather old-fashioned good manners. They called me ma'am and seemed rather shy. It is one of the most endearing things about Americans that they are naturally very courteous. (Except in New York, of course, which I love for entirely different reasons.) When I told my eldest daughter (she was fifteen) about my daily proximity to NBA hopefuls, she was beside herself with envy.

On the day of the presentation, loaded up with our storyboards, scripts, layouts and references, all eight of us boarded a minibus which was to drive us from Chicago, Illinois, to the client's corporate headquarters in neighbouring Wisconsin. I don't think it was a long journey in terms of actual distance, maybe equivalent to driving from Sydney to Katoomba, but the traffic on the twelve-lane highway had to be seen to be believed, and so we inched our way to the meeting. We knew when we had entered Wisconsin, however. As a state it was renowned for its dairy products and they weren't about to let you forget it. Every roadhouse we passed (and there were a lot of them) bore huge neon signs saying – very bluntly – CHEESE.

When we finally arrived, the compound lived up to its reputation. The central meeting room was enormous and had a vaguely Native American theme. I didn't have time to take much of it in, however, due to the fact that most of the room was taken up by a huge U-shaped table occupied by upwards of forty people. This was going to be the biggest presentation I had ever done. At the arse end of the enormous table there were just enough vacant seats for us creatives and our two American minders. Right at the apex sat the man whom I silently christened 'the big cheese' (it seemed appropriate). He immediately established that this was his meeting. He began to talk in a loud and authoritative voice. As he talked, it soon became clear that he was completely undermining the brief that we had been working on for the whole eight days. Everything he suggested he was looking for was the opposite of what we had been told. All that research, all that analysis, all that work, he tossed blithely aside. In fact, it sounded to me as if he hadn't even bothered to read the briefing document.

Frankly, we should have stood up, torn up our work and walked out. Instead, we listened quietly and then did the best we could to salvage the meeting. Our work was received politely but that was all. I was angry. Not just because we had lost some good work, nor because so much effort had been wasted, but because of the astronomical sum of money this big CHEESE had so lazily pissed up against a wall to feed his out-of-control ego. I can't begin to calculate how much it must have cost to fly all those people from all over the world (more than forty of them by my count) and put them up for eight days in a swish hotel for no result.

Worse, in the briefing we had been told just how big a problem the brand we were working on was facing and how urgent it was that we got a campaign to air. I went to that rumble in about 2005. Ten years later, I have still not seen any campaign for the brand we worked so hard over. In fact, I hardly hear of it at all. What a waste. Perhaps you can see why I am not nearly so enamoured of the much-vaunted efficiency of private industry as are so many of my more right-wing friends.

I had another international experience while working for the sad place that finally convinced me I had to get out of advertising once and for all. We were briefed to write a campaign to launch a milk product into the Australian market that was aimed at women over forty. The milk had a special formula that made it protective of bones, a particular issue for women as they approach menopause. In 2005, I was forty-eight years old, bang on the target market. My art director and I wrote a terrific campaign, using animated tarot cards where all the characters – the Empress, Wizard, Knights, even Death came to life but were horribly affected by osteoporosis, the message being that, whatever the future held, you would need strong bones.

We were proud of the work. It was different, beautiful, arresting and absolutely on brief. Off I flew to present to the big kahunas in Singapore. I presented the work to a room full of men – an Indian (he was the milk company's big cheese), some Japanese, some Singaporeans, South Africans and New Zealanders. I was the only woman in the room and the account director and I were the only Australians. My ideas went down like a lead balloon. This is always disappointing, but I was (and am) used to it. What really got my goat was that the big cheese and his cronies then proceeded to lecture me about what Australian women over forty would actually respond to – apparently we were all just waiting for some local minor female celebrity to give us the facts and we'd all obediently rush out to buy the milk she recommended. All my arguments to the contrary fell on deaf ears. It was during that outrageous bout of mansplaining that I finally made up my mind to leave advertising behind.

Advertising and its allied industries spend a fortune researching that poor bint they call 'the consumer'. Political parties do too. And, frankly, look where it's got them. Far from having a greater understanding of the human beings they are trying to talk to, they have never been more disconnected. I think this is because most research thrives on turning other human beings into strange zoological specimens to be examined through a microscope and wondered at. Far from bringing communications professionals closer, it actually distances the professional marketer from their audience. Successful communication does precisely the opposite. It closes the distance and creates connections. I recently worked for a wonderful client who did extensive market research in preparation for the advertising task that I was eventually asked to perform. Once the job was done, the ads written and produced, the client was ecstatic with the result. She turned to me after yet another successful showing of the ads to stakeholders (they were shared 44,000 times in just four days on social media) and expressed her delight and satisfaction.

'What really impressed me was how you took all that research – that huge document with hundreds of pages – and distilled it all down into these ads. It's an incredible skill.'

I didn't like to tell her I had written the ads long before I ever saw the research.

Mansplaining is a bit like that. It is often practised by people who are determined to keep their distance from you (many men are terrified of actually empathising with women in case it literally unmans them) by taking a superior position and telling you what you should do, how you should think and what your deepest drives and desires are. Yet with every word they reveal how little they know – not just about you, but about themselves. Most marketers, sadly, are the ultimate mansplainers. They just don't know what they don't know. Worse, they really don't care to find out, either.

twenty-seven

Polly and Charlotte were eighteen and fifteen by this time and Polly had just finished her HSC. Polly had come through her teenage rebellion stage and was becoming a pleasure to have around. Unfortunately, as is so often the way, as she improved, Charlotte grasped the rebellion baton and proceeded to embark on her defiant years. We struggled as all parents do when their children begin to assert themselves. I remember when Polly was in Year 9 (every teacher will tell you that this is the nightmare stage) going to her parent–teacher night. At that time, Charlotte was a lovely, biddable Year 7 and it was Ralph's turn to go to her parent–teacher interviews. Having drawn the short straw, I went from teacher to teacher, getting feedback, and it felt like being poked with little sharp sticks. Finally, I reached my second-to-last interview. It was her drama teacher. I introduced myself.

'Hi, I'm Jane Caro, Polly's mother.'

His facial expression in response to hearing her name said all that needed to be said (well, he was her drama teacher). Long story short, she was being a little bitch. Ouch.

When I reached her English teacher, I must have looked as bad as I felt, because before I had a chance to say a word, she reached out and patted my hand across the table.

'Never mind, the parent in front of you was in tears.'

Polly has more than redeemed herself since. (Indeed, both girls have.) At the end of Year 12 she suddenly had a change of career plan.

'Mum, I don't want to be a journalist anymore.'

'Don't you, darling? What do you want to do?'

'I want to be an English and drama teacher.'

'That's great, but why the change of plan?'

'Because if I can turn bad kids around like Mr Feros' (the previously mentioned drama teacher) 'and Mr Young' (her English teacher) 'did with me, well, that's what I want to do with my life.'

And people thought I was mad to send my kids to Mosman High.

Polly went on to get first-class honours in education from Sydney Uni. Charlotte, meanwhile, has graduated from the University of New South Wales with a degree in fine arts. Despite their neglectful mother and bog-standard public education, they appear to have turned out rather well. Polly has become something of an overachiever, in fact.

Towards the end of her degree, she was getting a lot of work as a substitute teacher, particularly at Canterbury Boys

High School. Canterbury Boys (John Howard's old school) has a hugely diverse student body that includes kids from Middle Eastern backgrounds, the Pacific Islands, Asia in general and Africa, including Sudanese and Somalian refugees, some of whom were once boy soldiers. Polly loved teaching there and was passionate about her students.

All very worthy, but even her excellent public school education couldn't iron out all the kinks: she was also an *Oprah* tragic. (Honestly, Paris Hilton? Oprah Winfrey? Oh well, there's no accounting for taste.) The year she was teaching at Canterbury Boys was the year Oprah came to Australia for the *Oprah Down Under* shows. Polly was determined to go. She put her name and mine (?) into the lottery for tickets. Our names did not come up and, while I was indifferent to the point of being relieved, she was really pissed off. Nursing her disappointment, she began tootling around the *Oprah* website and found this question: *What part of Australia would you like to show JayZ?* JayZ, for the uninitiated, is a mega-famous rapper, married to Beyoncé. Whatever I may think of his music, he is a very admirable person, having dragged himself up by his bootstraps from the housing projects in Brooklyn to international stardom. Polly is (sigh) also a massive fan of JayZ.

Polly answered the question on the *Oprah* site by saying she would like to show JayZ her boys at Canterbury Boys High School. She explained that because her students were like him when he was young, starting out with few opportunities, he would be an inspiration for them. She also talked about how proud she was of the boys she taught and how determined they were to overcome their disadvantages. She argued that they would also be an inspiration for JayZ. Then she hit send and thought little more about it.

A few weeks later, Polly came running into the room with a panicked expression. She was holding up her phone.

'Mum! Listen to this!'

She played the voice message she had just received.

'*Hello, Polly. This is Candy from* The Oprah Winfrey Show. *Can you call me back on . . .*' and she left a US number.

'What should I do?' She looked anguished.

But because mothers are very wise, I knew exactly what to do. 'Call her back.' I said. (I know – I am impressed with myself too.)

To cut a long story short, Polly called the producer back, and after a lot of rigmarole about them possibly doing a segment on education in Australia, it was finally decided that Polly and the whole school – every student and every staff member – would be bussed to the recording of Oprah's show at the Opera House on the following Tuesday. Polly was to announce this treat to the whole school on the Monday morning.

'And, oh,' said Candy, as an afterthought, 'could you bring your original email with you and read that out too?'

Polly was only too happy to agree. All she'd wanted was to be in the audience for the *Oprah Down Under* show, and if she had to take the whole school with her to do it, well, so be it.

On Monday morning (you can view this on the internet on Oprah's website), Polly stood on the steps of the quadrangle reading her email to the staff and students as requested. Suddenly the normally well-behaved boys started to go a bit wild. Polly looked up, then turned around. JayZ was standing behind her!

He spent the day at the school, jamming with the African drumming band, talking to the kids and generally proving to be a lovely person.

At 6 am on Tuesday morning, every single student arrived on time, many accompanied by their excited parents. They were all spruced up in their full school uniforms. They got on the three buses provided by Oprah and headed for the Opera House Concert Hall. They were beautifully behaved, but when they got to their segment – signalled by JayZ coming on stage – they understandably got very excited. They watched, as did millions around the world, an edited version of what had happened at their school the day before and Polly had the thrill of hearing her name said and her actions praised by her hero, Oprah Winfrey. Then, when the segment had finished, Oprah made the following announcement.

'And thanks to my good friends at Microsoft and Hewlett Packard, every student and staff member at Canterbury Boys High will receive a brand-new laptop computer. The school will receive fifteen state-of-the-art computers for the library and six state-of-the-art music computers for the music department.' It was a donation worth a million dollars – one of the single biggest donations ever made to a public school in Australia.

Well, everyone went ballistic, not least her proud but sobbing parents watching at home. For a few days, Polly was the darling of the media, something she handled with grace and aplomb.

'We need more teachers like you,' said the shock jock on 2GB who was interviewing her.

'But you have thousands and thousands of teachers like me, who are proud of their students and work hard on their behalf,' replied Polly. 'All I did was hit send.'

As I look at both my lovely, (relatively) well-adjusted, interesting, gainfully employed and contributing daughters, all I can think is – all this and no fees!

* * *

It was around this time that my life changed radically too, and for the better. In December 2005, I was sitting at my desk in the sad place contemplating my next move, when my phone rang. It was Adam Boland and he offered me a regular gig on *Sunrise* reviewing the daily newspapers. It meant starting work each day at 4.30 am, but the upside was I'd be finished by 8.30. I'd get paid, though not much. No matter, I'd fill the rest of my day with well-paying freelance work, I thought, so I jumped at the chance. Adam's offer had come at just the right time and was the push I needed to get out of working in ad agencies.

As it turned out, the *Sunrise* gig only lasted for three months, but it didn't matter. I was out of ad agencies and offers I hadn't expected were starting to come through the door. Ever since I'd left Saatchi I'd been feeling as if my world was closing down, and now it was opening up. I was writing my first book and my co-author Chris Bonnor and I had found a publisher. It had been my dream for as long as I could remember to be a published author.

I had also been working on a historical novel in spits and spurts for years. I'd started it in the monthly writing group I used to attend when the kids were small. I no longer went to the writing group, but I had kept writing that novel. Now I had time to really get stuck into it. And although I was sad when Adam rang to say he didn't think the gig was working out, I wasn't surprised. I hadn't felt it was either. I didn't quite know what they wanted from me and I also didn't feel I was allowed to be myself. I knew by that time that being myself was what I was best at. More than that, I had hated getting up at 4.30 am and had found the attendant exhaustion cumulative. I was sick of feeling as if I was pushing through treacle. I had a nap every afternoon at two and went to bed at nine, but I still felt groggy and exhausted every day. For weeks after the gig ended I dreamt of my alarm going off at 4.30 am and the sound of it – even in my dreams – made me feel ill.

When Chris asked me to write a book with him, just before I left the sad place, I had been thrilled. Chris had just retired as principal of Davidson High School and was in the middle of his term as the president of the New South Wales Secondary Principals Council. I had become a bit of a spokesperson for public education since I wrote that first cheeky article which got me published in *The Sydney Morning Herald*. The sector was desperate for a disinterested voice and when I spoke up – without quite realising it – I assumed the mantle. It helped that by this time Ann was the deputy principal of a public high school in Sydney's west. The stories she told me about the miracles people like her were expected to perform with tiny budgets and no support broke my heart and made me determined to do what I could to help. The staff in state schools cannot speak to the media without permission, but I could and so I did.

'Sometimes I feel like I am holding this school together with a roll of sticky tape and a ball of string!' Ann said to me after yet another round of budget cuts. It was particularly galling under the Howard government to watch enormous sums of public money going to already luxuriously resourced schools charging high fees while schools like Ann's struggled with the kids the private schools didn't want, while losing an average of 1 per cent of their funding annually – in real terms – over more than a decade.

I often say to people, if you want to find Australia's most efficient money managers, don't go to the private sector, pop round to your local public school and ask the principal how they manage to do everything they do for the money. Bloody miracle workers they are, particularly if they work in disadvantaged areas where it is virtually impossible to fundraise.

Chris and I wanted to write a book about Australia's education system as a wake-up call and our working title was *The Illusion of Choice*. Our publisher at New South, Phillipa McGuinness, didn't think much of that, so eventually we called the book *The Stupid Country: How Australia is dismantling public education*. Clearly, it pays to listen to your publisher. *The Stupid Country* came out in 2007 and it is still selling.

That book gave me some credibility and I began to receive invitations from all over the country to speak to public schools and public school organisations. Pretty soon, I had an agent and was beginning to earn quite decent money on the speakers' circuit. That's when I started to realise that you don't write books to make money, you write books to get you the speaking gigs that actually make you money.

My next foray into publishing was also with New South. This time my close mate Catherine Fox and I decided to write a book about the important part feminism had played in our lives as workers and mothers. Catherine and I had first met at the school bus stop and she lived at the end of the road. She was a journo with *Australian Financial Review* and was best known for her regular weekly column, 'Corporate Woman'. We both worked part-time and for years, every Friday, after seeing our girls off to school – between us we had five daughters – we'd have coffee and unload about our lives. It was these conversations that we now turned into a book. We called it *The F Word: How we learned to swear by feminism*. This time, Phillipa approved of the choice of title.

While all this was going on, I was still working on my novel and getting freelance advertising commissions, and I had begun working as a permanent part-time lecturer at the University of Western Sydney, teaching the Advertising Creative elective in their communications major. I was also getting frequent work as a speaker and, increasingly, appearing in the media and writing opinion pieces and articles for various publications. I had, it seemed, fallen on my feet. I was also being called by friends and ex-colleagues in the advertising industry and asked if I'd been contacted about something called *The Gruen Transfer*. I hadn't and a few people urged me to give the producers a call.

'They're desperately looking for women in the advertising industry for their show.'

I could understand their difficulty, but I still did not get in touch with the producers.

I had made a decision when I leapt into the dark after Adam's well-timed call about *Sunrise*. I knew I was taking a risk leaving the best-paid job I had ever had for the exact opposite, but I didn't feel particularly worried about it. The girls were almost grown. We'd had the good sense to send them to public schools so the financial pressures on us were not as onerous as they are for many people and Ralph was (I thought) secure in his job with the company he'd been with for twenty-five years. I decided it was now or never. I would take charge of my own destiny and I would do it my way.

My expectations were modest. I wanted to do interesting work. I did not want to set the world on fire. I also decided I would not chase anything; I would simply do what I did to the best of my ability. If something good came out of it, great; if not, so be it. I would not try to please others or seek their approval. I would not agonise or make myself miserable by yearning for things I could not have. I gave up trying to control what happened. I had learnt – very much the hard way, thanks to my decades-long anxiety neurosis – that I could not control outcomes. I knew that all I could control was inputs and that was what I put my time and energy into. It's still how I run my life. So when I was urged to call the producers of *Gruen*, I refused. I am easy to find, I told people. If they want me, they will call me.

And eventually they did. The show was co-created by Andrew Denton and Jon Casimir. When Jon rang and asked me if I would come in and do a workshop with some of the other potential panellists, I agreed and turned up at the ABC to be part of a mock episode. They then asked me to be on the panel for the pilot. The pilot never went to air but featured Dee Madigan and her art director doing the now-famous pitch segment, which is how she earned her regular place in the show, no doubt. Then I was asked to be in the launch episode.

The full story of the success of *The Gruen Transfer* will no doubt be told one day, but it should be told by the people who created, developed and produced the show. I was just lucky enough to be one of the regular talent. But even being a small part of those first few seasons was quite a phenomenal experience. The show launched to critical and popular acclaim. It averaged over a million viewers an episode, not least because it was such an original and fresh inkling for a TV show. However, I cannot claim to have had any inkling that it would be as successful as it turned out to be. Indeed, when Jon, in that initial phone call, told me it was a show about advertising, I remember thinking that it would never work. I couldn't imagine why anyone would want to watch a bunch of advertising people dissecting their work. Partly, perhaps, this was because I was still very disillusioned with advertising in general, but I suspect it was also because I did not realise just how refreshing advertising's concentration on audiences would be to . . . well . . . audiences. Yes, it was a show about advertising, but that meant it was also a show about all of us, because that is what advertising is about in the end. It is a mirror that reflects us back to ourselves as we really are. Not as we'd like to be, not an idealised version of ourselves, but us in all our narcissism, insecurity, small-mindedness, greed and, occasionally, glory.

I wasn't alone in my pessimism (which I kept entirely to myself, by the way). There was a lot of naysaying in the advertising community itself, some of it by people who were miffed they had not been included and some by those who feared it would either trivialise or further debase an industry that was already held in low esteem. Of course, the opposite happened. Advertising was suddenly cool again, thanks in part to *Gruen* but also to the launch of the HBO drama series *Mad Men*. The irony that I was suddenly famous for being in advertising just as I was trying to extricate myself from it was not entirely lost on me. Indeed, Jon had told me that the reason they waited so long to call me was because they wanted current practitioners in the show and they were not sure that I still fitted that description. Fortunately, my uni job, my continued participation in the AFA ethics board and my frequent freelance work got me over the line.

I say fortunately, because there is no doubt that *The Gruen Transfer* changed my life. It did that for all of us who were plucked from relative obscurity onto that panel. Weekly regulars

Todd Sampson and Russel Howcroft rocketed immediately into the celebrity stratosphere, and even those of us who only appeared every now and again found ourselves suddenly being recognised in public. I wouldn't say I became famous; rather, I found myself occupying a much nicer space in the public's mind. I became familiar.

What this meant was that people would often look at my face with recognition, and then they would smile at me. Sometimes they would ask me where they knew me from and I learnt pretty quickly to say they had probably seen me on the telly. I did this because otherwise they would go through their whole life story trying to discover where we might have met. Unfortunately, telling people they recognised me from their TV meant they invariably reacted with embarrassment and apologised. I responded that there was no need. It was (and still is) lovely to be familiar. People don't impinge on your ordinary life very much, but the whole world suddenly seems much more welcoming. I would hate to be really famous – I imagine that must be quite overwhelming – but I am glad I am still familiar, even though I haven't appeared on *The Gruen Transfer* for almost three years.

It also turned out to be extremely clever of me to have kept my own name when I married Ralph all those years ago. The girls have his last name not mine (I was keeping my identity, not starting a dynasty), so they have plausible deniability. If they don't want someone to know I am their mother, they do not have to tell them. I am sure it has helped Ralph, particularly now that he is a partner in his own wine business (yes, that twenty-five-year job we thought was so secure eventually also went pear-shaped), that he is not automatically associated with me. It also liberates me to be able to say whatever I want without having to worry about any effect it may have on them. (Keep your own name, ladies, the benefits of such little acts of independence can be unexpected.)

However, it moves me very much that my family seem to be rather proud of my unexpected late-onset public profile. If I am recognised or approached when we're together, they are pleased for me and take delight in passing on the nice things people have said to them when they realise their relationship to me. I don't know if they also hear nasty things. If they do, they are kind enough not to tell me.

I was also very glad that the naysayers and, indeed, my own pessimism were wrong. It is thrilling to be part of a successful television show. I was determined to stick with my new-found philosophy, though, and decided that I would not try to be anything I wasn't. I suspect my relaxed attitude infuriated some of the people who worked on the show. To their mind, I was too laidback and not trying hard enough. They didn't realise that I had long ago discovered that I am at my best when I am spontaneous and don't think about things too much in advance. I did my research and prepared thoroughly beforehand and then I simply took things as they came. I remember waiting in the wings one evening – *Gruen* was always filmed at 7 pm in front of a live audience – when Wil Anderson suddenly looked at me rather accusingly.

'You're not nervous, are you?'

'No. I'm not.'

'How come? How can you be so calm?'

'I look at it like this. I'll go out there and do my best. I'll answer your questions as honestly as I can and you and the audience will either like me or you won't. And if you don't, the worst thing that will happen is that you won't ask me back.'

I am not sure Wil believed a word I said, but I was telling the truth. It is how I do everything now. I don't anticipate; I deal with the next thing as it comes up. I don't agonise; I just try to be as truthful as possible. I don't have to be the star or the best. I don't worry about the outcome – how I appear to others; I just concentrate on the inputs – being as much myself as I can be. I don't have to be right. I don't have to win. I don't have to be the wittiest or the wisest. I just want to contribute. (This does not mean I never worry or feel insecure. Of course I do. I don't live in a permanent state of anxiety anymore, that's all. I did that for more than ten years and that is quite long enough.) If someone says something funny, I will laugh. I try to listen to what the others say so that I can respond appropriately and . . . well . . . that's it, that's all I try to do. One of the nicest things anyone ever said to me about my appearances on *Gruen* was when the director Mark Fitzgerald told me that whenever they wanted a reaction shot they always cut to me. He said, 'You are always in there reacting to what is going on.' I have learnt to live in the moment (thank you, anxiety) even when I am on the telly.

And there was another trick I had learnt in my three months as a daily regular on *Sunrise* (nothing is ever wasted). In the first few days of that gig, I had been warned a couple of times about not looking at the monitor. When you are on TV, especially live TV, there is a monitor that shows you what the audience is seeing – so you can see yourself, in my case double chin and all, in close-up. It is, as you can imagine, very distracting. The only way I could make myself ignore the monitor was to stare fixedly at whoever was talking. It became a habit. Now, whenever I am on any kind of TV program (and at the time of writing I make regular appearances on *Sunrise*, *Weekend Sunrise* and *The Drum*), I automatically look at whoever is speaking. It's a trick that has paid off in spades. I often get feedback from viewers about how much they like the way I listen intently to the other people on the panel. Little do they know that I am really just trying hard not to look at the monitor.

I don't always maintain full possession of myself, of course. I have occasionally allowed people on discussion panels to get under my skin, especially when the topic is something dear to my heart. I try to be extra vigilant when I know we will be covering public education or feminism or our (appalling) treatment of refugees and maintain my relaxed attitude. Sadly, if it really matters to me, I usually fail.

Only a few years after I had left ad agencies and struck out on my own, my life was as satisfying as I could ever have wished. I was earning very well. I had an infinite variety of interesting things to do. I had a professional reputation and even a small public profile that I could never have anticipated. I had two books published that had been greeted with respect and sold modestly well. None of this I had planned; I had simply gone out there, said yes to whatever came my way and concentrated on doing the task rather than worrying about how my efforts would be judged by others.

My (hard-won) relaxed attitude didn't endear me to everyone. I was called in to a meeting with a very important media person to discuss my career. He advised me to be more selective about what I agreed to do. I told him that I had a policy of saying yes to everything. He was not impressed. Just recently I was speaking on a panel at a writers' festival and a (male) member of the audience came up to me afterwards.

'You are much more intelligent than I thought you'd be,' he observed. (I think he thought that was a compliment.) 'You really shouldn't do so much of that celebrity comment.'

'I am just very grateful for every opportunity to contribute to the public conversation,' I said.

'My friends and I think you are selling yourself short.'

'I take my opportunities where I find them.'

And I do. I know that one day the phone will stop ringing, so I don't take any offer for granted. Nor will I pick and choose my audiences. In fact, I love getting an opportunity to put a different point of view to audiences that might not otherwise hear one. Of course, there are things I won't do, but I don't try to control what is pretentiously called 'my image'. I don't try to control how I come across. I learnt very painfully why that doesn't work for me and I am not going back there.

* * *

Meanwhile, I was still slogging away at my novel. When I finished the book I sent it around to a few publishers. They all sent it back saying they had enjoyed it very much but could not see how to place it in the Australian market. It was a historical novel about Elizabeth Tudor, who later became Elizabeth I. I had conceived the idea of writing a trilogy about Elizabeth's life years before at that writing group I mentioned previously. One of the other members, Lisa Storrs, had been writing a novel set during the wars between the Romans and the Etruscans and she was the only one of us to get a bit of interest in her project. Since that time, three of us have been published, including Lisa. Her good fortune got me thinking about the market.

If I was going to get a novel published, I would need to write a genre novel. Which genre should I choose? Detective? I wasn't clever enough at plots. Science fiction? Not interested. Romance? I'd rather kill myself. Historical? Yes, I could do historical. But what period and which personalities could I bear to spend years researching and then writing about? The answer was obvious. I had been fascinated by Elizabeth I since I was a child. I would love to write about her.

Young girls are very short of real female heroes to admire. I think that is why when I discovered Elizabeth Tudor – and I have loved her for so long I don't recall when that was – she so quickly became such a hero of mine. She is one of the very few women in history who is seen as having wielded power well. Moreover, she did it on her own. I think it was that sense of a powerful woman who did not come to a sticky end (most of the others did) and who took on the male world and more than matched it that filled me with not just admiration, but hope. Most of the women who were admired when I was young were self-sacrificing and self-effacing. I am afraid that was never a model of behaviour that did very much for me. I didn't want to be patronised and sentimentalised the way so many traditional heroines are (think Joan of Arc, Grace Darling, Edith Cavell – talk about sticky ends). I preferred to be respected like Elizabeth Tudor.

I conceived the idea of writing a trilogy in her voice. The first volume would be narrated by twenty-five-year-old Elizabeth on the night before her coronation, unable to sleep, passing the time by looking back over her life and asking herself how she had survived, what she had learnt and how she would rule.

The second volume would be told from the perspective of fifty-four-year-old Elizabeth while she suffered a four-day breakdown after the execution of Mary, Queen of Scots. She would obsessively ask herself how she had come to do the very thing she always said she would never do by killing an anointed queen.

The third would be narrated by sixty-nine-year-old Elizabeth, sitting on a cushion with her finger in her mouth for six days before she died (also historically accurate), silently contemplating her whole life and rule and wondering how she had fulfilled her destiny and how she would be judged by posterity.

A friend called the trilogy a big, hairy, audacious goal. It was looking as if I might never achieve it, if the judgment of the first couple of publishers to read the first volume was anything to go by.

Then I had another lucky interaction with an old colleague from my early days at Saatchi. Kate Hunter had come to see me when she was a young copywriter and I had liked her work. My recommendation had helped her to get a start at a good agency. She had since left agency life to have kids and had written and published her first novel. It was for young adults and was called *Mosquito Advertising*. Her publisher was Kristina Schultz at University of Queensland Press (UQP). While congratulating Kate for her achievement (I was actually eaten up with envy), I mentioned my own disappointments with my Elizabeth Tudor novel.

'Could it be a young adult novel?' Kate asked me.

'Well, yes, I suppose it could.'

'Send it to Kristina, then. She's lovely and will give you an honest and fair reading.'

Within a couple of weeks I had a publisher and *Just a Girl* was released in 2011. It was received very positively and, like *The Stupid Country*, was a 'Pick of the Week' for *The Sydney Morning Herald*. It has now been reprinted twice. The second volume *Just a Queen*, has just been released. Depending on its reception and how well it sells, I may just get a contract for the third volume, *Just Flesh and Blood*. If I do, I will have achieved that big, hairy, audacious goal.

I know that I am not a literary genius or a winner of prizes. I am just a good clear writer, a reasonable researcher and am able to tell an interesting tale. That is enough for me. It is a contribution and that is all I ever aim to make. Some people say that the good is the enemy of the great. I actually think the reverse – that the desire to be great stops people who would otherwise be damn good.

My first book, *The Stupid Country*, was published when I was fifty, and I don't think that is a coincidence. Getting older has had the effect of concentrating my mind. At forty-nine, I left advertising. At fifty, I published my first book. At fifty-eight, this memoir will be my eighth book in eight years. I know my time is limited (ten to twenty productive years left at best), so I am getting on with things. In 2013, Amanda Armstrong and I created, wrote and produced a six-part radio series for Radio National's *Life Matters* called 'For Better, For Worse' about long-lasting relationships. In 2015, as I write these final few paragraphs, I am in the middle of filming the TV version.

Yes, I get tired. Very tired sometimes. Yes, I am privileged and incredibly lucky. My girls are grown and, despite all dire predictions that their public education would destroy their opportunities, they both have university degrees, paid employment and are in longstanding successful relationships with lovely men. Was I a great or perfect mother to them? Not by any means. Was I a good enough mother? At the time of writing it would seem so. My luckiest break was in meeting Ralph and being smart enough to hang on to him. There is no doubt that he made up for my failings.

What have I learnt in my fifty-eight years on this planet? Just this: safety is an illusion and danger is reality. Terrible things can happen and they can happen to anyone. You are not special and nor is anyone else. Once I accepted the truth of that – not just intellectually but viscerally – I gave up trying to stay safe. I stopped battling to control the uncontrollable. I don't know when I stopped having intrusive thoughts. They appeared abruptly and I remember the exact moment when they did. They disappeared very gradually and I cannot recall when I finally realised I was free of them. They just lost their power over me and dwindled away.

When I experienced real fear and gave in to it, paradoxically I gave up anxiety. There is no way out of life except through death. I don't believe in a god or an afterlife. I assume that what happens after I die will be pretty much what happened before I was born. That doesn't frighten me in the slightest. After all, I don't remember oblivion being so terrible or anything much, for that matter. I know I am only here for a short time and I want to make the most of it, not by being brilliant or great or important, but simply by doing whatever it is that I can.

Acknowledgments

The first *thing* that I want to acknowledge is that this is a memoir. It consists of my memories. If you were present at some of the events I relate in these pages and your recollection varies, my apologies in advance. This is how I remember what happened. I have tried to be as truthful as I can be (see the title of this book) but memory is a notoriously unreliable instrument and it is entirely understandable that others might see the same event differently.

The first *person* I want to acknowledge is my publisher at Pan Macmillan, Ingrid Ohlsson. The fact that this book was written at all is entirely due to her. I had never dreamt of writing a memoir until she suggested it. In 2013 Ingrid published a book – *For God's Sake: An Atheist, Christian, Jew and Muslim Debate Religion* – that I co-wrote with three other authors (I am the atheist). She saw the germ of this book in some of the contributions I made to that one. I am (mostly) very grateful to her for gently prodding me into undertaking this daunting task.

I think it was Ross Gittins who said you have to be an egomaniac to write a memoir and I agree with him. I think that is why I was so hesitant. Not because I am not an egomaniac but because – like so many women – I was frightened of looking like one. Without Ingrid's sympathetic support and encouragement, I think I might have fallen at the first hurdle.

I also want to acknowledge my wonderful editor Libby Turner who has expertly sharpened and improved this book beyond recognition. She and Ingrid read the first draft and their suggestions about becoming more specific, telling more stories and – in Ingrid's words – allowing myself more 'rants' – means there is simply light years between the first draft and the final book. The improvements are entirely due to them.

Lara Wallace, the publicist on this book, also deserves acknowledgment for her patience, good humour and sheer hard graft. Any attention this book receives is due to her.

Peter Brew-Bevan who took the cover shot has worked miracles with not very promising raw material. Not only am I no model, I also have an aversion to having my photo taken. I'd much rather appear on live TV or speak in front of thousands than stand in front of a camera. Peter was ably assisted by make-up artist Paul Bedggood and together they helped me both look good and feel good.

Lastly, I would like to thank everyone who appears in this book and many who – despite their impact on my life – have not. Whether my memories of you are good or otherwise,

I learnt from you and you have helped shape the story of my life.

Particular gratitude must go to my long-suffering family. My parents Kate and Andy, my siblings Ann, Robert and Ruth and, of course, my husband Ralph and children Polly and Charlotte. It has not been possible to write this story without mentioning them (sorry Ann) because they are so much a part of it. I hope each of them feel I have told the truth and been fair. I thank them for for trusting me to tell it.